D0126214

▷ This Bumper Book of London
belongs to

- - - - - - - - - - - - - - - - - -

CONTENTS

לאָנדאָן
Yiddish

Lundúnir
Icelandic

Reondeon
Korean

런던

LUNNAINN
Scots Gaelic

Luân Đôn
Vietnamese

Rondon ロンドン
Japanese

Պասեստավկոդսած Լյուքեր
Armenian

ლონდონი
Georgian

לונדון
Hebrew

Landan
Arabic

กรุงลอนดอน
Thai

Londër
Albanian

LONDEN
Afrikaans

ЛОНДОН
Russian

LUNDENWIC
Anglo-Saxon

Londhíno
Dutch

LLUNDAIN
Welsh

Londain
Irish

Λονδινο
Greek

London
Azeri

Londona
Latvian

Londinas
Lithuanian

Londinium
Latin

Londra
Albanian, Italian, Maltese, Romanian, Romansh, Turkish

Lontoo
Finnish

Londýn
Czech, Slovak

Londyn
Polish

Лёндан
Belarusian

Londres
Catalan, French, Portuguese, Spanish, Ladino

* London is the CAPITAL city of England and Great Britain
* London is the sixth RICHEST city in the world
  London is made up of two cities: WESTMINSTER and the CITY OF LONDON
* London is its own county called GREATER LONDON
* London has a reputation for being a RAINY city but in fact it is one of the DRIEST capitals in Europe
* MORE PEOPLE live in London than in any other city in Europe
* If London were a country, it would be the 35TH BIGGEST in Europe
* 53 countries in the world are SMALLER than London
* Almost a quarter of Londoners are CHILDREN AND TEENAGERS
* TEXT SPEAK for London is LDN

London by numbers

* **1 BILLION** passengers travel on the Tube every year
* **25 MILLION** visitors come to stay in London every year
* **13 MILLION** people go to London's theatres every year
* **7.7 MILLION** people live in London
* **5.6 MILLION** go to the British Museum every year
* **3.5 MILLION** passengers take the Tube each day
* **1,213,870** children go to school in London
* **36,000** people run the London Marathon

Random places called London . . .

. . . a village on **CHRISTMAS ISLAND** in the Pacific Ocean
. . . a city in **ONTARIO**, Canada. The river that flows through it is called the Thames!
. . . a city in **SOUTH AFRICA** called East London
. . . eight towns in the **USA**:
  London, Arkansas • London, California • London, Kentucky • London, Minnesota
  • London, Ohio • London, Pennsylvania • London, Texas • London, West Virginia

What's in a name?

- The Celtic word **LOND** means **A WILD PLACE**. **DON** means **FORTRESS OR HILL FORT**.
- The Latin word **LAUNDUN** means **CITY OF THE MOON** and London had a temple devoted to the goddess Diana, associated with the moon.
- The Anglo-Saxons called the abandoned Roman city **LUNDENBURH**, which means **LONDON FORT**.
- **LUNDENWIC**, the Saxon settlement at Aldwych, means **LONDON TRADING TOWN**.
- Geoffrey of Monmouth wrote in 1136 that London was called London after **LUD**, a pre-Roman King of Britain. **LUDGATE** is one of the old gateways into the City of London.

London has . . .

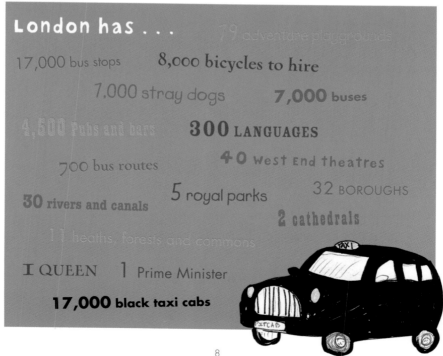

79 adventure playgrounds
17,000 bus stops   8,000 bicycles to hire
      7,000 stray dogs   7,000 buses
4,500 pubs and bars   300 LANGUAGES
  700 bus routes   40 West End theatres
30 rivers and canals   5 royal parks   32 BOROUGHS
                          2 cathedrals
11 heaths, forests and commons
1 QUEEN   1 Prime Minister
17,000 black taxi cabs

How far from
London to . . . ?

NEW YORK – 5,536 kilometres (3,440 miles)

9,585 kilometres (5,956 miles) – TOKYO

8,148 kilometres (5,063 miles) – BEIJING

MEXICO CITY – 8,898 kilometres (5,529 miles)

9,540 kilometres (5,928 miles) – BANGKOK

10,872 kilometres (6,756 miles) – SINGAPORE

AUCKLAND – 18,352 kilometres (11,404 miles)

5,494 kilometres (3,414 miles) – DUBAI

17,007 kilometres (10,568 miles) – SYDNEY

CASABLANCA – 2,092 kilometres (1,300 miles)

9,673 kilometres (6,011 miles) – CAPE TOWN

LONDON MONOPOLY

There are twenty-two streets of London on the Monopoly board.
There is only one street in south London: Old Kent Road.
Angel is the only 'street' on the board that is not actually a London street.
The people who created the London version of the game would meet over
tea at Lyon's Corner House at the Angel.
There are only four railway stations in Monopoly: Liverpool Street,
Fenchurch Street, Euston and Marylebone.
Vine Street is a tiny dead-end alleyway in Piccadilly, of no significance at all.

London calling

- The first telephone directory was published by the London **TELEPHONE COMPANY** in 1880. It was just six pages long and had 255 names.
- The first name in the first phone directory in London was John Adam and Co. at 11 Pudding Lane. The phone book listed only the name and address of the person who had a telephone, not the phone number – you had to call the **OPERATOR** to ask to be put through by name.
- **SELFRIDGES** department store had number one as its phone number.

Before 1966, telephone numbers were not written all in numbers: a telephone dial had letters as well as numbers on it. You began by dialling letters from the place where a person lived, for example WIM for Wimbledon, followed by numbers.

FAMOUS LONDON PHONE NUMBERS

Buckingham Palace – VICtoria 6913
Winston Churchill – PADdington 1003
Alfred Hitchcock – FRObisher 1339
Scotland Yard – WHItehall 1212

If you want to call a friend in London you have to dial 020 first.

RANDOM THINGS CALLED LONDON

- The London Equation is a scientific theory created by two brothers called Fritz and Heinz London in 1935. It relates to the electromagnetic fields around a superconductor.
- 8838 London is a main belt asteroid, discovered on 7 October 1989 by E.W. Elst.

DID YOU KNOW?

* The Royal Mail is giving London's new Queen Elizabeth Olympic Park the same E20 postcode as the fictional borough of Walford in the television soap opera *EastEnders*.
* The previous highest postcode was E18; there is still no E19.
* A new postcode, N1C, has been created for King's Cross.

A postcard addressed simply as 'The BEST HATTERS in the World, London' was delivered to the door of LOCK & CO. at 6 St James's Street, SW1. Amazing!

London first: postcodes

The first system of postcodes in the world was devised for London in **1856**.

The codes originally covered a circular area of 12 miles radiating out from the central post office at St Martin's Le Grand, near St Paul's Cathedral. This was divided into **TEN POSTAL DISTRICTS**: EC, WC, N, NE, E, SE, S, SW, W and NW. (NE was later merged into E and S was spilt between SE and SW.) In 1917, as a wartime efficiency measure, the districts were subdivided with a number applied to each sub-district. Within each section the most central post district was given the number 1. The Post Office allocated the other numbers alphabetically. As the city has grown the system has become more complex.

London needed postcodes because so many streets had the same name. It was suggested that street names could be changed instead but several wealthy families protested, as they lived in streets named after their ancestors.

Decode your postcode

Postcodes are often used as shorthand to describe the sort of people who are thought to be typical of a particular area.

NW3	**HAMPSTEAD**	Liberal, intellectual, bohemian
W1	**WEST END**	Smart, glamorous, moneyed
N1	**ISLINGTON**	Lawyers, journalists, socialists
SW3	**CHELSEA**	Sloane rangers, Tories, Americans
W11	**NOTTING HILL**	Celebrity media people, trustafarians

★ LONDON LINGO ★

★ People always say that they are 'travelling *up* to London', no matter where in England they are coming from.

★ London is referred to in two distinct areas: north of the river and south of the river.

★ Eastenders are people who live east of the City of London.

★ The West End is anything west of the City as far as Marble Arch. People who live here are not called Westenders.

The Shard is London's tallest building

Height of Shard: 310 metres/1,017 feet
Speed of erection: 30 cm/12 inches an hour

The highest point in London

Hampstead Heath at 134 metres/440 feet

London's most popular museums and galleries

The British Museum • The Science Museum •
The National Gallery • Tate Modern •
The Natural History Museum

The London Eye is London's most visited tourist attraction

The centre of London

A plaque on the ground in Trafalgar Square by the statue of Charles I marks the centre of London.

The population of London

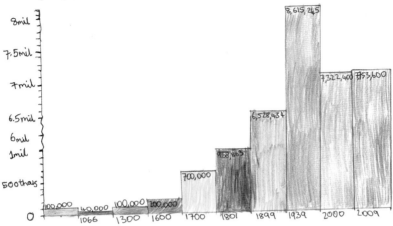

Take a butchers at this ...

- Londoners are known as **COCKNEYS**. Technically, only people born within the sound of the Bow bells qualify as cockneys. These are the bells of St Mary-le-Bow on Cheapside.
- The name cockney was coined by people from the countryside who thought that Londoners were ignorant, as they knew nothing about country ways.
- The word cockney comes from **COCK'S EGG**, a Middle English expression meaning 'a deformed, rather small egg'. It describes an ignorant person or simpleton.
- Cockneys speak in a disitinctive way, with a London accent. They also have their own secret code: cockney **RHYMING SLANG**.
- **MOCKNEY** is a term used to describe people who are not real cockneys but who chose to speak in a cockney accent to seem cool.

count to ten in cockney ...

½ = Lamb (and calf)

1 = Lost (and won)

2 = Bottle (of glue)

3 = Holy (see)

4 = Stand (in awe)

5 = Scuba (dive)

6 = Fiddle (–sticks)

7 = Exeter (in Devon)

8 = Fartoo (late)

9 = Coal (mine)

10 = Foxes (den)

ROMAN LONDON
AD 43–450

Two thousand years ago, on the banks of the Thames, the Roman Emperor Claudius set up camp in damp, marshy ground. He had successfully beaten back the half-naked, **BLUE-PAINTED CELTS** who had occupied Britain for the preceding 500 years, using elephants to terrify them. Close to the sea but safely upstream and easy to defend, the ground was a great spot for a new trading post, and soon a small town started to thrive. This was the beginning of London. In its heyday, the waterfronts along the river of Roman Londinium were packed with warehouses and docks. Ships arrived laden with cargoes of wines, fish, dates, **FIGS AND OLIVE OIL** and returned to Rome carrying wool, hides, tin and slaves.

Under repeated attack from the Celts and Britons, the Romans built a wall 5 metres (16 feet) high around their city using 85,000 tons of Kentish ragstone brought up the Thames on barges. The wall was heavily guarded, with impenetrable entrance gates and catapult towers.

By AD 100 **LONDINIUM** was the capital city of Roman Britain. It had imposing stone buildings, temples, a fort, an amphitheatre and a marketplace. There were public baths at Cheapside and Upper Thames Street. The vast forum and basilica was the largest Roman building north of the Alps. The homes had central heating, piped water, public baths, a sewage system, education, art and culture. The city was wealthy and sophisticated, home to soldiers, administrators, traders, **SLAVES** and people drawn from the surrounding area who came to make their fortune.

The Romans built a network of roads from the city across England and the first London Bridge over the Thames, almost exactly where it is today. Their **OCCUPATION** was to last for more than 400 years, until the end of the Roman Empire, when the city was left empty and abandoned to dogs.

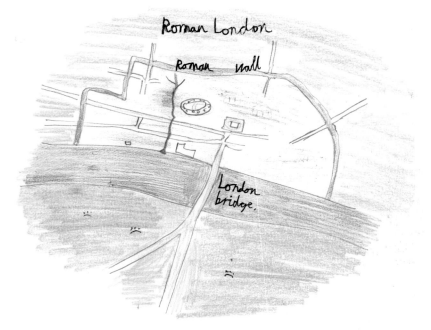

Cornhill, Cheapside and Poultry in the
City of London are all Roman roads.

ROMAN LONDON FIRSTS

✸ The first ever picture of London is on a Roman gold coin, called the Arras Medallion, dug up in a great hoard of treasure in 1922. It dates back to AD 296 and shows a man on horseback carrying a spear being welcomed with open arms by a woman in front of the gates of a walled city: London. It is the only portrait of Roman London that exists.

✸ Romans were the first Londoners to wear bikinis. Archaeologists found a perfect pair of first-century leather bikini bottoms in a Roman well in Queen Street in 1953. Roman women wore bikini bottoms for performing acrobatics and sport.

✸ The first Roman archaeological discovery was found by workmen rebuilding St Paul's Cathedral after the Great Fire of London in 1666. They found a Roman kiln used for firing pots.

Ssshhh!

SECRET ROMAN LONDON

- Roman London was formed between two hills: Cornhill and Ludgate Hill.
- The only surviving part of the once glorious Roman basilica can be seen down in the basement of a hairdresser's at 90 Gracechurch Street.
- There is a precious Roman mosaic hidden in the basement of 11 Ironmonger Row. Knock on the door and ask politely to be taken to see it.
- Fragments of a child's shoe, small leather slippers, bone whistles and other toys belonging to Roman children have been found in London.
- Roman finds are kept safe at the Museum of London.
- There is a detailed handmade model of what Roman London would have looked like in the crypt at the church of All Hallows by the Tower.
- At the bottom of some steps just off Surrey Street, Aldwych, is a public bath that is said to be Roman. We know it was still in use 100 years ago, as Charles Dickens went there from time to time.
- An office in Lower Thames Street, Centennium House, has a Roman bath in its foundations.
- Tombstones of Roman children have been found in London, one of a boy called Onesimus, a 'well-deserving' son.

A child's life . . .

Once the Romans arrived, there was no more running around HALF NAKED smearing yourself with mud. A Roman child was expected to learn Latin and Greek and the art of public speaking and debate, train to be a lawyer or wield a sword. Children practised spellings with ivory letters. HOMEWORK was done on a soft wax tablet. Rich girls were tutored at home until they were thirteen, when they married. At sixteen, boys wore togas to show they were grown up. Favourite snacks were snails fattened on milk, PEACOCK'S BRAINS and flamingo tongues. Children were expected to help look after chickens, piglets and bees.

Children had games to play with: toy boxes were filled with toy soldiers, rattles, doll's houses, carts, board games with pebbles for counters and wooden dolls. Dogs, birds and MONKEYS were popular pets.

roman coin

London's oldest place of worship . . .

The underground **TEMPLE OF MITHRAS** was discovered in the 1950s. Roman soldiers from the nearby Watling Street barracks once held candlelit feasts and rituals inside it. Exquisite sculptures were found here and are now in the Museum of London. The ruined temple is now unceremoniously exposed in Queen Victoria Street.

London's one and only Roman amphitheatre

Roman London's great amphitheatre was unearthed with much excitement under Guildhall Yard in 1988. Archaeologists had been searching for it for over 100 years and in the end they stumbled across it by accident. It is the only Roman amphitheatre found in London.

The amphitheatre was big enough to hold 6,000 people, a quarter of Roman London's population. It was 80 metres (262 feet) wide and the centre of the arena was filled with sand to soak up the **BLOOD** from the savage battles held there. Public **EXECUTIONS** and wild animal fights also took place here. The remains of the amphitheatre lie underneath Guildhall Yard in the City.

GLADIATORS were sometimes prisoners of war, slaves or criminals condemned to gladiator school. Some gladiators were sons of rich men looking for fame or poor men hoping to win great prize money.

Gladiators were thrown in to the arena to fight hungry wild animals, such as **BEARS** and bulls, or to fight against each other to the death.

Women gladiators were very rare. They were given the name **GLADIATRIX** and were usually teenage girls. Archaeologists were delighted when they dug up a grave in Great Dover Street in 2000 to find the body of a gladiatrix. It was a twenty-year-old woman who had made her **FORTUNE** fighting in the Roman amphitheatre. Pictures found in her grave tell the story of her life.

Gladiator

★ LONDON LINGO ★

Latin was the language of the Roman Londoners.
We still speak Latin sometimes without even realizing it.

Ad hoc (towards this) = For this purpose
Ad infinitum (to infinity) = Never ending, indefinitely
Ad nauseam (to sickness) = Continuing to the point of being sick
Caveat emptor = Let the buyer beware
Circa = Around
In flagrante delicto (with the crime blazing) = Caught red handed
In vino veritas (in wine there is the truth) = Drinking wine loosens the tongue
Modus operandi = Way of operating or working
Non sequitur = Does not follow on, illogical
Paterfamilias = Head of the house
Quid pro quo = An exchange of favours
Status quo = The present state of affairs
Verbatim = Word for word

The story of Boudicca, the Celtic warrior queen

Boudicca was a fierce warrior queen of the Celtic Iceni tribe. In AD 60, with red hair flaming and knives in the wheels of their chariots, she and her daughters attacked Londinium, riding over muddy lanes and marble pavements, slicing up Roman soldiers on the way. She rallied the thousands of Celtic tribesmen who fought alongside her with the words 'Win the battle or perish; that is what I, a woman will do.'

Seventy thousand Londoners were slaughtered, ships blazed on the Thames and the whole city was set alight, burning to ashes in a terrible fire.

Archaeologists have found the remains of burnt buildings and shattered objects and even layers of oxidized earth that indicate how fiercely Boudicca's fire burned.

But in the end Boudicca was defeated by the Roman army. She fled with her daughters to Epping Forest, where they drank a poisonous potion and died. Londoners believe Boudicca is buried under platform 10 at King's Cross railway station.

London folklore

In a wall on Cannon Street opposite the station, hidden behind a metal grille, is the **LONDON STONE**, thought to be a Roman milestone. It is said to be the point from which the Romans measured all distances to and from London. It has become part of London's mythology and is sometimes said to be where King Arthur drew his sword Excalibur. Like the ravens at the Tower of London, it is superstitiously linked to the safety and success of the city itself.

Sunken cargo

- In 1910, a Roman ship laden with scores of PRECIOUS coins was discovered in the Thames at Westminster Bridge.
- A Roman ship built by the Celts in AD 150 was found in the bed of the river Thames off BLACKFRIARS in 1962. It was 14 metres/46 feet long, built of oak with a sailing mast, and had no keel. When it was pulled out of the river it was still laden with its heavy cargo of building stone. It is known as the BLACKFRIARS BOAT.

TOP TEN ROMAN THINGS TO SPOT IN LONDON

✳ The AMPHITHEATRE at Guildhall

✳ Statue of EMPEROR TRAJAN at Tower Hill

✳ Model of ROMAN LONDON at All Hallows by the Tower of London

✳ Roman MOSAICS at the British Museum

✳ TEMPLE OF MITHRAS on Queen Victoria Street

✳ Roman TREASURES at the Museum of London ✳ MOSAIC FLOOR at No 11 Ironmonger Row ✳ The LONDON WALL at Moorgate

✳ Roman BASILICA at 90 Gracechurch Street

✳ LONDON STONE at Cannon Street

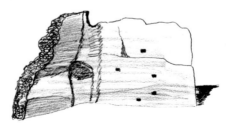

Saxon and Viking London
450-1066

After the Romans left, Danish and German invaders settled on the marshland and in the fields alongside the river Thames, outside the abandoned Roman city, which was now a ghost town. They were the Middle Saxons; the county name Middlesex comes from them. Angles and Jutes came too. The tribes intermarried and became known as the ANGLO-SAXONS.

Over the years a small market town grew up where Covent Garden is today. Evidence of this town, which was called LUNDENWIC, has been found underneath the Royal Opera House.

In AD 787 the peaceful farming life of the Anglo-Saxons came to an end: the VIKINGS attacked. For the next 350 years marauding Vikings from Sweden, Denmark and Norway came seeking wealth and land to grasp and pillage. They sailed up the river Thames to London in terrifying raids. With little to protect them, the Anglo-Saxons were at the mercy of these fearsome Vikings until in 866 the King, Alfred the Great, became thoroughly fed up and moved his people behind the crumbling protection of the walls of the old Roman city. He cleared out the rubble and restored the city, creating a royal plan for the streets between Cheapside and the Thames that is still visible today. London steadily grew and became richer. Meetings of the Witan, the council of wise men that advised the king on matters of government, were increasingly held in London. King ETHELRED THE UNREADY issued the Laws of London from here in 978. However, in 1016 the Danish King CANUTE won the battle for London and he and his sons ruled over the city until 1042, when the Anglo-Saxon EDWARD THE CONFESSOR became king.

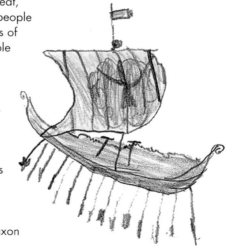

The word VIKING is Norse for PIRATE RAID

★ LONDON LINGO ★

★ The Germanic languages of the Saxons and Angles merged into Anglo-Saxon. When the Norse language of the Vikings was mixed in with Anglo-Saxon it became what we call Old English. Viking words often have 'sk' sounds in them. Words like score, fellow, take, skin, sky, dregs, birth, cake, feckless, ransack, sister, smile, ugly, anger, are all Viking.

★ Some of the days of the week are named after Viking gods:
Wednesday is named after Woden (or Odin), the father of all Viking gods.
Thursday is named after Thor, Odin's warrior son.
Friday is named after Freya, Odin's beautiful wife, who made all things grow.

★ Lots of street and place names in London come from the Anglo-Saxons:
Aldwych = Ealdwic (old city)
Borough = Burh (fortress)
Southwark = Suth-weorc (southern defence)

DID YOU KNOW?
LONDON FACT · LONDON FACT · LONDON FACT · LONDON FACT

England was divided into many kingdoms. London and Winchester were some of the most important Saxon cities in England. London was part of the kingdom of Essex.

A child's life

Saxon Londoners were farmers, and children worked hard with their parents on the farm. Sometimes boys would be left to keep a lookout for **WOLVES**, still common around London back then. Clothes were made of animal skins and wool that was spun at home. To ward off sickness and **EVIL SPIRITS**, babies were given a Thor's hammer charm to wear. Toy whistles were made from bones; dolls and toy long boats were carved in wood.

At night, families would sit around the fire **SINGING SONGS**. They would tell stories and poems about their great leaders, daring adventures, fierce battles and powerful gods.

saxon and Viking London Firsts

The first documented mention of London Bridge is a description of the drowning of a witch there in AD 970. The woman was accused of attempting murder by sticking nails into a puppet. A doll with pins sticking in it was found during a search of her house and was used as evidence against her.

Ssshhh!

SECRET SAXON AND VIKING LONDON

There is a plaque on Southwark Bridge to King Alfred that celebrates the resettlement of the Roman City in 899. It is here that a new harbour and markets were established to help London thrive once more.

Who reigned?

The Saxon kings
Egbert (802–39)
Aethelwulf (839–55)
Aethelbald (855–60)
Aethelbert (860–6)
Aethelred (866–71)
Alfred the Great (871–99)
Edward the Elder (899–925)
Athelstan (925–40)
Edmund the Magnificent (940–46)
Eadred (946–55)
Eadwig All-Fair (955–9)
Edgar the Peaceable (959–75)
Edward the Martyr (975–8)
Ethelred the Unready (978–1016)
Edmund Ironside (1016)

The Viking kings
Svein Forkbeard (1013–14)
Canute the Great (1016–35)
Harald Harefoot (1035–40)
Hardicanute (1040–42)

The Saxon kings, again
Edward the Confessor (1042–66)
Harold II (1066)

Edward the confessor

The Saxon word for strong leader is cyning, like our word king.

Ethelred the Unready had a funny name that does not mean he was never ready. Unready actually means 'poorly advised'. It is a twist on his first name, Ethelred, which means 'good advice'.

London folklore

Harold Harefoot, son of King Canute, was King of England for just three years, 1037–40. After his death, his body was exhumed from Westminster by his angry half-brother, Hardicanute, gruesomely beheaded and thrown in the Thames. It is said that Danish FISHERMEN caught his body in a net and buried him secretly at St Clement Danes Church on the Strand.

All you need to know about Saxon and Viking kings

- There were five important Anglo-Saxon kingdoms in AD 600. These were Northumbria, Mercia, Wessex, Kent and East Anglia. The strongest king would sometimes be the ruler of all Britain.

- ALFRED THE GREAT is the most important Saxon king. He was a valiant king and he defended England from fierce Viking invaders. He has been known as 'the Great' ever since. He is famous for being so worried about his kingdom that he let some cakes burn in the oven.

- Seven Saxon kings were crowned at Kingston upon Thames. They were Edward the Elder; Athelstan; Edmund the Magnificent; Eadred; Eadwig All-Fair; Edward the Martyr; and Ethelred the Unready. The CORONATION STONE used in the ceremony is now outside the Guildhall in Kingston. There is a coin from each king at its base.

- The Saxon kings liked to collect relics of saints, such as their BONES.

- Saxon rule was interrupted by the VIKINGS, who took over the throne for twenty-six years.

- The Viking king HAROLD HAREFOOT got his name because he was fast and skillful at hunting.

- The Saxons returned to power with EDWARD THE CONFESSOR in 1042. Edward the Confessor built Westminster Abbey and the Palace of Westminster in London.

- Edward the Confessor's death in 1066 sparked the invasion of England by the Normans. WILLIAM THE CONQUEROR killed Harold II, who laid claim to the throne, at the Battle of Hastings, by firing an arrow into his eye.

- Edward the Confessor was the first king to be buried at WESTMINSTER ABBEY.

The story of King Canute . . .

King Canute was a Danish warrior who became the undisputed Viking King of England in 1016. He had invaded England, raising a force of over 10,000 men. In April 1016, he sailed up the Thames on a Viking warship and laid siege to London. King Ethelred the Unready was so shocked by the invasion that he had a heart attack and died.

London Bridge is falling down . . .

OLD NORSE STORIES tell of the great Viking battles in London. A Norse poet, Ottar Svale, wrote about the pulling down of London Bridge, in the saga of **OLAF HARALDSON**. The story goes that, in 1014, the Viking warrior Olaf sailed up the Thames to come to the aid of **ETHELRED** and the English, who were being attacked by fierce Danish invaders. The Danes had captured London Bridge, so Olaf Haraldson sailed underneath it. The Danes pelted arrows from above and Olaf's soldiers protected themselves with shields carried above their heads. Once under the bridge, they tied great ropes to the legs of the wooden bridge. With a great heave, Olaf and his Viking soldiers pulled on the ropes and forced London Bridge to collapse into the water. The unfortunate Danes tumbled in after it. A version of the old nursery rhyme 'London Bridge is Falling Down' appears in the saga of Olaf Haraldson.

St Clement Danes Church

London Bridge is falling down,
Falling down, falling down,
London bridge is falling down,
My fair lady!

The Strand, the centre of Lundenwic
for many years, was called
Densemanestret or the Street of Danes.
The church at the top of the Strand
at Aldwych is called St Clement Danes,
after the Danish who settled there.

TOP TEN SAXON AND VIKING THINGS TO SPOT IN LONDON

✳ Edward the Confessor's **TOMB** at Westminster Abbey
✳ St Clement Danes **CHURCH** on the Strand ✳ Coronation Stone of the **SAXON KINGS** at Kingston Town Hall ✳ Statue of **BOUDICCA** at Westminster Bridge ✳ The **GREAT HALL** at the Palace of Westminster ✳ A gold leaf and garnet **SAXON BROOCH** at the Museum of London ✳ **ANCIENT WOODLAND** at Epping Forest ✳ Sutton Hoo **TREASURES** at the British Museum ✳ **VIKING BATTLEAXES** in the Museum of London ✳ The **ANGLO-SAXON CHRONICLE** at the British Library

MEDIEVAL LONDON
1066-1485

By the Middle Ages London was a thriving, wealthy city within the old Roman walls. To enter the City, you had to cross a **DRAWBRIDGE** and walk under a raised portcullis at one of the seven London gatehouse entrances. Once you were inside, the streets were narrow: in places you could stretch out your arms and touch the houses on either side.

By the 1300s, luxuries such as **SILKS, JEWELS,** sugar and spices were being sold on London's streets. Merchants traded with Arab and Turkish ships, from as far away as India, Africa and China.

Sailing barges, called shouts, carried heavy cargo up the Thames and for two pence you could take a ferry to Gravesend in Kent for a day out in the country. The river teemed with fish; hot dishes were served in the streets; young men jousted at Smithfield; **FEAST DAYS** were celebrated with dancing and singing around London's maypoles; banners and flags were hung from the houses; and bonfires were lit in the streets.

Religion was very important to Londoners and parish churches were opening on every street corner: there were 126 churches in the square mile of the City by the end of the twelfth century. **MISSIONARY FRIARS** came to London from the Continent and opened new priories: Blackfriars, Greyfriars, Whitefriars, Austin Friars and the Crutched Friars. St Paul's Cathedral, topped by a towering wooden steeple, was the City's main landmark. The large, comfortable houses of the rich were cheek by jowl with the jumble of **HOVELS** and slums of the poor: the Black Prince, son of Edward III, had a house on Fish Street Hill; the Duke of Suffolk lived by the fish sellers on Ducksfoot Lane.

By the end of the fifteenth century, the nobility had begun to move west, out of the old City, along the Strand towards the new Palace of Westminster.

MEDIEVAL LONDON FIRSTS

The first English parliament, known as the Mother of Parliaments, was held on 26 March 1257 in the Chapter House at Westminster Abbey. Henry III gathered together bishops, knights, townsmen and barons in a great council. Parliament did not move to the Palace of Westminster until 1547, nearly 300 years later.

RANDOM MAD MEDIEVAL FACTS

❋ Men wore very pointy shoes called poulaines
❋ Women wore long dresses and pointy hats called wimples
❋ Only the very rich were allowed to wear silk and fur
Everyone drank ale, even the children
❋ Fresh water was hard to come by and so no one washed much:
King John was thought rather peculiar because he had eight
baths in six months

A load of rubbish
By 1400 there
was a weekly rubbish collection in London
by RAKYERS, who took the refuse to
LAY-STALLS outside the city gates.

Medieval
Shoes

A child's life

Ordinary London children slept on a bare earth floor, ate with their
fingers from a wooden platter and weed into a pot. They never washed
or brushed their teeth, and probably had only one hot meal day. The
children of nobles and rich merchants snuggled up on a feather mattress
behind tapestry curtains draped round a four-poster bed, drank from a
pewter tankard and dined handsomely.

Children played chess, cards, dice, marbles, dominoes,
blind man's buff (called Hoodman Blind) and conkers (called
cobnuttes). Their toys included kites, rattles, hoops, rocking
horses, spinning tops and dolls. Boys wrestled, played
shuttlecocks, bowls and went ice skating at Moorfields,
strapping animal bones to their feet as skates.

DID YOU KNOW?

❋ Minster means church. The great church of London was
always St Paul's in the City in the east. When Edward the
Confessor built a new abbey, west of the City, he called it
Westminster.
❋ In 1393, Richard II decreed that all pubs must hang signs
outside them so that the examiner of ale would know the location of
every pub in London. Pubs still hang painted signs outside today.

Who reigned?

The Normans
William I the Conqueror (1066–87)
William II Rufus (1087–1100)
Henry I Beauclerc (1100–35)
Stephen (1135–54)
Empress Matilda (1141)

The Plantagenets
Henry II Curtmantle (1154–89)
Richard I the Lionheart (1189–99)
John Lackland (1199–1216)
Henry III (1216–72)
Edward I Longshanks (1272–1307)
Edward II (1307–27)
Edward III (1327–77)
Richard II (1377–99)

House of Lancaster
Henry IV Bolingbroke (1399–1413)
Henry V (1413–22)
Henry VI (1422–61, 1470–1)

House of York
Edward IV (1461–70, 1471–83)
Edward V (1483)
Richard III Crookback (1483–85)

Richard I

The first known painting of any English king is of the teenage Richard II. It can be seen at Westminster Abbey.

The story of the princes in the Tower ...

In May 1483, the young Edward V was brought to the Tower by his Uncle Richard to await his coronation. Four weeks later his little brother was brought to join him. They were sometimes seen playing in the grounds, but one day they disappeared and were never seen again. Uncle Richard was crowned King of England. Speculation was rife: it was rumoured that assassins climbed the Tower early one morning and crept into the room where the boys were sleeping. One was suffocated with a pillow, the other stabbed to death. The bodies were buried under a pile of stones. Two hundred years later the bones of two young children were found at the Tower of London and they are believed to be remains of the royal princes. Charles II gave them a royal burial at Westminster Abbey.

All you need to know about medieval monarchs

- The **NORMANS** were descendants of Vikings who had settled in northern France.
- The first Norman king of England was William the Conqueror, crowned on **CHRISTMAS DAY 1066** at the newly built Westminster Abbey.
- Londoners were not happy to have this French invader, William, as their king and tried to stop him by blocking **LONDON BRIDGE**. To keep Londoners happy, William granted the City special financial privileges.
- William the Conqueror built the **TOWER OF LONDON**.
- **RICHARD THE LIONHEART** led the Crusades to Jerusalem. He lived in France most of the time, and spoke no English.
- King John signed an important document called the **MAGNA CARTA** in 1215.
- Edward I spent his time trying to bring Scotland and Wales under his control and captured the ancient Coronation Stone of Scotland, the **STONE OF SCONE**, and brought it to Westminster Abbey.
- The fifteen-year-old Edward III started the **HUNDRED YEARS WAR** against the French in 1337. It actually lasted 116 years.
- Richard II was only ten when he succeeded his grandfather, Edward III, as king in 1377. His father, **EDWARD, THE BLACK PRINCE**, had died the previous year.
- Henry V won a great victory at the **BATTLE OF AGINCOURT, 1415**.
- Henry VI was just a one-year-old baby when he came to the throne. He went on to lose his throne in the **WARS OF THE ROSES** (1455–87).
- The thirteen-year-old Edward V ruled for two months before being **IMPRISONED** with his little brother Richard in the Tower of London.
- Richard III took over the throne after the disappearance of the **PRINCES IN THE TOWER**.
- Henry Tudor killed Richard III at the **BATTLE OF BOSWORTH FIELD, in 1485**.

King John and the Magna Carta

On 17 May 1215, the rebel barons of England captured London in a struggle with King John. This act forced the weak king to give the barons more power, which he signed away in a document called the **MAGNA CARTA** at Runnymede on the Thames on 10 June 1215. Seven copies were made, two of which are now in London's British Library. The document contained a special clause about London that still holds true today. It gave the City special rights and privileges, allowing it to become even **RICHER** and more powerful in the years that followed.

A Medieval Crown

How to be a knight

Respectable families wanted their sons to become knights. Seven-year-old boys were sent away to live with the family of a knight as a page. They were taught about religion, good manners and cleanliness. There were lots of **STRICT RULES** to follow.

If things went well, at fourteen you became a squire, a personal servant to a knight. You would learn to ride a horse and wield a sword. You would go hunting and hawking in the nearby forests of Epping and Richmond.

If you were worthy, at eighteen you would be knighted in a special and elaborate ceremony and swear to abide by the knights' **CODE OF CHIVALRY**. A true knight would promise to be brave in battle, keep his promises, defend the Church and treat women politely.

THE GOLDEN RULES

* say 'good speed' when entering a room and greet everybody cheerfully
* walk in to a room calmly with your head held high and then kneel on one knee to your lord
* speak when spoken to and make sure you bow whenever you speak to your lord

Richard II held a magnificent JOUSTING TOURNAMENT in 1390 at Smithfield, with over sixty knights taking part. Each night the knights and their ladies feasted at the King's expense and danced till daybreak.

Richard the Lionheart

Groups of Crusader knights, who were also monks, joined Richard the Lionheart to fight in the CRUSADES to win Jerusalem in the Holy Land for the Christians. One of the most important groups in London were the Knights Templar, who built a church in 1185 in a part of London we call TEMPLE. It is a round church, designed to look like the Church of the Holy Sepulchre in Jerusalem. Inside are the life-size tombs of the greatest knights of all.

Medieval Celebrities

Wat Tyler (1341-81) was one of the leaders of the Peasants' Revolt of 1381, when workers rebelled against cruel exploitation and high taxes. Peasants from Kent and Essex marched to London and young apprentices in the City opened the gates to welcome them in. In the riots that followed, houses and palaces were looted and burned, ministers were slaughtered, the fourteen-year-old Richard II was blockaded in the Tower and the Archbishop of Canterbury was beheaded at Tower Hill.

On 15 June, in an effort to bring the trouble to an end, a meeting was held at Smithfield between the King and the peasants' leaders. But things went very badly. Wat Tyler was pulled off his horse, stabbed and killed. The rebel army was in uproar. At this point the young King showed great courage. Shouting 'You shall have no captain but me', he led the rebels off, calmed them with promises of reforms and persuaded them to disperse. However, once the nobles had re-established control the King's concessions were revoked and the leaders of the revolt were hanged.

The dagger that killed Wat Tyler is kept safely at Fishmongers Hall and it is said that this dagger is the one shown on the City of London's coat of arms.

William Caxton (about 1422-92) brought the first printing press to London. He printed the first books in 1476 from his press at Westminster, in Dean's Yard behind the abbey. This was a revolution in book publishing. Before the printing press, every word had to be written out by hand, usually by monks who dedicated their lives to writing out religious books in beautiful script. But even the printing press wasn't exactly fast: Caxton printed only 110 books in his life.

Geoffrey Chaucer (1343-1400) came from a family of London wine merchants, known as vintners. He worked as a tax collector at the gates of the City at Aldgate, where watching the comings and goings of Londoners was good inspiration for the characters in his books. He is most famous today for writing *The Canterbury Tales*, a collection of stories told by pilgrims on their way to Canterbury. Every night, one of them would tell a tale to entertain the others.

The Canterbury Tales are funny and sometimes quite rude. Chaucer had planned to write 120 tales, but only 24 were finished. Each story is called after the person who tells it: *The Miller's Tale*, *The Knight's Tale*, *The Cook's Tale*, *The Wife of Bath's Tale* and so on.

They were some of the first stories written in English and some of the first books to be printed on Caxton's press. Chaucer wrote in a London dialect of a version of English that we call Middle English. Because no one had ever written many of the words down before, he was free to spell them however he liked.

The name Chaucer is from the French word for shoemaker, *chausseur*.

★ LONDON LINGO ★

Ordinary Londoners spoke English, albeit a different English from the one we speak today. When spoken, it would have sounded a little bit like someone speaking with a northern accent. There are lots of Middle English words whose meanings are still recognizable if you say them out loud:

Alderbest = All the best
Bitwixen = Between
Certes = Certainly
Eek = Also
Goostk = Ghost

Noonk = No
Namok = No more
Seydek = Said
Ynoghk = Enough

PRINTER'S DEVIL was the name given to an apprentice printer.

The story of Queen Eleanor's cross . . .

When Queen Eleanor, wife of Edward I, died at Lincoln in 1290, the broken-hearted King had her body carried across England to London, a journey of twelve days. He decreed that a cross be built to mark each overnight stop. The final stopping place was at the top of Whitehall, where the last of these 'Eleanor crosses' was erected. The next day she was buried in Westminster Abbey, at the foot of her father-in-law Henry III's grave. Her heart was buried at the Dominican priory in Blackfriars. The medieval cross was destroyed in 1647, but a replica was commissioned by the Victorians in 1865, and erected on a new site by Charing Cross station. The word charing is usually thought to come from the Old English *cierran* for 'turn', because the river bends there. But some people believe it is from the French *chère reine* – 'darling queen'.

X marks the spot

The place where Eleanor's cross originally stood is the official centre of London, from which all distances are measured. A plaque on the ground marks the spot, below the statue of Charles I in Trafalgar Square, at the top of Whitehall.

★ LONDON LINGO ★

★ Thirteenth-century London was trilingual.
The three languages used were French, Latin and English.
Kings, queen and nobles all spoke French. Latin was the language of the
Church and English was the language of the people on the street.
★ Thousands of French words entered the English language.
English words of French origin include:
diamond, embroidery, jewel, pearl, petticoat, bacon, biscuit, feast, grape, mackerel,
mutton, salmon, vinegar, geometry, grammar, medicine, painting, poet, romance.
★ The Lord Chancellor opened the 1362 Parliament with a speech in the English
language for the first time since Saxon times. It had taken almost 300 years,
since 1066, to oust French as the language of government.
★ There are still French phrases that are used in government today.
The Queen says 'La Reine le veult', which means
'The Queen wills it', every time she passes an
Act of Parliament.

London's oldest . . .

- The cloister garden at Westminster Abbey is the **OLDEST GARDEN** in England. Medieval monks grew herbs, soft fruit trees and grape vines to make wine. Until 1300, London had a warmer, sunnier climate and these plants grew easily.

- St Bartholomew the Great at Smithfields is the **OLDEST SURVIVING NORMAN CHURCH** in London, built in 1123 by William the Conqueror's son, Henry I.

- The Norman spill holes in the walls of the White Tower at the Tower of London are London's **OLDEST LOOS**.

- Britain's **OLDEST DOOR** is at Westminster Abbey and dates back to 1050.

London wipeout: the Black Death

When a **TERRIBLE PLAGUE** struck medieval London in the late summer of **1348**, a third of Londoners died in a matter of months. Through the winter, 200 people a day were buried, in graves stacked **FIVE BODIES DEEP**. By 1349, the graveyards were so overflowing that the Mayor of London bought 13 acres outside the City wall, where Charterhouse Square is today, to bury more dead. An estimated **50,000 LONDONERS** were thrown into the pits. The devastating plague was called the **BLACK DEATH**.

ssshhh!

SECRET MEDIEVAL LONDON

* The grand entrance of St John's Gate, off Clerkenwell Road, is the only surviving part of the medieval Priory of the Knights of St John of Jerusalem and a reminder of London's monastic part, built in 1504. It was heavily restored by the Victorians.
* Very little of medieval London remains, but hidden in the basement of an office block on Magpie Alley is the crypt of the Whitefriars monastery. It was lost for hundreds of years, deep in the coal cellar of an old house.
* There are big medieval knights' tombs at St Martin-in-the-Fields Church on Trafalgar Square.
* A large black slab in the southern cloister of Westminster Abbey probably covers the remains of the Abbot of Westminster and twenty-seven of his monks, who were all taken by the Black Death.
* Westminster Abbey's Chapter House has the best medieval tiled floor in London
* Crosby Hall in Cheyne Walk, Chelsea, is the hall of a medieval manor house that was moved from Bishopsgate and rebuilt brick by brick in 1910.

TOP TEN MEDIEVAL THINGS TO SPOT IN LONDON

* The **MAGNA CARTA** at the British Library
* **CORONATION CHAIR** at Westminster Abbey
* The **JEWEL TOWER** at the Palace of Westminster
* The **WHITE TOWER** at the Tower of London
* Crusader **KNIGHTS' TOMBS** at Temple Church, Inner Temple Lane off Fleet Street
* The **CLOISTER GARDENS** at Westminster Abbey
* **ST ETHELDREDA'S** Church, Ely Place
* St Bartholomew the Great **CHURCH** at Smithfield
* **MEDIEVAL ARMOUR** the Wallace Collection
* The City of London **SHIELD**

33

TUDOR AND ELIZABETHAN LONDON
1485–1603

I n 1485, London was two cities: one to the east around St Paul's and one to the west in Westminster. Open countryside lay in between, much of it owned by the monasteries. There was still only one bridge across the Thames, old London Bridge. Ferrymen taxied people across to the **THEATRES** in Southwark for a penny.

Coal boats from Newcastle and boats laden with trading goods sailed up the river all the way to Westminster, and up the Fleet River to Holborn. Shipbuilding yards opened in Deptford and Woolwich to build boats for the expanding navy.

London's merchants unloaded cargoes of fine cloth, silks, carpets, wines, spices, sugar, jewels, saltpetre for guns, **POTATOES AND TOBACCO**. Adventurers set sail from the Thames to trade in the newly discovered Americas. Explorers, such as Sir Francis Drake, sailed off in search of Spanish gold.

Mansions graced the banks of the Thames from Hampton to Greenwich. Chelsea became known as **THE VILLAGE OF PALACES**. Wealthy Elizabethan men would spend the morning sauntering in the aisles of St Paul's, flirting with women

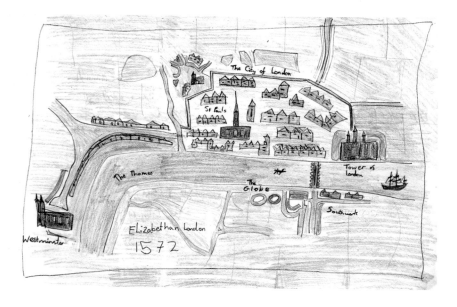

and showing off their new clothes. The City's narrow cobbled streets were crowded with merchants, milkmaids, blacksmiths and entertainers. There were big markets at **CHEAPSIDE** and Leadenhall, and City men drank at the Pope's Head Tavern on Cornhill, where a pint of beer and a **HUNK OF BREAD** cost a penny. In 1577 a man called William Lamb put up a new water pipe for Londoners in Bloomsbury, on what is now Lamb's Conduit Street.

London was growing fast: in 1563, it had a population of 90,000 people. By the end of the Elizabeth I's reign in 1603, over 200,000 people lived in London. England was the richest and most powerful country in Europe, and London was its influential capital. It was felt to be a **GOLDEN AGE**.

Ssshhh!

SECRET TUDOR AND ELIZABETHAN LONDON

* There is a portrait of every Tudor king and queen at the National Portrait Gallery, Trafalgar Square.
* Sutton House in Hackney is the oldest house in east London, dating back to 1535.
* The black-and-white half-timbered Staple Inn, on High Holborn, is the only Elizabethan shopfront left in London, dating back to 1586. It was once where wool was weighed and taxed.
* The seventeenth-century George Inn, off Borough High Street, is the only London pub that still has a galleried yard, where plays were once performed.
* Richmond Green was one of the most famous jousting spots of Tudor London, just next to Richmond Palace.
* Queen Elizabeth's Hunting Lodge in Epping Forest is a very tall building where from the top floor she and her courtiers could watch the hunt in progress and fire their crossbows.
* There is a monument to the Elizabethan writer John Stow at St Andrews Undershaft Church. On 5 April each year in a special ceremony the Lord Mayor replaces the statue's feather quill pen with a fresh one. The old quill is given to a child who has written the best essay on London.

Tudor and Elizabethan schooldays

Before 1400, education was left mostly to the **CHURCH** and many children were taught by **MONKS**. Rich boys and girls were educated by tutors at home in languages, music, history, art and mathematics. When Henry VIII closed the monasteries, London needed more schools.

Elizabethan boys went to a petty school from ages five to seven, where they were taught **GOOD MANNERS**, prayers and basic lessons. Books were made of horn, etched with the alphabet and the Lord's Prayer and strapped to wooden boards. From seven to fourteen, some children went to **FREE** grammar schools. There they learnt to read and write, and studied mathematics, grammar, Latin, Greek and history. They translated the classic works of Ovid, Horace, Virgil and Cicero. Children were expected to speak **LATIN** at all times.

Schools were very religious and children studied the Bible, the Creed and the **TEN COMMANDMENTS**. They were expected to learn the Catechism by heart, a book that detailed the workings of the Christian faith. Writing was done on a **WAX TABLET**. Schools were strict and serious places. The day started at six in the morning and ended at five in the evening. Sunday was the only day off. **PUNISHMENTS** were severe and children were **CANED** for disobedience. Fifty strokes were commonplace. If you were rich enough, you could pay another child to take your beating for you. He was called a **'WHIPPING BOY'**.

In his play *As You Like It*, William Shakespeare described an Elizabethan boy on his way to school: 'the whining school-boy, with his satchel and shining morning face, creeping like snail, **UNWILLINGLY** to school'. Boys went to university as young as fourteen.

Girls were rarely educated outside the domestic skills of sewing and cooking. The poor did not go to school at all and few learnt to read or write.

School rules

London schools had lots of rules: 'no running, no jumping, no chattering or playing, no carrying of sticks or stones or bows, no tricks upon passers-by, no laughing or giggling', which didn't leave room for much fun.

Spoil sports

Londoners played so many games that in 1512 a law was passed to stop ordinary people playing lots of their favourite games, like dice, cards and skittles, so that they would work harder and longer. They were only allowed to play games on Christmas Day.

London's oldest schools

London's wealthy, including merchants and the guilds, opened new schools across the city throughout the fifteenth and sixteenth centuries:

WESTMINSTER SCHOOL	Founded in 1179 then famously refounded in 1560 by Elizabeth I
CITY OF LONDON SCHOOL	Set up by the Town Clerk of London, John Carpenter, in 1442 to educate four boys from Guildhall Chapel
MERCHANT TAYLORS'	Established in 1561 by the Merchant Taylors' Company, one of London's livery companies
CHRIST'S HOSPITAL	Set up by the Lord Mayor in 1552, in Newgate, for boys and girls
ST PAUL'S SCHOOL	Founded in 1509 by the Mercers' Company at St Paul's Cathedral
DAME ALICE OWEN'S	Founded in 1613 by Dame Alice and the Worshipful Company of Brewers for 30 Islington boys

The Tudor and Elizabethan **ALPHABET** contained only twenty-four letters, not the twenty-six we have today. U and V were the same letter, as were I and J.

DID YOU KNOW?

* Sir Walter Raleigh started the first London club at the Mermaid Tavern in Bread Street.

* Elizabeth I loved fashion and she introduced silk stockings to London ladies. When she died, she left 3,000 dresses and 80 wigs.

* Cathedrals were once places where Londoners met and did business. In 1553, an Act was passed to forbid the walking of horses and mules through the middle of St Paul's Cathedral, and a proclamation was issued banning the drawing of swords inside.

Tudor & Elizabethan Celebrities

Thomas More (1478-1535) Henry VIII's Lord Chancellor was born in Milk Street, London. At the age of twelve he was sent to Lambeth Palace to work as a page for the Archbishop of Canterbury. He coined the word utopia when in 1516 he published a book about an ideal imaginary island called Utopia. Thomas More refused to swear an oath recognising Henry VIII as head of the Church and so was taken to the Tower of London, where he was tried and executed for treason.

John Stow (1525-1605) was the son of a tallow maker and became an apprentice tailor. As a boy, he would fetch milk from a farm just outside Aldgate for his mother. He went on to become a writer and famously wrote a detailed history book called *Survey of London* in 1598 about the houses, customs and social conditions of Elizabethan Londoners.

William Shakespeare (1564-1616) lived in London for much of his life, in Southwark and Blackfriars. He is regarded as the greatest writer in the English language. He came to London from Stratford-upon-Avon to work as an actor and became a playwright in an acting company called the Lord Chamberlain's Men. William Shakespeare invested in the theatres and had a share in one called the Globe in Southwark. New plays were needed to feed the demand of the new theatres and in his lifetime Shakespeare wrote thirty-eight plays: histories, comedies and tragedies. His most famous plays include *Macbeth*, *King Lear*, *Romeo and Juliet*, *The Tempest* and *As You Like It*. The plays were extremely successful and Shakespeare died a very rich man.

Shakespeare

A man called Francis Bacon, a writer, scientist and Lord Chancellor in 1618, is thought by some to have written parts of William Shakespeare's plays. There is little evidence to prove this. There is a statue of him in South Square in Gray's Inn.

Who reigned?

House of Tudor
Henry VII Tudor (1485–1509)
Henry VIII (1509–47)
Edward VI (1547–53)
Lady Jane Grey (1553)
Mary I Tudor (1553–8)
Elizabeth I (1558–1603)

Rose of the
House of Tudor

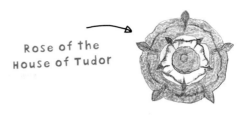

All you need to know about the Tudor monarchs

- The first Tudor king was a nobleman called Henry Tudor, who defeated Richard III at the **BATTLE OF BOSWORTH FIELD** in the Wars of Roses in 1485. He was the last English king to win the Crown on a battlefield.
- **HENRY VIII** loved to hunt and play music. He lived in some of London's finest palaces: Hampton Court, Whitehall, St James'.
- Henry VIII forced London's monasteries to close when he married Anne Boleyn and broke away from the **CATHOLIC** Church.
- Henry VIII's son, **EDWARD VI**, became king at just nine years old. He was sickly and died young.
- **LADY JANE GREY** was on the throne for just nine days in 1553.
- Edward's half-sister, the Catholic Mary I, was nicknamed **BLOODY MARY** because she burned alive more than 300 Protestants at Smithfield.
- Mary I imprisoned her **HALF-SISTER**, Elizabeth, in the Tower of London. Mary died, childless, in 1558.
- **ELIZABETH I** reigned for 45 years. She imprisoned her Scottish cousin Mary, Queen of Scots for 19 years before executing her for treason.
- Elizabeth I and Mary I share a tomb at **WESTMINSTER ABBEY**.

London first . . .

The **PREMIERE** of Shakespeare's **TWELFTH NIGHT** was held at Middle Temple Hall in 1602 by candlelight for Elizabeth I and her court.

Curtain Up!

One of London's earliest theatres was opened by James Burbage in 1576. Imaginatively called the Theatre, it was in **SHOREDITCH**. But in 1599 it was taken down and the wood was ferried across the Thames to Southwark and used to build the **GLOBE** theatre. Designed in the style of the galleried pub yards where most plays had been put on before, the new theatres were wooden, **FIVE-SIDED** buildings surrounded by galleries. Shakespeare described the design as a **WOODEN O**.

The open cobbled yard in front of the stage was for **GROUNDLINGS**, people who paid just a **PENNY** to stand and watch the show. The audience was noisy and rough: fights and brawls broke out, and people gambled and drank as they watched, breaking out in raucous applause after exciting **SWORD FIGHTS**. The galleries were more expensive and had seats. Ticket-holders who sat here looked down on the groundlings below.

More theatres were built on the edge of the City of London, often invested in by the acting troops themselves. Like the Globe, the Swan and Rose Theatres were on the **SOUTH BANK** at Southwark. Londoners were summoned across London Bridge with blasts of **TRUMPETS** and flying flags announcing that a play was soon to begin. Crowds would stream across the bridge or take a ferry across the river to enjoy the show.

The Globe famously went up in flames in 1613 in the middle of a performance of Shakespeare's play Henry VIII, when a **CANNON** shot a blazing cannon ball into the thatched roof.

Ticket money was kept in a LOCKED BOX in the theatre. This became known as the BOX OFFICE.

The Globe theatre

The sad, sad story of Lady Jane Grey . . .

Lady Jane Grey was Queen of England for just nine days. She was a young cousin of Edward VI and was crowned queen four days after his death. She sailed in a stately procession by river from Syon House to the Tower of London, wearing a green velvet gown stamped with gold. It was the custom for a new king or queen to live in the Tower of London. In the meantime, Edward's sister Mary had rallied her supporters, and she threw Lady Jane into prison. She charged her with high treason at Guildhall. She was asked to choose the manner of her death, by being either burned alive or beheaded. She chose to have her head cut off and was taken to be executed on Tower Green on 12 February 1554, aged seventeen. She tied a cloth over her eyes and stumbled as she approached, unable to find the chopping block. A kindly onlooker guided her to the block and her head was duly severed.

London folklore

Henry Grey was executed two weeks after his daughter, Lady Jane. His mummified head is said to be hidden in a glass-topped box in the church of St Botolph-without-Aldgate.

All the fun of the fair

Londoners loved fairs, singing, dancing and playing music. Southwark Fair and BARTHOLOMEW FAIR were held every year, with puppet shows, CONJURORS, fire eaters, jugglers and other amusements. They loved to feast, and on coronation days a fountain near the Great Hall at Westminster would flow with French wine for everyone to drink. Londoners also loved watching BEAR BAITING, dog fighting, cock fighting and bull fighting, often held in Southwark's playhouses and theatres. Even Elizabeth I loved to watch these BLOODTHIRSTY sports. Wealthy merchants would organize great river pageants, complete with barges decked with banners, music and fine robes.

ELIZABETHAN PERFUMES AND DELICIOUS SMELLS

In Elizabethan London people hardly ever bathed or washed their hair. To mask their bad odours, perfumes and room scents were popular. These were made out of natural ingredients such as flowers, spices and oils.

Make rose petal perfume

6 handfuls of rose petals
10 drops rose essential oil

3 tbsp vodka
4 drops glycerine

- Put 500ml/1 pint water in a large saucepan and bring it to the boil.
- Add the rose petals and cover with a lid. Simmer for 2 hours.
- Strain the liquid through a muslin-lined funnel into a bowl.
- Measure out two mugs of this rosewater into another bowl.
- Add the vodka, glycerin and rose oil, and stir. If you want a stronger scent, add more drops of rose oil.
- Pour the perfume into glass bottles.

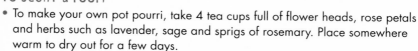

Make potpourri

Pot Pourri is a dried herb and flower mixture to scent a room

- To make your own pot pourri, take 4 tea cups full of flower heads, rose petals and herbs such as lavender, sage and sprigs of rosemary. Place somewhere warm to dry out for a few days.
- Raid the cupboard for strong smelling spices such as nutmeg, cinnamon sticks and cloves.
- Dry out some strips of orange or lemon peel.
- Put everything together in a pretty bowl.
- To make the smells last longer, add drops of essential oil such as rose or lavender.

Make an orange pomander

Tie some narrow ribbon around the middle of an orange. Then stick in cloves one by one until the orange skin is completely covered. You can do this in a pattern or just randomly. Hang the orange in a room and it will release a lovely spicy scent.

This sporting life

Many of London's royal parks are former **HUNTING** grounds of the Tudor kings and queens. Only the rich were allowed to hunt deer. Farmers could hunt foxes. The poor were only allowed to hunt hares and rabbits.

Henry VIII would sometimes spend five hours a day in the saddle. His daughter Elizabeth I also loved to hunt and was often to be seen riding on a fine horse in Epping Forest and Richmond Park.

Henry VIII enjoyed playing **TENNIS** and built courts at several of his palaces. The tennis he played was real tennis, which is one of the oldest racquet sports and was played indoors with a large net.

JOUSTING TOURNAMENTS were popular in Tudor times. Only the rich were allowed to joust: it was a sport for knights and lords. Heralds organized the joust, with opposing knights challenging each other. Riders fought in pairs, wielding lances, swords and axes. They were aiming not to kill each other but to destroy each other's weapons. Thousands would watch a joust, at 12 pence a ticket, and bet money on who would win. Henry VIII had a Tilt Yard for jousting especially built at Whitehall Palace.

TOP TEN TUDOR THINGS TO SPOT IN LONDON

✹ **TOMB** of Elizabeth I and Mary I at Westminster Abbey

✹ The **GLOBE THEATRE** on the South Bank

✹ King Henry VIII's **ARMOUR** at the Tower of London ✹ the **KITCHENS** at Hampton Court Palace

✹ **MIDDLE TEMPLE HALL**

✹ **STAPLES INN** High Holborn

✹ **TUDOR GALLERIES** at the National Portrait Gallery

✹ **DEER** in Richmond Park

✹ The **GOLDEN HINDE** at Borough

✹ The **ROYAL FUNERAL EFFIGIES** at Westminster Abbey

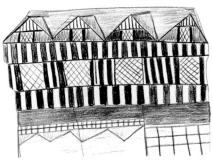

STUART LONDON
1603–1714

. . . .

By the 1600s, London was becoming a big and important city. But it was also a turbulent time. Londoners were to witness the execution of their king and live under the strict PURITAN rule of Cromwell's Parliament until 1660, when the monarchy was restored to the throne.

In 1665 a particularly virulent plague swept through London, wiping out a fifth of the population. It was called the GREAT PLAGUE. It was followed in 1666 by the GREAT FIRE OF LONDON, which razed the medieval City to the ground.

The City was rebuilt with stone houses, wider streets and a magnificent cathedral at St Paul's. A new wave of development began to the west around Covent Garden, Strand and Whitehall. The richer nobility abandoned the old City to live in more FASHIONABLE PARTS of west London in newly built grander houses. It was said that 'no gentleman ever went east of the Gaiety', a theatre at Aldwych.

Women rode in carriages, dressed in the latest fashions; men wore powdered wigs and tall hats. Londoners carried posies of rosemary and jasmine to mask the terrible smells of London's streets. The first CHOCOLATE shops and coffee houses were opening up. The diarist Samuel Pepys wrote of street market stalls piled high with nuts, GINGERBREAD, oranges and oysters.

London was a growing financial centre and the Bank of England was founded in the Mercers' Hall in Cheapside in 1694. The streets were lit for the first time: a new law in 1680 ruled that every tenth London house hang an OIL LAMP outside its front door to light the way. Elegant new stone buildings were built at Greenwich, Whitehall and Covent Garden. There was a new grandeur to the city.

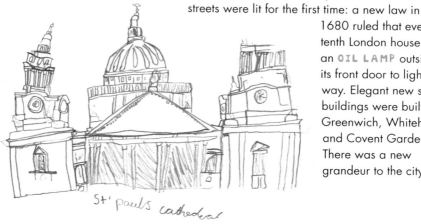

St' pauls cathedral

The English Civil War (1642-51) was between
PARLIAMENT and the royal family. CHARLES I was an extravagant king who argued with Parliament about money and in 1629 decided to rule the country without it. Parliament was furious and eventually a civil war broke out. Those on the side of the King were called the CAVALIERS; those on the side of Parliament and OLIVER CROMWELL were called the ROUNDHEADS.

Londoners sided with Parliament against the King. Charles I fled to safety and to rally support. He set up a rival capital city in Oxford from where he plotted his campaign. When he returned to invade London with his Cavaliers, he found it fortified against him: 6,000 tailors, 5,000 SHOEMAKERS, and 5,000 cappers and felt makers, along with their wives and children, had picked up shovels, dug trenches and raised DEFENCES across London to keep him out. A huge fortification was built at Piccadilly; guns were placed on every approach to the city. Even noble ladies lent a hand in the trenches.

Poor Charles lost the war in 1649 and was sentenced to death. He spent his last night in St James's Palace and walked through St James's Park with his little dog to Whitehall Palace, where his head was CHOPPED OFF on a public scaffold.

London, once a fun and flamboyant city, full of theatres, pleasure gardens, coffee houses and gambling, became an austere and serious place. Cromwell frowned on fun: theatre dancing, singing and celebrations, like CHRISTMAS, were banned and the bears in the bear pits were shot.

roundhead

There was once a grand 30-metre/100-foot maypole garlanded with flowers at the Strand. It was pulled down by Cromwell's Puritans, along with all the other maypoles in London.

The gruesome end of Oliver Cromwell

When Charles II was crowned king, and the monarchy was restored, he dug up Cromwell's body from his grave in Westminster Abbey. Although Cromwell was long dead, Charles ordered his body to be ritually hanged at Tyburn. The body was left hanging in chains. Later, Cromwell's head was cut off and stuck on a spike at the Palace of Westminster until 1685. His body was thrown into a pit.

Who reigned?

The Stuarts
James I (1603–25)
Charles I (1625–49)

The Commonwealth
Oliver Cromwell (1649–58)
Richard Cromwell (1658–9)

The Stuart Restoration
Charles II (1660–85)
James II (1685–8)

House of Orange
William III, Mary II (1689–1702)

The Stuarts
Anne (1702–14)

King Charles I

All you need to know about the Stuarts

- James I was the first **KING OF ENGLAND** and **WALES** who was also King of **SCOTLAND**. He was the son of Mary, Queen of Scots.
- James I passed a law forcing everyone to go to **CHURCH** on Sundays and commissioned an English translation of the Bible in 1611.
- Charles I was an extravagant king who had his **HEAD CUT OFF**.
- Oliver Cromwell was known as **LORD PROTECTOR** and ruled for nine years.
- Cromwell's son, Richard, took over for just nine months. He resigned and left the way open for Charles I's son to come back to England and claim the throne.
- Charles I's son returned from exile and walked back into London on 29 May 1660 to be crowned Charles II. This is known as the **RESTORATION**.
- Charles II was nicknamed the **MERRY MONARCH** and famously had a mistress who was a London actress called Nell Gwyn.
- Charles II's reign was dogged by terrible events: the **GREAT PLAGUE 1665** and the **GREAT FIRE OF LONDON 1666**.
- Charles II's brother James II succeeded him and was deposed by his own daughter, Mary, and her hunchback husband, William of Orange. This was part of the **GLORIOUS REVOLUTION** of 1688.
- **QUEEN ANNE**, Mary's sister, was the last Stuart monarch. She had eighteen children, but they all died when they were little, so she had no heir to inherit the throne.

Oak Apple Day

After the Battle of Worcester in 1651 the future Charles II had to hide in an **OAK TREE** to avoid capture by Cromwell's Roundheads. Ever since then, he has been associated with the oak. The oak symbol is on the helmets of the soldiers who guard the monarch. Every year at the Royal Hospital in Chelsea, they celebrate Oak Apple Day on 29 May to commemorate the **RESTORATION** of Charles II to the throne of England in 1660.

The number two on the clock at Horse Guards in Whitehall is painted black to commemorate the hour at which Charles I was executed in 1649.

It's a dog's life

This little dog is named after Charles II, who was often to be seen out walking his spaniels in St James's Park. King Charles spaniels were very fashionable among the English nobility. Ladies would use them as hot water bottles, holding them on their laps to keep them warm in winter as they drove in open carriages through London's streets.

King Charles Spaniel

RANDOM ROYAL FACTS

* Every day 86 tables were laid at Whitehall Palace for Charles I and his court. Enormous quantities of food were consumed. In one year, the palace chefs prepared a staggering 3,000 carcasses of beef, 7,000 sheep, 7,000 lambs and 24,000 birds.
* An extra throne was specially made for the coronation of William and Mary as they were both crowned. They are the only joint monarchs in British history. The spare throne is now kept in the undercroft at Westminster Abbey in a glass case.
* The unpopular William III died when his horse slipped on a molehill. Londoners were delighted and raised a glass to toast 'the little gentleman in black velvet'.

The story of Guy Fawkes and the Gunpowder Plot

Remember, remember the fifth of November,
Gunpowder, treason and plot,
I know of no reason
Why the gunpowder treason
Should ever be forgot.

Down in the cellars beneath the House of Lords, back in 1605, Guy Fawkes and his friends, angry about the treatment of Catholics in England, laid down barrels of gunpowder in an attempt to blow up the House of Parliament and kill the Protestant Stuart King James I. But Guy Fawkes was caught in the act and was duly tortured, hanged, drawn and quartered, his head placed on a spike on London Bridge for all to see. That night, 5 November, bonfires were lit across England to celebrate the survival of the King. Bonfire Night has been celebrated on 5 November every year since then, with effigies of Guy Fawkes traditionally burnt on top. Even today, the cellars of the Houses of Parliament are searched before the Queen enters the building to make sure there is nothing lurking below stairs.

Toilet trouble

Ordinary folk went to a privy (a hole in the ground over a pit) in the garden or in the basement of their house. Samuel Pepys wrote on 20 October 1660: 'Going down to my cellar . . . I put my foot into a great heap of turds'. Every night, a night-soil man would come to empty the privies.

Stuart Celebrities

christopher wren (1632-1723) is famous for rebuilding London after the Great Fire. He was very good at mathematics and was a scientist and an astronomer. He loved inventing things. He was also one of Britain's most important architects at a time when new kinds of design and new ways of building things were being worked out.

In 1675, Christopher Wren was given a Royal Warrant by the King to start his work rebuilding London. He took the footprint of the old medieval city and over the next thirty-five years, he slowly built fifty-one new churches, the Monument and the magnificent St Paul's Cathedral. Wren himself laid the first stone of the cathedral on 21 June 1675 and was sometimes hoisted up in a basket to see how the work was progressing throughout its construction. He would often visit the cathedral and was very upset to see that a safety rail had been placed around the dome. On one last visit, he caught a chill and died, aged ninety. His son wrote the epitaph for his tomb in the crypt of St Paul's: 'Lector, si monumentum requiris, circumspice', which translates as: 'Reader, if you seek his monument, look around you.'

> Never a cleverer dipped his pen
> Than clever Sir Christopher, Christopher Wren.

Daniel Defoe (1659-1731) was the son of a tallow chandler and was born in the slums of Cripplegate. He is famous for writing the great adventure book *Robinson Crusoe*, the story of a man shipwrecked on a desert island. It was one of the first novels to be written in English.

He also published fascinating accounts of two major historical events of the time: *The Journal of the Great Plague*, and *The Storm*, which recorded a terrible hurricane of 1703 that damaged swathes of London. He is buried in Bunhill Fields near the Barbican.

Samuel Pepys (1633-1703) was born in Fleet Street and grew up to witness some of the most momentous events in London's history. He wrote about them in great detail in his diary. Because of him, we know exactly what London was like at the time and how Londoners felt, what they thought and how they lived. He started writing when Charles II came to the throne in 1660. He documented the Great Plague and the Great Fire of London. His diaries were written in a secret code and were only deciphered about 200 years ago.

Samuel Pepys

The Great Plague

Outbreaks of plague were a constant threat and could wipe out thousands in one go. The disease was spread by **FLEAS**, carried by rats to every nook and cranny. In 1665, bubonic plague ravaged London on a scale no one had seen before, killing at least 70,000 Londoners and perhaps as many as 100,000. It was so bad that it was called the Great Plague.

It all began in a village just outside the City, **ST GILES-IN-THE-FIELDS**, where eleven people were taken ill. The disease spread quickly. The sick were shut in their houses and **RED CROSSES** were painted on their doors with the words 'Lord have mercy on us' to warn people away. Guards were placed at the doors to keep watch. Plague nurses visited the sick.

London's markets were closed down, schools, pubs and theatres were shut and a **CURFEW** was imposed so that people could not spread the plague from one to another. Only important people were allowed to travel. Those who could – the rich and the royal – left London. Charles II and his court **DESERTED** to Richmond Palace. Only urgent mail was delivered.

The authorities ordered **CATS AND DOGS** across London to be slaughtered, which sadly just made matters worse: the rats thrived, as there was nothing to kill them, and so did the fleas. What's more, it was a hot summer. Nothing could stop the plague in its tracks: at its peak 7,000 people a week were dying. The dead were loaded on to carts and thrown into great **PLAGUE PITS** dug on the outskirts of the City. The chances of surviving if you caught the plague were almost nil. There was no treatment or **CURE**. A cold winter brought the plague to an end. By February, the King and his Court dared to come back to London.

PLAGUE POTIONS

These are some of the things Londoners did to try and keep the plague at bay

✲ Hanging lavender and cloves around the house ✲ Making sweet-smelling pomanders ✲ Smoking tobacco ✲ Drinking alcohol ✲ Wearing a mask ✲ Wearing a good luck charm ✲ Purifying the air with bonfires

These are some of the things doctors did to try to cure people sick with plague

✲ Cutting the patient to bleed out the sickness ✲ Blistering the skin with red-hot irons or boiling water ✲ Giving them herbal potions ✲ Administering strange poo and clay mixtures ✲ Putting a toad in a bag on their stomachs ✲ Resting a live chicken's bottom on their sores

London's first . . .

The first recorded **DEATH FROM THE GREAT PLAGUE** in London was of a woman called Rebecca Andrews, on 12 April 1665.

London treacle

In the mistaken belief that it would protect them from the **HORRORS** of the plague, Londoners sniffed a **VILE** concoction of gunpowder, oil and sack (a kind of wine) up their noses. It was called London treacle.

Ring a ring o'roses is a nursery rhyme about the plague. A symptom of the plague was a red ring appearing on the skin. A posy of flowers protected you from others who were sick or the **SMELL OF DEATH**. The sneezing and the falling down refer to the disease taking hold and doing its worst. Children, holding hands, dance round in a **CIRCLE** chanting the rhyme, tumbling to the ground at the end.

> Ring a ring o'roses
> A pocket full of posies
> Atishoo, atishoo
> We all fall down.

RANDOM STUART FACTS

* Mary Ramsey, the woman who is said to have brought the Great Plague to London, is buried in St Olave's Church, Hart Street, in the City. The gate to the churchyard is guarded by stone skulls and bones. Charles Dickens called it the 'churchyard of Saint Ghastly Grim'. Samuel Pepys, the diarist, and his wife are buried there too, though they both survived the plague.
* Prince Henry's Room on Fleet Street is one of the oldest surviving houses in London. Inside is a small museum about Samuel Pepys.
* Ham House on the river at Richmond has the best-preserved Stuart interior in London.
* World-famous London hatters Lock & Co. started business in the City in 1676, moving to St James's, Piccadilly, a few years later, following fashionable Londoners who were rebuilding their lives away from the smoking ruins of the City after the Great Fire.

The Great Fire of London

In the middle of the night on **SUNDAY 2 SEPTEMBER 1666**, a fire broke out at the King's bakery on **PUDDING LANE** in the City. The fire took hold as none ever had before and raged out of control. The first person to die was the baker's maid who, too scared to jump out of the window to safety, perished.

The fire spread fast, gutting warehouses full of highly flammable pitch, tar, oils and cloth and destroying everything in its wake. A **STRONG EASTERLY WIND** fanned the flames along the narrow streets of timber houses. By breakfast time on Sunday morning, **300 HOUSES** had been destroyed. Every Londoner helped fight the fire: there was no fire brigade in London at the time. Boys from **WESTMINSTER SCHOOL** carried buckets of water to quench the flames of a burning church. Charles II rode through the streets on horseback, encouraging the people in their efforts and handing out money as a reward.

Thousands of Londoners fled to the country villages of Islington and Highgate. Others camped on the banks of the Thames. Some buried what possessions they could not take with them. Samuel Pepys, the diarist, famously hid his best **PARMESAN CHEESE** and a flask of wine in his garden in Seething Lane. Prisoners from London's prison at Newgate were evacuated across the Thames, many escaping along the way. **TWO HUNDRED CHILDREN** from Christ's Hospital School were evacuated to Clerkenwell. It took four long days and nights to put out the fire. By the end, four-fifths of the **CITY OF LONDON** had been destroyed – almost everything that lay between the Tower of London and the Temple, and as far north as the Roman wall; and 100,000 people were homeless and **HUNGRY**. The Tower of London was saved. Miraculously, **ONLY SIX** people died.

Writer John Evelyn walked to Highgate and Islington to see the homeless lying in heaps with their belongings and described them as 'ready to perish from hunger and destitution'.

DID YOU KNOW?

* The Olde Watling pub on the corner of Bow Lane and Watling Street was the first building in the City to be rebuilt after the fire.
* The scorch marks on the statue of London poet John Donne in St Paul's Cathedral are from the flames of the Great Fire. The statue was the only thing to survive the burning-down of the cathedral.
* The bones of an old watchmaker, Paul Lowell, who vowed he would never leave his house on Shoe Lane, were found in his cellar along with his keys.

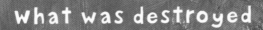

what was destroyed

13,200 houses

87 parish churches   St Paul's cathedral

BRIDEWELL PRISON   6 chapels

NEWGATE PRISON

3 CITY GATES

4 stone bridges   THE CUSTOM HOUSE

The Royal Exchange

52 livery company halls

London landmark: the Monument

The Monument is the tallest, isolated stone column in the world, standing 61 metres/200 feet tall. It was built so that no one would forget the horror of the Great Fire of London. Its height is the exact distance from where it stands on Fish Street Hill to where the fire started in Pudding Lane.

The Monument is crowned, like a giant candle, by a golden flame, symbolizing the fire. At the bottom there is a frieze that tells the story of the fire. The north side records London's destruction, and the south, its restoration. For many years, the Monument towered high above the skyline of the City.

There are 311 steps up the spiral staircase inside the Monument at Pudding Lane. If you climb to the top, you are rewarded with a certificate.

Rebuilding London

After the fire, the King decreed that London houses had to be made out of BRICK as well as wood, overhanging upper floors and thatched roofs were no longer allowed. London's first stone pavements were laid and STREETS were widened to stop fire spreading so rapidly ever again.

TOP TEN STUART THINGS TO SPOT IN LONDON

✳ BANQUETING HALL, Whitehall ✳ STATUE of Charles I, Trafalgar Square ✳ The MONUMENT, Fish Street Hill ✳ St Paul's CATHEDRAL ✳ A Cavalier King Charles SPANIEL ✳ GHASTLY GRIM CHURCHYARD, St Olave's Church, Seething Lane ✳ The Great Fire of London EXHIBITION at the Museum of London ✳ ROYAL HOSPITAL, Chelsea ✳ HAM HOUSE, Richmond ✳ The HOUSEHOLD CAVALRY MUSEUM at Horse Guards, Whitehall

ST PAUL'S CATHEDRAL

The magnificent St Paul's Cathedral, in the heart of the City, was built to replace Old St Paul's which burnt down in the Great Fire of London 1666. The new cathedral was modelled on the fashionable domed cathedrals of Europe: Sir Christopher Wren, the architect who designed it, had travelled to Paris and admired what he saw. One of Sir Christopher Wren's designs for the new St Paul's included a stone pineapple 18 metres (60 feet) high on top of the dome.

Charles II chose the final design and it took another thirty-five years to complete. The cathedral was officially declared finished in 1710. Wren was the first architect in the world, since 587, to see his cathedral finished in his lifetime.

fantastic facts

- The first cathedral on the site of St Paul's was built about 1400 years ago.
- St Paul's was the first triple-domed cathedral in the world.
- The great dome is the second largest in the world, after St Peter's in Rome.
- The great dome of St Paul's weighs as much as 65,000 elephants.
- The golden ball and cross on top weighs 7 tonnes and has room inside for ten people.
- The organ has over 7,000 pipes. Some of them are large enough for children to crawl through.
- Wren's St Paul's Cathedral cost £7,000 to build, the equivalent of £85 million today.
- The finished cathedral is as high as twenty-five double-decker London buses piled on top of one another.
- The foundations of the cathedral are only 1.3 metres/4½ feet deep.
- St Paul's Cathedral is said to have been built on the site of a Roman temple to Diana.
- 528 steps lead up to the Golden Gallery and a fine view of London.

The Whispering Gallery, underneath the lip of the dome, has special sound-travelling qualities: someone whispering into the wall on one side of the dome can be heard loud and clear from the opposite side.

Georgian and Regency London
1714–1837

B y the 1720s, London was getting smarter and **GRANDER**. Fine squares such as Bloomsbury, Cavendish, Mecklenburgh and Fitzroy were built around a central garden and edged with graceful terraced houses. Front doors were raised from street level with steps so that a lady could step into her carriage without muddying her large hooped skirt or dainty shoes.

Posts marked the way for pedestrians. Every house that looked on to the street had to light a **LANTERN** from six in the evening till eleven at night between Michaelmas and Lady Day. But the side streets and alleyways were still dark and dangerous and were the hangouts of London's thieves.

Country merchants owned London houses and shopkeepers and craftsmen came to town to serve the gentry. **FINE PASTRY SHOPS** and elegant grocers such as Fortnum & Mason graced the streets of Mayfair and St James's to serve the new rich and nobility of west London. Ladies spent their days playing cards and arranging parties. It was fashionable to ride in a carriage on a summer's evening to the new **SERPENTINE LAKE** in Hyde Park, the upper classes' favourite place to meet. Coffee houses were the favourite places for men to gather and talk about business and the politics of the day. Gentlemen **DUELLED** with swords to settle their arguments, in the Field of the Forty Steps behind the British Museum.

Rich men wore brightly coloured waistcoats in the latest designs, breeches, long jackets and buckled shoes. Women wore **ENORMOUS HATS** and low-cut dresses. Both men and women wore wigs; the men's were long and powdered. Daily newspapers started for the first time, passed from hand to hand and read aloud in taverns and coffee houses.

By the end of the century, nearly a million people lived in London. It was now the **LARGEST** city in the world.

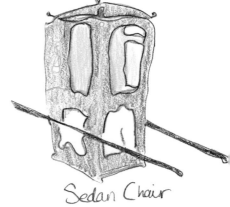

Sedan Chair

Who reigned?

House of Hanover
George I (1714–27)
George II (1727–60)
George III (1760–1820)
George IV (1820–30)
William IV (1830–37)

All you need to know about the Georgian monarchs

- Queen Anne had died without an heir, so **ROYAL COUSINS** were summoned from Germany to take over the English throne.
- The first King George didn't show much interest in England and did not even bother to **LEARN ENGLISH**.
- **GEORGE II** could manage a few English **SWEAR WORDS** that he used rather too often.
- **GEORGE III** was twenty-two years of age in 1760 when he became king.
- George III lost control of the American colony in the **AMERICAN WAR OF INDEPENDENCE (1775-83)**.
- George III reigned for sixty years. His nickname was **MAD KING GEORGE** because in old age he suffered from an illness called porphyria, which made him lose his mind and behave oddly.
- His son, also called George, was **PRINCE REGENT** for many years while his father was ill and took over the affairs of state. This was called the Regency Period (1811–20) and lots of London built at that time is named after him: Regent Street, **REGENT'S PARK** and Regent's Canal.
- When he finally became king, George IV reigned for just ten years.

DID YOU KNOW?

- George III and Queen Charlotte stopped their carriage to wave at nine-year-old Wolfgang Amadeus Mozart as he walked through St James's Park with his father.
- The London May Fair was held every year for over two weeks at the place we now call Mayfair.
- Street lighting was so unusual in European cities at this time that a visiting German prince thought the streets of London had been lit especially for his visit.
- Gin was the favourite alcoholic drink of Georgian Londoners.

★ LONDON LINGO ★

★ In eighteenth-century London, men wore vast wigs.
The higher and larger the wig, the more important you were.
Very important people were known as big wigs.
★ A Tyburn top was a kind of wig with the fringe brushed forward to
hide the face, worn by somewhat dodgy characters on London's streets.

A child's life

All well-to-do Georgian children wore **DRESSES** until the age of five, whether they were a boy or girl. Boys would exchange their dresses for breeches in a coming-of-age tradition called breeching. From then on boys dressed just like their fathers. Wealthy girls had to wear tight corsets, **IRON COLLARS** and backboards to improve their posture. There are accounts of girls who were so tightly laced that their ribs began to grow into their **INTERNAL ORGANS**.

As well as playing with the usual ball and hoop, cards and dolls, children played some rather mean games. Popular ones were **CONQUERING SNAILS**, where snails were smashed against one another, or catching mayflies and threading them together to stop them flying away. Pets were popular and might include a song thrush caught on Hampstead Heath or a **MARMOSET MONKEY** dressed in clothes.

Tough times

Unlucky children worked as SERVANTS and were sometimes cruelly treated. Famously, fourteen year old MARY CLIFFORD joined the household of ELIZABETH BROWNRIGG in 1766 in Fetter Lane. She was SAVAGELY BEATEN and starved and kept locked in a dark cellar at night. She was found locked in a cupboard with terrible injuries and died at St Bartholomew's Hospital. Elizabeth Brownrigg was HANGED at Tyburn in 1767. Her body was dissected at Surgeon's Hall and her SKELETON was left to hang there as a permanent exhibit. She was known as the CRUELLEST MISTRESS IN LONDON.

One of the first books just for children was
published, called *A Little Pretty Pocket-Book*,
which was sold with a ball for boys and
a pincushion for girls.

Parish orphans Some orphans were looked after by a church parish. The children were often NAMED after the places where they were found. Covent Garden parish registers are filled with names like MARY PIAZZA and PETER PIAZZA, after the market square.

The story of the Foundling Hospital

London was full of poor people and lots of families had more children than they could look after. Returning sea captain Thomas Coram was so shocked to see homeless and hungry children on the streets of London that he set up the Foundling Hospital at Coram's Fields in 1739. Mothers handed over their new-born babies to the hospital. A lottery system was set up as demand was so high, and each mother would have to pluck a coloured ball out of a bag to see if her child would be taken. Every baby was given a new name: boys were given names inspired by heroes or from the Bible; girls were given virtuous names like Hope, Faith and Charity.

Treasured tokens left by the mothers of the abandoned babies are on display at the Foundling Museum in Bloomsbury.

Toilet trouble

Most people had a chamber pot or a GUZUNDER (goes under the bed) for night-time emergencies. If you were very well-to-do, you could get your servants to bring your CHAMBER POT to you, so that you could go even while you were enjoying a meal with friends at the dinner table. This was a fine eighteenth-century tradition. Filled pots were left in panelled cupboards in dining rooms for removal later.

Georgian London firsts

* The first London attempt at hot-air ballooning was from Moorfields when an Italian called Signor Vincent Lunardi took to the skies on 15 September 1784.
* One of London's first postal systems was at Fortnum & Mason on Piccadilly, set up in 1794. It had letterboxes where post was collected six times a day. This system lasted until 1839.
* The first purpose-built art gallery in England was founded in 1811 in Dulwich.
* The first London University was established in 1826, when University College opened. It was set up to welcome students of any religion. The universities of Oxford and Cambridge only admitted students who were Protestant at that time.

London's pleasure gardens

Pleasure gardens were created at **VAUXHALL** and at **RANELAGH** in Chelsea for entertaining Londoners of all kinds. These were extravagant and **EXOTIC** places, where for a shilling, you could enter a **MAGICAL WORLD**. At Vauxhall, the trees were hung with lamps, **FOUNTAINS** were illuminated, orchestras played and people feasted together. You could stroll down the dimly lit Lover's Lane, visit the Hermit's Cottage or the **CHINESE TEMPLE**, or gaze at shows under the Umbrella, a giant canopy. Musicians hid in bushes playing **FAIRY MUSIC**. On special days, there were **HOT AIR BALLOON** ascents, fireworks, **ROPE WALKERS** and jugglers. Ranelagh Gardens was an altogether more upmarket pleasure garden. Prime Minister Horace Walpole was heard to say, 'You can't set your foot without treading on a Prince, or the Duke of Cumberland.' In 1765, the nine-year-old Mozart performed in the Rotunda at Ranelagh Gardens.

The story of Madame Tussauds

Marie Tussaud came to London from Paris with a travelling show of wax models of public heroes and rogues that she had made herself. She had escaped execution in the French Revolution of 1789 and proved her allegiance by making wax death masks of the executed nobles and her former employers, the King and Queen of France. Madame Tussauds opened in 1835 on Baker Street as a permanent exhibition for her growing collection of waxworks, which people could see for sixpence a ticket. A separate room where gruesome relics were displayed was named the Chamber of Horrors. Later Madame Tussauds moved to Marylebone Road.

Georgian Celebrities

George Frideric Handel (1685-1759) was one of the great Georgian composers. He was German, but he loved London so much that he lived here, in Brook Street. Handel's *Water Music* was played for the first time on a barge on the Thames for George I. The King was delighted and he insisted the musicians repeat the whole piece three times until they were exhausted. His work *Zadok the Priest*, composed for the coronation of George II, is still played when a monarch is crowned. Handel often organized fundraising concerts for Thomas Coram's Foundling Hospital and he left the rights to *The Messiah* to it in his will.

William Blake (1757-1827) a poet, painter and print maker was born at 28 Broad Street (now Broadwick Street) and was the son of a draper. When he was eleven years old he went to Par's Drawing School in the Strand and he became an apprentice engraver. An eccentric and radical thinker, his work was not appreciated and he was buried in an unmarked grave at the dissenters' burial ground at Bunhill Fields. Now he is recognized as a great London artist and his art is on display at Tate Britain.

Mary Wollstonecraft (1759-97) Born in Spitalfields, she was one of the first women to write about the unfairness of how women were treated. She was best known for her book *A Vindication of the Rights of Woman* (1792), in which she argued that men and women should be treated equally. She set up a school for girls in Newington Green and travelled to Paris shortly after the French Revolution. She fell in love with the philosopher William Godwin. They lived next door to each other in two houses in Somers Town, Camden. She died after giving birth to his daughter, the future Mary Shelley, author of the famous horror story *Frankenstein*.

William Hogarth (1697-1764) was a printmaker, engraver, artist and cartoonist who drew lively, often comic pictures of London street life. He was born at Bartholomew Close, son of a poor Latin teacher. His father had opened an unsuccessful coffee house where the customers could only speak Latin and he went to the debtors' prison for five years as a result. Familiar with the rougher side of life, William Hogarth drew scenes of poverty and gin drinking on London's streets. His self-portrait (1745) with his pug dog hangs in Tate Britain. He spent his last days in his country house at Chiswick and is buried in St Nicholas's Churchyard.

Dr Samuel Johnson (1709-84) is famous for writing one of the earliest dictionaries of the English language in the attic of his house in Gough Square. It took him nearly nine years. If he didn't like the usual meaning of the word he changed it. He is remembered for coining the phrase 'When a man is tired of London, he is tired of life.' He had a cat called Hodge and was often found drinking at Ye Olde Cheshire Cheese, a pub near his house. His favourite chair is still at the pub. He would often meet a writer called Boswell in coffee houses in Covent Garden. Boswell later wrote Dr Johnson's biography.

★ LONDON LINGO ★

Dr Johnson's dictionary definitions:

Jobbernowl = Blockhead
Lexicographer = A writer of dictionaries, a harmless drudge
Pastern = The knee of a horse
(This is wrong and when asked how he managed to make such a mistake he said,
'Ignorance, madam, pure ignorance.')
Kickshaw = A dish so changed by the cookery that it can scarcely be known
Far-fetch = A deep stratagem, a ludicrous word
Oats = Food given in England to horses,
and in Scotland, to men

London's best Georgian houses to snoop around

- John Soane's House, Lincoln's Inn Fields • Dr Johnson's House, Gough Square
- Handel House Museum, Brook Street
- Queen Charlotte's Cottage, Kew Gardens • Keats' House, Hampstead
- Dennis Severs' house, Spitalfields • Kenwood House, Hampstead
- Hogarth's House, Chiswick

Ssshhh!

SECRET GEORGIAN LONDON

- Queen Anne's Gate is the finest Georgian street in London.
- There is a pub on Charles Street in Mayfair, an important area in Georgian London life, called the Only Running Footman.
- Wolfgang Amadeus Mozart was living at 80 Ebury Street when he composed his very first symphony.
- Burlington Arcade off Piccadilly was Britain's very first shopping arcade. It opened in 1819.
- Hatchards bookshop on Piccadilly is the oldest surviving bookshop in Britain, founded in 1797.
- A perfect example of a Georgian shop in London can be found at 56 Artillery Lane, Spitalfields. Back in 1756, it was a luxury shop selling silks made by the Huguenot weavers who lived and worked there.
- Dennis Severs' meticulous restoration of a Huguenot weaver's house at 18 Folgate Street in Spitalfields is a magical and atmospheric treat.

A poem about London . . .

COMPOSED UPON WESTMINSTER BRIDGE

Earth has not anything to show more fair:
Dull would he be of soul who could pass by
A sight so touching in its majesty:
This City now doth like a garment wear
The beauty of the morning; silent, bare,
Ships, towers, domes, theatres, and temples lie
Open unto the fields, and to the sky,
All bright and glittering in the smokeless air.
Never did the sun more beautifully steep
In his first splendour, valley, rock, or hill;
Ne'er saw I, never felt a calm so deep!
The river glideth at his own sweet will:
Dear God! the very houses seem asleep;
And all that mighty heart is lying still!

William Wordsworth, 1802

Coade stone Lion

Steak and ale pie

Londoners loved to eat pies. Here is a traditional recipe.

1.25kg/2.2lb cubed beef
plain flour
salt and pepper
250g/8oz chopped mushrooms
2 large chopped onions
2 cloves of crushed garlic
vegetable oil
50g/2oz butter

400ml/14fl oz brown ale
300ml/10fl oz beef stock
2 bay leaves
2 sprigs of thyme
a handful of parsley, chopped
1 tbsp tomato purée
1 tbsp Worcestershire sauce
500g/1lb puff pastry

- Coat the beef in flour seasoned with salt and pepper.
- Soften the mushrooms, garlic and onions in oil and half the butter. Set aside.
- Fry the beef to brown and seal. Add the ale, the mushrooms, garlic and onions, the beef stock, bay leaves, sprigs of thyme, tomato purée and Worcestershire sauce to the beef. Stir and bring to the boil. Then simmer with a lid on it for 2 hours.
- When the stew is ready, use a slotted spoon to place the ingredients in an ovenproof pie dish. Reduce the remaining liquid, and when it has thickened to a gravy pour it over the other ingredients with the chopped parsley. Leave to cool.
- Preheat the oven to 200°C/400°F/gas mark 6. Roll the pastry to fit the top of the dish and top the stew with it. Put the pie in the oven to cook for 30 minutes.

LONDON AND THE SLAVE TRADE

For hundreds of years London was one of the most important slave ports in the world. Ships left the city carrying goods to trade, such as cotton, guns, gunpowder ammunition, ironware, alcohol and trinkets. These were exchanged in West Africa for slaves, who were brought back to London before being sold and transported in ships in terrible conditions. Up to 12 million African people were traded as slaves across the globe. 3000 slave ships left London's ports.

Many of the slaves ended up on plantations in America. There the now empty ships loaded up with cargoes of sugar, tobacco, rice, cotton, tea, ginger, sugar, pearls and hides, to sell to London merchants.

By the eighteenth century, many people were reacting with horror to the scale and inhuman cruelty of the slave trade. The philanthropist William Wilberforce led the campaign to stop this terrible trade in human life. The slave trade was finally abolished in Britain in 1807.

Slave child

There is a plaque on the wall of St Margaret's Church, Westminster, commemorating the baptism of a fourteen-year-old boy called OLAUDAH EQUIANO on 9 February 1759. He was a slave who was kidnapped in Nigeria and worked on a plantation in America. He came to London as the slave of a kindly Englishman, who taught him to read and write and allowed him to buy his freedom. He wrote a book called *The Interesting Narratives of the Life of Olaudah*, published in 1789. It caused a sensation, as it revealed the full horror of slavery. It shocked Londoners to the core and helped bring slavery to an end.

DID YOU KNOW?

* After the American War of Independence, in 1783, slaves from the United States came to London hoping for a better life.
* There were as many as 1,100 black Americans living in London in 1786.
* 400 black Londoners who were freed slaves settled in Sierra Leone, Africa, in 1787. They built a new home called Freetown.

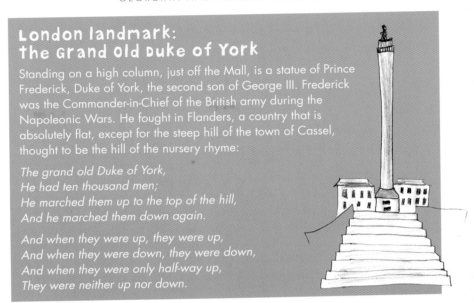

London landmark: the Grand Old Duke of York

Standing on a high column, just off the Mall, is a statue of Prince Frederick, Duke of York, the second son of George III. Frederick was the Commander-in-Chief of the British army during the Napoleonic Wars. He fought in Flanders, a country that is absolutely flat, except for the steep hill of the town of Cassel, thought to be the hill of the nursery rhyme:

The grand old Duke of York,
He had ten thousand men;
He marched them up to the top of the hill,
And he marched them down again.

And when they were up, they were up,
And when they were down, they were down,
And when they were only half-way up,
They were neither up nor down.

World's first museum

A wealthy doctor called Hans Sloane lived in Bloomsbury Place. He was a collector of objects from all over the world and was visited by the great and the good. He was outraged when the composer GEORGE FRIDERIC HANDEL came to tea and put a BUTTERED MUFFIN on one of his precious books. He collected so many things that he moved to a big house in Chelsea. Sloane Square is named after him. On his death in 1753, he left over 71,000 books, natural history specimens, coins and medals to the nation, the first collection of the new BRITISH MUSEUM. Its doors opened in 1759, as the first national public museum in the world. Entry was free to 'all studious and curious persons'.

TOP TEN GEORGIAN THINGS TO SPOT IN LONDON

✸ SERPENTINE LAKE, Hyde Park ✸ FORTNUM AND MASON, Piccadilly ✸ QUEEN ANNE'S GATE, Westminster ✸ ROYAL ACADEMY OF ARTS, Piccadilly ✸ FOUNDLING MUSEUM, Coram's Fields ✸ SUGAR AND SLAVERY at the Museum of London, Docklands ✸ YE OLDE CHESHIRE CHEESE pub, Fleet Street ✸ DULWICH PICTURE GALLERY ✸ GEORGIAN CLOTHES at the Victoria and Albert Museum ✸ REGENT'S CANAL at Regent's Park

Victorian London
1837–1901

T he population of London exploded from 1 million to almost 7 million people in 100 years. London was BURSTING at its seams: the houses were overcrowded and three-quarters of Londoners were horribly poor. Almost half the London funerals in 1830 were for children under ten.

Victorian Londoners tried to make the best of life. Business was booming. Children watched puppet shows, acrobats, organ grinders and jugglers and grown-ups visited the PENNY GAFF to see a show or dancing. Dozens of new theatres were springing up in the West End, and plays by playwrights such as Oscar Wilde delighted audiences. The GREAT EXHIBITION in 1851 brought the wonders of the world to London. The Natural History Museum, the Science Museum and the Victoria and Albert Museum opened soon afterwards on the Cromwell Road. Harrods department store flourished and was employing 100 people by 1880.

London was becoming an ever more civilized place: pavements were now everywhere, streets were widened, and the first ELECTRIC STREET LAMPS lit the way. Fine embankments were built on the Thames and the world's first Tube trains rattled their way underneath them. A complex system of SEWERS was built under London for the first time and new bridges straddled the the Thames. Grand railway stations were opened at Cannon Street, Victoria, St Pancras, King's Cross and Waterloo. Hospitals, schools, public baths and libraries sprang up across the city. London was the GLOBAL CENTRE of trade and finance. It was undoubtedly the most important city in the world.

St Pancras Station

Who reigned?

Victorians
Queen Victoria (1837–1901)

All you need to know about Queen Victoria

- Victoria was born at Kensington Palace on 24 May **1819**.
- The young princess was christened in a private ceremony in the Cupola Room of **KENSINGTON PALACE** and spent a restrictive and unhappy childhood there.
- When she was a child she had a King Charles spaniel called **DASH**.
- Victoria was only **EIGHTEEN** when her uncle, William IV, died and she came to the throne. She was an only child.
- The Hanoverian monarchs also reigned over a small part of Germany called Hanover. They did not allow women to rule their land, so Victoria was only Queen of **GREAT BRITAIN** and the Empire.
- The Queen was the first monarch to live at **BUCKINGHAM PALACE**.
- Victoria is the **LONGEST REIGNING** monarch in British history.
- There were several **ASSASSINATION** attempts on her life.
- Victoria used the newly discovered pain-relieving **CHLOROFORM** for the birth of her eighth child, Leopold, in 1853. She was so pleased with its results she used it for the birth of her last child, Beatrice, as well.
- When her dear husband, **ALBERT**, died in December 1861, Victoria was devastated. She wore black clothes as a sign of mourning for the rest of her life. She hardly ever stepped foot in London again.

Places named after Queen Victoria in London

VICTORIA PARK   Victoria station

VICTORIA AND ALBERT MUSEUM

VICTORIA EMBANKMENT

Queen Victoria Street   Victoria Tube line

VICTORIA ROAD   Victoria Street

Victoria Tower, Houses of Parliament

Royal Victoria Dock

Queen Victoria

DID YOU KNOW? · LONDON FACT · LONDON FACT · LONDON FACT ·

Black painted railings are everywhere in London. But they haven't always been black. The Victorians painted them all sorts of colours: bronze, dark blue and red were fashionable but green was the standard colour. When Prince Albert died in 1861 London railings were painted black, along with door frames, doors and window frames, as a sign of mourning his death. London's railings have stayed black ever since.

Not so deadly assassins

There were several bungled attempts on Queen Victoria's life: in 1840 a man called Edward Oxford fired two shots of his gun at the Queen while she was out horse riding on Constitution Hill with Prince Albert. He missed and was seized by onlookers. He was sent to a hospital for the insane called Bedlam.

Two years later Queen Victoria was riding in a carriage along the Mall when a man called John Francis pulled out his gun and pointed it straight at her. He didn't fire. The next day when she passed in her carriage he took aim and shot at her but was arrested by a policeman and convicted of high treason.

Two days later a man called John William Bean also fired a pistol at the Queen but this time it was loaded only with paper and tobacco. His crime was punishable by death but Prince Albert thought this too harsh and he was sentenced to eighteen months in jail.

RANDOM VICTORIAN FACTS

* The grim, forbidding exterior of one of London's most famous workhouses for the poor can be seen in St Pancras Way near King's Cross, now the St Pancras Hospital.

* The white marble monument built in 1911 to honour Queen Victoria, which stands right outside Buckingham Palace, is nicknamed the Wedding Cake.

* The Victorian toyshop Pollock's continues as a magical toy museum at 1 Scala Street, Fitzrovia. There is a new Pollock's shop in Covent Garden that sells old-fashioned toys, theatres and puppets.

* In the pavement in front of many old London houses are round metal coal-hole covers. At a time when houses had real fires in every room to keep them warm, the coal man would regularly tip sackfuls of coal directly down into the cellar, without coming into the house. Many of the covers are etched with the names and dates or just interestingly decorated with patterns. Some of the best are around Gordon Square, Bloomsbury.

London's Eiffel Tower

In 1880, Sir Edward Watkin ran a competition to design a tower for London that would compete with Paris's new Eiffel Tower. He called it the **GREAT TOWER OF LONDON**. The winning design was to be 46 metres/150 feet higher than the Eiffel Tower and was to be called the Watkin Tower. Sadly, the money and enthusiasm to build it ran out when only a fraction of it had been built. Its **FOUNDATIONS** are underneath Wembley Stadium.

stink bombs

Some Victorian street lamps were fuelled by gas from the sewers below the city, burning off the terrible smells at the same time. There is still a Webb Patent Sewer lamp on Carting Lane near the Savoy Hotel.

Victorian London firsts

* The first London Underground train travelled on the newly built Metropolitan line on 10 January 1863.
* The first escalator in London started moving at the up-market department store Harrods in 1878. A footman stood by with brandy and smelling salts to comfort those disorientated by the experience.
* The first successful UK telephone call was made from Brown's Hotel, Mayfair, by the telephone inventor Alexander Graham Bell in 1876.
* The first woman doctor in Britain was the daughter of a Whitechapel pawnbroker, Elizabeth Garrett Anderson, born in 1836. At the time, women were banned from medical school and she had to fight to get her training. She set up a hospital for women in 1872.
* The first pillar boxes in London were put up in Fleet Street, Strand, Pall Mall, Piccadilly and Portland Gate on 11 April 1855. The idea of post boxes was a new one, dreamed up by author and postmaster Anthony Trollope, a decade after the first postage stamps and penny post service began. Originally painted green, post boxes have been painted a distinctive bright red enamel since 1874. There are more than 150 different designs of post box. One of the prettiest is the hexagonal-shaped Penfold.

Victorian Street Urchin

A child's life

Well-to-do children were strictly brought up, were seldom seen and rarely heard. Looked after in a nursery by a **NANNY**, they were kept away from the family and were fed on food deemed suitable for children like boiled vegetables and **MILK PUDDINGS**. They were brought to see their parents in the afternoon for an hour.

Victorians freely gave children medicines and **POTIONS** to keep them quiet. They were dosed with Mrs Winslow's Soothing Syrup and Godfrey's Cordial, made of laudanum (a drug), alcohol and syrup.

Schoolboys were often **BEATEN** by their teachers. Boys at Temple Grove school in East Sheen would clutch a Latin grammar book between their teeth to stop themselves **SCREAMING** while they were being beaten.

children at play

Parlour games were popular and included word games, memory games, board games, cards, hide and seek, blind man's bluff and **HUNT THE SLIPPER**. Poor children would make their own toys, like spinning tops and rag and peg dolls. Rich children shopped at the new **HAMLEYS** Noah's Ark Toy Warehouse and other similar shops, bursting with new toys such as wind-up **CLOCKWORK SOLDIERS**, train sets, china dolls, jigsaw puzzles and jumping jacks. They played with shadow puppets and cut out **PAPER THEATRES** bought from Mr Pollock's amazing new toy store in Hoxton.

The writer Robert Louis Stevenson went to Benjamin Pollock's toy shop and wrote, 'If you love art, folly, or the bright eyes of children, speed to Pollock's!'

children at School

London's barefooted poor children did not go to school, as it cost a penny a day. Reformers wanted to change this. **DR BARNARDO** was a doctor who came to London's East End to treat the sick and was so shocked by the number of orphaned street children, starving and homeless, that he bought some canalside warehouses and in 1876 set up a free school called the Copperfield Road Ragged School to teach them. It became the largest **RAGGED SCHOOL** in London. Other ragged schools were set up across the city to teach children reading, writing and simple maths. They were also given food to eat: breakfast and dinner. Classes were huge, with 200 children to one teacher. Children left school at the age of ten. By 1870, a law was introduced to make sure all young children went to school for free.

Children at work

Most London children had to work to bring in some money for the family: three-quarters of Londoners were VERY POOR. From the age of four, children could be put to work in factories for SIXTEEN HOURS a day, six days a week. It was boring, hard, DANGEROUS, dirty and exhausting. Children did whatever they could to earn a penny: sweeping the streets, opening the doors of gentlemen's carriages or selling muffins, fruit and vegetables from a barrow from dawn 'till dusk.

The unlucky ones were CHIMNEY SWEEPS, forced up London's tall, narrow, crooked and sooty chimneys. Sometimes when children were too scared to climb them, their masters would light FIRES underneath them to make them move. Little match girls made and sold matches, coating them in POISONOUS phosphorus, which made them sick. Adventurous children worked as tumblers, street ACROBATS and entertainers. Tens of thousands of children lived on the streets and worked for gangs of thieves, like Fagin's gang in Charles Dickens's story *Oliver Twist*, PICKPOCKETING and stealing from the rich.

Muddy mudlarks

Mudlarks were mostly boys and girls between the ages of eight and fourteen who scavenged on the muddy banks of the Thames at low tide to see if they could salvage anything worth selling. They would pick up SCRAPS of metal and coal, pieces of canvas and wood. Mostly orphans, they would sleep rough in barges and sheds. What clothes they had were RAGGED, torn and patched – many didn't have a shirt or shoes to help keep them warm. If they were lucky they got a hunk of bread at breakfast and a pint of beer whenever they could afford it. They rarely had an evening meal.

Flower Girls

On a sunny summer Sunday as many as 400 girls would be on the streets selling posies of violets, primroses, wallflowers, stocks, pinks and carnations bought at London markets such as COVENT GARDEN. These are the words of a young flower seller recorded by the journalist Henry Mayhew:

'I pay 1s. for a dozen bunches . . .
Out of every two bunches I can make three, at 1d. a piece. We
make the bunches up ourselves. We get the rush to tie them
with for nothing. We put their own leaves round violets. The
paper for a dozen costs a penny, sometimes only a halfpenny.
The two of us doesn't make less than 6d. a day.'

Violets

Wall of heroes

Tucked away behind Little Britain at Smithfield is POSTMAN'S PARK, home to a special memorial called the Wall of Heroes. Each beautiful hand-painted tablet was put up to commemorate the heroic deeds of ordinary people. The artist William De Morgan designed the first plaques to be put up in 1900. These are the words on the tablet remembering the last acts of a very brave London boy:

SOLOMON GALANAN

Aged 11 Died of injuries Sept 6 1901 After saving his little brother from being run over in commercial Street.

MOTHER I SAVED HIM BUT I COULD NOT SAVE MYSELF.

The story of Henry Mayhew (1812–87)

One of seventeen children and the son of a London lawyer, Henry Mayhew cared a great deal about the poor and destitute in London. He spent months interviewing all kinds of ordinary Londoners: beggars, street entertainers, market traders, mudlarkers, children and adults alike. He described everything: their clothes, how and where they lived, their entertainments and customs, and the way they earned a living. He wrote it all down in his book London Labour and the London Poor, published in 1851. This had a big influence on the novelist Charles Dickens as well as on the politicians in government. As a result, new laws were brought in to protect children and the poor. Here is his eyewitness account of a Victorian London market:

Little boys, holding three or four onions in their hand, creep between the people, wriggling their way through, and asking for custom in whining tones. Then the tumult of the thousand different cries of the eager dealers, all shouting at the top of their voices, is almost bewildering. 'So-old again,' roars one. 'Chestnuts all'ot, a penny a score,' bawls another. 'An 'aypenny a skin, blacking,' squeaks a boy. 'Buy, buy, buy, buy, buy–bu-u-uy!' cries the butcher. 'Half-quire of paper for a penny,' bellows the street stationer. 'An 'aypenny a lot ing-uns.' 'Twopence a pound grapes.' 'Three a penny Yarmouth bloaters.' 'Who'll buy a bonnet for fourpence?' 'Pick 'em out cheap here! three pair for a halfpenny, bootlaces.' 'Now's your time! beautiful whelks, a penny a lot.'

★ LONDON LINGO ★

Footpad = A thief

Pickpocket = Someone who steals from passers-by

Smuggler = Someone who brings in goods from abroad without paying custom duties

Highwaymen = Someone who held up coaches at gunpoint to rob the passengers

Thief takers = Someone who was hired privately to catch criminals

Hanging judges = Judges who decided if you were to hang for your crimes

Mudlark = Someone who braved the mud of the Thames in search of things of value

Toshers = Children who scoured the sewers for things they could sell

Lurker = Someone who copied the handwriting of the rich to forge their letters

Dredger = Someone who dragged dead bodies out of the Thames

Forgers = Someone who makes fake documents and papers

Scapegrace = A rogue or rascal

Peeler, bobby = Policeman

The Story of the Pearly Kings and Queens

A boy called Henry Croft, raised in a Victorian workhouse orphanage on Charles Street, St Pancras, ran away at the age of thirteen to work as a road sweeper and rat catcher. He would watch the fruit sellers, called costermongers, with their pearl buttons sewn on to the seams of their trousers, and decided to make his own costume. He used as many pearl buttons as he could find, and covered his clothes from top hat to tails. People came from all over London to see this young man in his fabulous costume. He asked them to make donations, which he gave to the orphanage where he had grown up.

The costermongers thought this was a great idea. They sewed more and more pearl buttons on to their clothes to raise money for charity and called themselves the Pearly Kings and Queens. There are twenty-eight costermonger families who are Pearly Kings and Queens, one family from each borough of London. You can only be a Pearly King or Queen if you are a member of one of these families.

London's Pearly Kings and Queens still hold huge gatherings at St Martin-in-the-Fields church, Trafalgar Square, on the third Sunday in May and at the Pearly Harvest Festival in October.

LONDON'S GREAT EXHIBITION 1851

London's Great Exhibition was the most exciting show the world had ever seen. Opened by Queen Victoria on 10 June 1851, it lasted for five months and fifteen days. It was held in a **DAZZLING GLASS PALACE** in Hyde Park. The inspiration of Queen Victoria's husband, Prince Albert, it was to celebrate the best of the new inventions of the industrial age and the greatness of the British Empire.

Everybody flocked to see the extraordinary **CRYSTAL PALACE**. Famous visitors included Charles Darwin, George Eliot, Charlotte Brontë and Lewis Carroll. Ordinary people came in their thousands, including one old lady who walked all the way from Penzance in Cornwall and the captain of a Chinese junk ship moored in the Thames, dressed in full Mandarin robes.

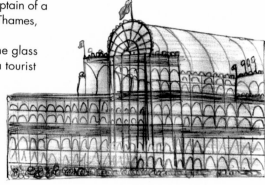

At the end of the exhibition, the glass palace was sold and set up as a tourist attraction in a park in Sydenham in south London. The Crystal Palace burnt down in 1936 and today nothing remains except a display of giant model dinosaurs in Crystal Palace Park.

fantastic facts

- Six million people visited the Great Exhibition.
- There were 100,000 objects on display.
- The exhibition displays stretched for 16 kilometres/10 miles.
- The glass palace was six times the size of St Paul's Cathedral.
- The centrepiece crystal fountain was made of 4 tonnes of pink glass and was 8 metres/27 feet high.
- Tickets were £3 for gentlemen and £2 for ladies for the first month, and then 'One shilling a head for the masses'.
- Tightrope walker Blondin thrilled the crowds with his daring rope act high above their heads.
- The exhibition made £186,000 profit, which was used to buy land for London's new Victoria and Albert Museum on the Cromwell Road.

The expression 'to spend a penny' was coined at London's Great Exhibition in 1851. Ladies and gentlemen made their way to the 'retiring rooms' to use the first public lavatories for the cost of one penny.

What everybody ate . . .

1,092 bottles of lemonade and ginger beer

36,000lb potted meat

37,700lb biscuits

33,456lb savoury pies

Five extraordinary exhibits

- The Koh-I-Noor DIAMOND, the biggest in the world, now part of the Crown Jewels
- A PRINTING MACHINE that could print 5,000 copies of the *Illustrated London News* in an hour
- A FOLDING PIANO
- The first FAX MACHINE
- An EXPANDING HEARSE

London landmark: The Royal Albert Hall

In the post-Great Exhibition rush to educate Londoners in the arts and sciences, the Royal Albert Hall in Kensington Gore was built in 1871. It was nicknamed the Nation's Village Hall. This round building famously had dreadful acoustics. It was once said it was the only place in Britain where a composer could be sure of hearing his work twice, because of the echo.

There were over 50,000 horses on London's Victorian streets, creating over 1,000 tonnes of smelly manure every single day.

Toilet trouble: the Lavender Men

For centuries most Londoners went to the loo in something called a **PRIVY**, usually a hole in the ground which drained into a cesspit. By the early eighteenth century nearly every house had a cesspit beneath the floors. **NIGHT-SOIL MEN** would come after dark to scrape dung from the cesspits and the streets and pile it high on their carts. It would then be taken away on barges from Whitehall pier to market gardens in Pimlico, or sold to families outside the city for fertilizer. The night-soil men were nicknamed the **LAVENDER MEN**, as they wore bunches of lavender around their necks to disguise the disgusting smell.

Ever since 1388 it had been illegal to dispose of human waste in any ditch or public waterway. But in 1815 the ban was lifted to enable waste to be carried to the Thames by way of open sewers. Human waste was dumped in the Thames and the contaminated water was pumped back for drinking, cooking and bathing.

By the 1850s there were more than 200,000 privies in London. The cesspits were overrunning and the river was becoming **SMELLIER AND SMELLIER**.

The GREAT Stink

By 1858 things in London had gone from bad to very smelly indeed. The hottest summer on record made the stench intolerable. The brand-new Houses of Parliament had opened on the river, but the putrid whiff was so great that nobody could bear to go near them. The curtains had been soaked in **CHLORIDE OF LIME** to disguise the smell, but this made little difference. The government made plans to move out to Hampton Court; the Law Courts planned to move to Oxford. The terrible odour became known as the **GREAT STINK**.

Members of Parliament decided that enough was enough: something must be done. They hired a man called Joseph Bazalgette as chief engineer to design and build London's first proper sewage system. Huge pipes would be built to carry the sewage well away from the city, up river, to the mouth of the Thames.

He began his great plan by building new embankments on the muddy tidal shore of the Thames, narrowing the river and reclaiming acres of land. He created a whole new road for London, parallel to the Strand, and shifted back the Thames from London. Underneath the Victoria Embankment he built an underground railway line, the District line, and below that, a fine sewer system. It was a remarkable feat of **VICTORIAN ENGINEERING**.

fantastic facts: sewers

- The engineer Joseph Bazalgette built six main sewers covering 160 kilometres/100 miles.
- 318 million bricks were used to build the sewers.
- 2.5 million cubic metres/88,286,666 cubic feet of earth were shifted.
- The sewers were built for a London population of 2½ million people.
- 4 million Londoners were using the sewers by the time they were finished in 1868.
- The shores of the Thames were reclaimed as embankments to avoid tunnelling under the smart West End.
- The granite used in the new embankments was from Lamorna Cove in Cornwall.
- Embankments on the Thames were first proposed by Christopher Wren in the 17th century.
- The Victoria Embankment and the Chelsea Embankment are on the north bank and the smaller Albert Embankment is on the south bank.
- There is a statue of Joseph Bazalgette in the Embankment Gardens.

Water Closet

HAHA!

THOMAS CRAPPER

London's sparkling new sewers led to a huge demand for water closets, the old-fashioned name for lavatories, and it became a golden age for the plumbing trade. One of the most famous was a man called Thomas Crapper (ha!ha!), who set up a company, Crapper and Co., to mass-produce lavatories and bathrooms at a price more people could afford.
The name Crapper can be seen on manhole covers in Westminster Abbey.

Victorian Celebrities

Charles Dickens (1812-70) was a hugely popular writer of stories that depict the Victorian London he knew and loved. As a child, he was forced to work in a blacking factory by the Thames while his family lived in the debtors' prison, Marshalsea. He saw all sides of life, walking for many long hours through the city as a young man. He worked as a lawyer's clerk, a court reporter and a journalist before writing his books. Many of his stories tell of the desperately hard lives of London children. He cared about social reform and justice. He lived in Doughty Street in Bloomsbury with his wife, Catherine Hogarth, and their ten children. He was so famous when he died that his grave at Westminster Abbey overflowed with flowers and mourners took two days to pay their respects by passing by his coffin. His novels have never been out of print. Particularly good ones about London are *Oliver Twist, The Old Curiosity Shop, A Christmas Carol, Martin Chuzzlewit, Little Dorrit, A Tale of Two Cities* and *Great Expectations*.

William Morris (1834-96) was an artist, designer, writer and publisher who founded the Arts and Crafts movement. Its followers wanted to get away from the new factory-produced goods that were flooding the shops and go back to the old ways of making and doing. Born in Walthamstow, as a boy he rode about in Epping Forest in a toy suit of armour and learnt all about nature, which he loved. His designs for wallpapers and fabrics feature flowers and leaves. He lived on the river at Hammersmith at Kelmscott House.

Kate Greenaway (1846-1901) was a famous illustrator of children's books. Her drawings of children in pantaloons, smock frocks, pinafores, mob caps and straw bonnets were so charming that the famous department store Liberty's of Regent Street copied the clothes to sell. Kate lived in Islington and Hampstead and is buried in the cemetery there.

Charles Darwin (1809-82) is famous for his book *On the Origin of the Species,* written in 1859. As a young man he was an avid collector of plants, insects and geological specimens. He travelled to the Galapogos islands on a ship called the *Beagle* as a naturalist and his study of finches there helped him to develop his theory of natural selection. His new ideas sent a shockwave through religious Victorian society. His work is the basis for the scientific theory of evolution.

★ LONDON LINGO ★

Victorian Londoners came up with the idea of speaking in a
secret code. This is called cockney rhyming slang. The code is
to use a phrase that rhymes with the word you mean to say.
In most cases the rhyming word is then dropped;

Apples and pears = Stairs – 'Up the apples'
Adam and Eve = Believe – 'I don't Adam and Eve it!'
Alan Whickers = Knickers – 'Keep your Alans on!'
Artful dodger = Lodger – 'My artful pays half the rent'
Barn owl = Row – 'I had a barny with my mate'
Brown bread = Dead – 'He was brown bread'
Rabbit and pork = Talk – 'He rabbits on a lot'
Plates of meat = Feet – 'Put your plates up and have a rest'
Ruby Murray = Curry – 'I'm so hungry I could murder a Ruby'
Two and eight = State – 'He was in a right old two and eight'
Whistle and flute = Suit – 'Do you like my new whistle?

christmas firsts

The Victorians absolutely loved Christmas and introduced for the first time many of
the traditions we still love today. In 1843 Charles Dickens wrote a story called *A
Christmas Carol*, which captured the spirit of Christmas in Victorian London.

- Largely thanks to Dickens, a new tradition of eating turkey for Christmas took off.
  The turkeys came to London on foot from Norfolk farms with their webbed feet
  wrapped in leather to protect them on the long walk. They had to set off in October
  to get to the city in time to be fattened up again for the Christmas table.
- Christmas trees were popular in Germany and in the royal family but didn't
  appear in London until Queen Victoria, Prince Albert and their children were
  pictured in the *Illustrated London News* in 1848, gathered around a beautifully
  decorated Christmas tree. Soon every wealthy family had one of their own to
  decorate with candles, sweets, fruits, gingerbread and small presents.
- Christmas cards became fashionable to send after a London art shop owner,
  Henry Cole, designed the first one in 1843.
- Crackers were pulled for the first time when they were
  invented by London sweet shop owner, Tom Smith. He
  created them in 1846, wrapping up his sugared almonds in
  a colourful twist of paper. He added love notes and mottoes,
  and made them go bang. Everybody loved them.

The eighth wonder of the world

Isambard Kingdom Brunel built London's – and the world's – first underwater tunnel in 1843. Deep under the Thames, running from Rotherhithe to Wapping, a tunnel like this had never been dug before. His father, MARC BRUNEL, had invented a new tunnelling shield technology to prevent tunnel collapse, and they were determined to try it. Even so, sewage seepage and flooding were a constant threat and Isambard came very close to DROWNING when the tunnel almost collapsed. Six men died in the terrible accident.

The tunnel took twenty years to build and was nicknamed the GREAT BORE, as Londoners lost faith that it would ever be finished. To cheer things along, Isambard once hosted a grand banquet in the repaired tunnel for his friends.

The THAMES TUNNEL was a huge hit with tourists and Londoners alike and the American travel writer William Allen Drew described it as 'the eighth wonder of the world'. But when it came to actually using it, few liked the idea of walking under the Thames and the tunnel was a financial disaster. Though it was designed for horse carriages, it was only ever used by people on foot. Damp and dark, it became a place where London's LESS DESIRABLE characters hung out. It was sold off to the East London Railway Company in 1865, much to everyone's relief, and is used by mainline trains today.

Isambard Kingdom Brunel's (1806-59) engineering feats have made him the most famous engineer in British history. He built the first propellar driven transatlantic steam ship; the first major railway line in Britain, the Great Western Railway; the first tunnel under the Thames and the first suspension footbridge across it at Hungerford. He also built Paddington station.

Henry Brunel, Isambard's baby son, was the first person to go through the Thames Tunnel when the connection was made between the northern and southern bores.

DID YOU KNOW?

✱ The sphinxes at the base of Cleopatra's Needle were positioned the wrong way round: they face the Needle, instead of looking away from it to guard it.

✱ There are winged sphinxes on the arm rests of many of the benches on the Victoria Embankment.

CLEOPATRA'S NEEDLE

Close to Blackfriars Bridge there is a distinctive Egyptian obelisk called Cleopatra's Needle, flanked by two sphinxes. It was given to London by an Egyptian ruler to celebrate Lord Nelson's naval victory at the Battle of the Nile in 1798, but it was not until 1877 that a generous man called Sir William Wilson stumped up the huge sum of £10,000 to pay for it to be finally shipped to London.

Encased in an iron cylinder, Cleopatra's Needle itself was turned into a small ship, with a rudder and a deck, called the *Cleopatra*, and was towed across the oceans by a bigger ship. But it was a perilous journey: there was a terrible storm in the notorious Bay of Biscay and the *Cleopatra* capsized. Six sailors lost their lives, but in a heroic rescue Cleopatra's Needle was saved from sinking to the bottom of the sea by a passing Spanish trawler. When it finally sailed up the Thames to London on a paddle tug called the *Anglia*, the city's excitement was so great that the children of Gravesend were given the day off school to celebrate its long-awaited arrival. It was 21 January 1878.

Cleopatra's Needle was taken to the new Victoria Embankment and erected for all to admire. Chillingly, it is said to be haunted. Ghoulish screams have been heard, and the ghost of a naked man leaping into the Thames has been seen by it.

BURIED TREASURE

A secret cache of treasure is buried under cleopatra's Needle:

A baby's bottle

Copies of the Bible in many languages

Children's toys

Some tobacco pipes

Some weights and measures

A BOX OF HAIRPINS

12 photographs of the prettiest English women of the day

A PIECE OF GRANITE FROM THE OBELISK   A portrait of Queen Victoria

A Whitaker's Almanac   A SET OF BRITISH COINS AND A RUPEE

Dr Birch's translation on parchment of the inscriptions on the obelisk   A map of London

THE STORY OF THE OBELISK'S JOURNEY TO LONDON

A BOX OF CIGARS   A shilling razor

A Bradshaw's Railway Guide   A bronze model of the obelisk

Copies of ten newspapers   A hydraulic jack and some wire cables used to raise the obelisk

The story of the bowler hat

The bowler hat is as much a symbol of London as the Post Office Tower. It was created in 1850 by Lock & Co. of St James's. A gentleman called William Coke commissioned a special new hat to protect his gamekeepers' heads while on horseback, as the top hats they usually wore were always being knocked off. Coke tested the strength of the hat by jumping on it to see if it would withstand his weight. It did and the gentleman was delighted.

The hat was originally called the Coke, in the age-old tradition of Lock & Co., who always called a new hat after the customer who commissioned it, but it soon became known as the bowler hat after the Southwark brothers Thomas and William Bowler, who manufactured it. At the height of the bowler's popularity 60,000 a year were sold. Essential wear for the Victorian working-class man, in the twentieth century it became popular with everyone from taxi drivers to landowners. It was seen as less posh than the top hat but more respectable than a felt hat, and no city gent was properly turned out without a pinstripe suit, a rolled-up umbrella, a briefcase and a bowler hat.

Immortalized by Charlie Chaplin, the detective twins Thomson and Thompson in the Tintin books, Mr Banks in Mary Poppins and Prime Minister Stanley Baldwin, the bowler has become an icon around the world. Bizarrely, though no longer fashionable in the streets of London, it remains to this day the favourite hat of Quecha and Aymara women in Peru and Bolivia. They have worn it since the 1920s, when it was introduced to Bolivia by British railway workers.

TOP TEN VICTORIAN THINGS TO SPOT IN LONDON

- CHARLES DICKENS'S HOUSE, Doughty Street
- ST PANCRAS STATION, Euston Road
- the ALBERT MEMORIAL, Kensington Gardens
- A Victorian PILLAR BOX
- BAKER STREET tube station
- WILLIAM MORRIS'S HOUSE, Hammersmith
- QUEEN VICTORIA'S BEDROOM at Kensington Palace
- CLEOPATRA'S NEEDLE, Embankment
- BRUNEL'S MUSEUM Rotherhithe
- Great Exhibition DINOSAURS at Crystal Palace Park

Edwardian and early Twentieth-Century London

I n 1900 London was the capital of the world's largest empire. It was the largest city in the world, bigger than rivals New York and Paris. London had changed beyond recognition in the space of just 100 years: it now had electric lights, cars, bicycles, railways, underground trains, public transport, sewers, clean water. It was a modern, enlightened city, and an exciting place to be. The glamorous RITZ HOTEL opened on Piccadilly in 1906, a far cry from stuffy Victorian life.

In 1914, the FIRST WORLD WAR broke out and the government called for men to enlist. There were already 80,000 Londoners in the armed forces but more were needed. Rallies were held in Trafalgar Square and to the chant 'Wake up, London!' columns of soldiers marched through London's streets to attract recruits.

London suffered bombardment by German aircraft, which dropped more than 900 bombs on the central area. 28,000 women were taken on to work at the Woolwich Arsenal armaments factory, replacing the men who had gone to war.

As the war ended, in 1918, a FLU EPIDEMIC raged over the world. In London, it killed 3,000 people in one week.

In the 1920s, London bounced back. Nightlife flourished in the West End, with jazz clubs, dancing and FLAPPER GIRLS. The new wireless radio broadcast for the first time from London's BBC studios. Cinemas were springing up on every street corner to screen the latest 'talkie' movies such as Alfred Hitchcock's *39 Steps*. Electric trains extended out to the suburbs, which were nicknamed METROLAND, the home of the new Londoner, the commuter.

London was lucky enough to largely escape the GREAT DEPRESSION that devastated the lives of many people in the rest of Britain. In 1936 ship builders marched from the river Tyne to the Thames to draw attention to their plight as unemployment soared. This was called the Jarrow March. At that time no work meant no money – there was no welfare state. Fascism in Europe was growing and the clouds darkened as the threat of a second world war loomed.

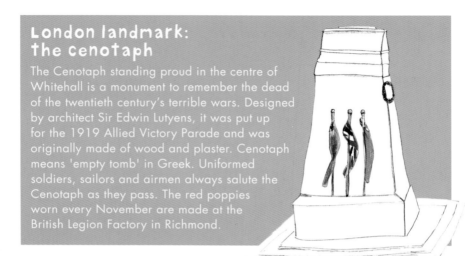

London landmark: the Cenotaph

The Cenotaph standing proud in the centre of Whitehall is a monument to remember the dead of the twentieth century's terrible wars. Designed by architect Sir Edwin Lutyens, it was put up for the 1919 Allied Victory Parade and was originally made of wood and plaster. Cenotaph means 'empty tomb' in Greek. Uniformed soldiers, sailors and airmen always salute the Cenotaph as they pass. The red poppies worn every November are made at the British Legion Factory in Richmond.

Who reigned?

House of Saxe-Coburg-Gotha
Edward VII (1901–10)

House of Windsor
George V (1910–36)
Edward VIII (1936)
George VI (1936–52)

Hyde Park corner was the codeword used to inform the government of George VI's death.

All you need to know about the Royals . . .

- EDWARD VII was the son of Queen Victoria. He was very fashionable and sociable, a sharp contrast to the reclusive old lady who had ruled for so many years.
- In 1917, during the First World War, when anti-German feeling was running high, GEORGE V changed the royal surname from the German Saxe-Coburg-Gotha to WINDSOR.
- George V made the first King's CHRISTMAS radio broadcast in 1932.
- His son, EDWARD VIII, was king for just 327 days in 1936. He wanted to marry an American divorcee, Wallis Simpson, but the Government and the Church of England would not allow it. So he abdicated, much to the disappointment of many Londoners.
- His brother, GEORGE VI, became king after the ABDICATION. He had not been expecting to rule.

The King's speech

George VI suffered from a bad stammer, which made it difficult for him to speak in public. An Australian speech therapist called Lionel Logue solved his problem with the use of exercises such as tongue-twisters. The King recognized Lionel Logue's help and friendship by awarding him the Royal Victorian Order.

Try a tongue-twister

Feeling footloose, fancy-free and frisky, this feather-brained fellow finagled his fond father into forking over his fortune. Forthwith, he fled for foreign fields and frittered his farthings feasting fabulously with fair-weather friends.

The story of the suffragettes

In 1907, 3,000 women trudged through the grimy streets of London to demand the right to vote. Back then women were not entitled to vote in a government election and they were not happy about this. The march became known as the Mud March and the women who protested were called the suffragettes. One of their leaders was Emmeline Pankhurst.

London was the focus of their anger. They threw stones at the windows of the Prime Minister's house, 10 Downing Street, and chained themselves to the railings on Whitehall. To draw attention to their cause, the suffragettes deliberately got themselves arrested and thrown into prison, and went on hunger strikes in protest. Cells under Mansion House in the City were used to imprison suffragettes. They burned buildings, broke shop windows in Oxford Street and damaged paintings in public art galleries. In 1913, Emily Davison threw herself in front of the King's horse at the races to draw his attention to their cause and was killed. Six thousand women marched through the streets of London to St George's Church in Bloomsbury to attend her funeral. Finally, in 1918, Parliament agreed to give wealthy educated women the vote. It wasn't until 1928 that all women were given the same political rights as men.

London landmark: the Oxo Tower

This old power station was given a makeover in the 1920s. It was owned by the makers of the Oxo Cube and they wanted to advertise their product on the side of the tower. Planning permission was declined but rather cleverly the architect came up with the idea of building four sets of three vertically aligned windows, which each happened to be in a different shape: a circle, a cross and a circle. Londoners have called it the Oxo Tower ever since.

The first nursery school

in Britain opened in a deprived part of Deptford in 1911. Two sisters, Rachel and Margaret McMillan, had new ideas about the importance of play for children and put them into practice at their open-air school.

The streets of London are paved with gold

Phyllis Pearsall, a determined woman who had the idea of publishing the first map of London's streets, spent the 1930s pacing the pavements, sometimes walking 29 kilometres (18 miles) a day. She kept her notes in cardboard boxes in her Dulwich home. When the book was complete no publisher wanted to print it so she published it herself, delivering the first copies to W.H. Smith in a wheelbarrow. She made her fortune: the book of maps was called the A-Z and is still the Londoner's bible for getting round the city.

20th-century London Firsts

* 1909 Britain's first aeroplane factory opened in Barking.
* 1912 The first non-stop flight from London to Paris.
* 1920 The first Imperial War Museum opened at Crystal Palace to display material about the Great War.
* 1928 London's first automatic telephone exchange opened in Holborn.

London's first red telephone box

The first London phone box was designed by an architect called Sir Giles Gilbert Scott in 1924. He won a Post Office competition to design a new telephone box to replace the ugly concrete kiosks called K1. All the entries were made up in wood and put on display outside the National Gallery. Scott's dome-shaped design was inspired by a mausoleum in **OLD ST PANCRAS** churchyard. He wanted the boxes to be painted silver on the outside with a greenish blue on the inside but they were painted red so they could be seen easily.

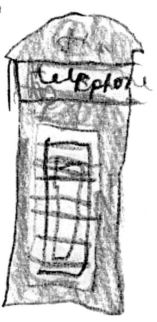

His winning design, called **THE K2**, has a perforated crown at the top for ventilation, is made of cast iron and has eighteen panes of glass on three sides. It was so expensive to make, at a cost of £50, that it was used only in London. A new design, the K3, was used in the rest of the country. There are just over 200 K2s left in London. The most common red phone box on the streets now is **THE K6**, which has an **EMBOSSED** crown rather than a perforated one.

One of Gilbert Scott's original London telephone boxes stands at the entrance to the Royal Academy of Arts, Piccadilly.

LONDON FACT · DID YOU KNOW? · LONDON FACT

✻ The writer George Orwell slept among tramps and shaved in the fountains at Trafalgar Square while researching for his book *Down and Out in Paris and London*, published in 1933.

✻ Until 1935, London's parks, commons and green spaces were regularly used for grazing sheep and cattle.

✻ The base of Cleopatra's Needle on the Embankment still bears the scars of the bombing Blitz on London in the First World War.

LONDON AT WAR 1939-44

London was an enemy target during both world wars. Much of London was blasted to smithereens and reduced to stones and dust by enemy bombing raids. During the Second World War George VI and his family stayed at Buckingham Palace in London throughout the Blitz, famously stating that if Londoners had to stay, so should they. The East End of London was the area most savagely attacked by the German bombers: 2,500 bombs were dropped on the docks and factories of the city. The royal family narrowly escaped death when a bomb exploded in the courtyard of Buckingham Palace, and the Queen declared: 'I'm glad we've been bombed. Now we can look the East End in the face.'

When Eleanor Roosevelt, wife of the American President Franklin D. Roosevelt, came to London during the war and stayed with the royal family, she complained about the tiny portions of rationed food, the limited bathwater and the lack of heating at the blacked-out Buckingham Palace.

Bombs and blackouts

The BLITZKRIEG is the German word for the lightning war that the Nazis waged on London. Londoners called it the Blitz. It is hard to imagine how people lived through this terrible assault on London. The city was bombed for 76 consecutive (with one exception) nights by the Germans from 7 SEPTEMBER 1940 to 10 May 1941. On the first night of bombardment the sky blackened with a swarm of 348 bombers and 617 FIGHTER PLANES. That night alone 448 Londoners were killed. As the nightly sirens sounded, terrified Londoners fled into SHELTERS in their basements and gardens. Children slept under iron tables at night. Some left London altogether and camped in Epping Forest to escape the terror. People were so scared that they stormed the TUBE STATIONS and demanded to be sheltered underground. While the bombs flew overhead, families would tell stories and sing songs to take their minds off the terror.

Strict BLACKOUTS were imposed every night, creating a darkness that Londoners were completely unused to. The daily bombing raids and broken nights took their toll on Londoners. Shops were LOOTED and bombed houses stripped of their valuables. Nonetheless, Londoners kept going with what became known as the Blitz spirit. To protect one of London's most precious symbols, and boost the city's morale, Prime Minister WINSTON CHURCHILL stationed special volunteer forces at St Paul's Cathedral to watch over it, day and night.

By the end of the Blitz over 20,000 PEOPLE had been killed and 1.4 million people had been made homeless.

Fascinating facts

- The worst night of fire bombs was 29 December 1940.
- The Houses of Parliament were bombed on the last night of the Blitz.
- Pied Piper was the code name for the evacuation of children from London to the safety of the countryside.
- A special suit was made for Prime Minister Winston Churchill by London tailors Austin Reed. Called the Siren Suit, it was an all-in-one suit he could pull on in under a minute so he could address the nation fully clothed at any time, night or day.

Pots and pans propaganda

Londoners donated their pots and pans, and even the railings in front of their houses, for the war effort, to be turned into weapons. This was in fact a propaganda exercise to boost morale: much of the metal was dumped in the Thames.

Ssshhh!

UNDERGROUND LONDON IN WARTIME

- Eight deep-level shelters were built in London's Underground during the Second World War to keep Londoners safe at night. Toilets, washing facilities and wooden bunk beds were built on the platforms and in tunnels and a Refreshment Special Tube train ran each night, delivering food and drink. The shelters are used as Tube stations today:

  - Belsize Park • Stockwell • Camden Town • Clapham North • Goodge Street
  - Clapham South • Chancery Lane • Clapham Common

- One of the most horrific events of wartime London happened in Bethnal Green Tube station while it was being used as a shelter. On 3 March 1943 a raid caused a panic among families rushing to safety. A woman tripped on the narrow stairs, causing the crowd to fall on top of her. 173 people, 62 of them children, were crushed to death.
- Goodge Street shelter was used by General Eisenhower as he prepared for the Normandy landings and the Allied invasion on D-Day, 6 June 1944.
- The Prime Minister and his cabinet worked from a secret bunker under Whitehall, known as the Cabinet War Rooms, instead of 10 Downing Street, because London was so dangerous.

children at war

If you lived in London and were of school age you
might well have been evacuated from London
to get away from the bombs dropping on the
city. This meant leaving your family and being
sent to stay in the country, most often with people you
didn't know at all. If you were very little, your mother could
go with you. If you were evacuated, you would have had a label
attached to you, just like a parcel. You would have been taken to a **RAILWAY
STATION** and put on a train with hundreds of other children to an unknown
destination. You would have had to be quite brave.

Once there, you would have been taken to the village hall to be picked by a
family who wanted you to come and stay with them. You might not have stayed
with your brothers and sisters. Some children were **BADLY TREATED** and made
to work hard, but some had a lovely time and didn't want to come back to grimy
London after the war. Every child had a **SWEET RATION** to keep their spirits up.

Lots of people didn't want to be evacuated. Even Princess Elizabeth and her
sister Princess Margaret stayed near London, at Windsor Castle. When asked why
she wouldn't send her children to safety, the Queen said, 'The children won't go
without me. I won't leave without the King. And the King will never leave.'

WHAT GIRLS HAD TO PACK:

A VEST   a pair of knickers   6 handkerchiefs   a cardigan   a blouse
a petticoat   TWO PAIRS OF STOCKINGS   a slip (like a very long vest)

WHAT BOYS HAD TO PACK:

a jumper   TWO PAIRS OF SOCKS   a pair of trousers
6 handkerchiefs   2 pairs of pants   2 VESTS

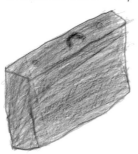

WHAT BOTH HAD TO PACK:

Coat   COMB   Wellington boots
TOWEL   facecloth   SOAP
toothbrush   shoes   PLIMSOLLS
SANDWICHES   packet of nuts and raisins
BISCUITS   barley sugar   an apple

children's writer Nina Bawden was a London child
living in the East End who was evacuated during
the war. She tells the story of what it
was like in her book *Carrie's War*.

Great escape

Nine months before the Second World War started, in 1938, England opened
its borders to 10,000 children, mostly Jewish, fleeing the **NAZI REGIME**.
The children were sent, without their parents, from Austria, Germany, Poland
and Czechoslavkia. Thousands of them arrived by a special train, called the
KINDERTRANSPORT, at London's Liverpool Street station.

Every year since 1947 the people of Norway have sent
Londoners a christmas tree, to say thank you for
Britain's support during the Second World War. This is
always displayed in Trafalgar Square.

War child

If you stayed in London and you were a **BOY SCOUT** or a **GIRL GUIDE**, you
would have helped in the war effort by collecting aluminium foil to be sent to
a munitions factory and made into guns; or you might have helped guide fire
engines towards fires created by the **FALLING BOMBS**. London children loved to
play in the rubble of the bombed-out houses during and after the war.

The story of the battle of Cable Street . . .

In 1936 the Black Shirts, a group of Fascists led by a man called
Oswald Mosley, decided to march through the streets of the East
End of London to galvanize support for the newly set-up British
Fascist movement. This was a deliberate and provocative move
against the Jewish people who lived here at a time when the Nazis
were threatening German Jews. 300, 000 East Enders – Jewish,
Irish, socialists and communists, men, women and children alike –
fought against the Fascist marchers and the police, throwing sticks,
rocks, chair legs, rubbish and even the contents of chamber pots at
them. Gathering at Leman Street, Cable Street and Aldgate, they
overwhelmed the marchers and forced them to turn back. It was a
victory for Londoners against the Fascist movement.

Post-war London
The rebirth of the city

A fter the Second World War much of London was a bombsite. One million houses in London had been destroyed. The city needed to be rebuilt. High-rise tower blocks replaced the bombed-out Victorian slums. All over London brand-new homes filled the gaps between the old terraced houses, complete with all the modern conveniences like bathrooms and indoor lavatories. It was a great opportunity for London to reinvent itself.

Who reigned?

House of Windsor
Elizabeth II (1952—)

All you need to know about Elizabeth II
- Elizabeth II became queen at the age of twenty-five in **1952**.
- She is the **FORTIETH MONARCH** since William the Conqueror.
- Elizabeth II was born at 17 Bruton Street, W1. She grew up at 145 **PICCADILLY**.
- Elizabeth II is the **OLDEST** ever reigning monarch of Britain.
- She is the second longest serving **HEAD OF STATE** in the world, after King Bhumibol of Thailand.
- Her favourite dogs are **CORGIS**.
- To celebrate the Queen's Jubilee in 1977 **TOWER BRIDGE** was painted red, white and blue.
- The first televised Royal **CHRISTMAS MESSAGE** from the Queen was in 1957.
- The Queen has **FOUR CHILDREN**: Charles, Anne, Andrew and Edward.
- She hosts three **GARDEN PARTIES** at Buckingham Palace every year, which over 30,000 people attend.

Royal break-in

In 1982, the Queen woke up at Buckingham Palace to discover a strange man at the end of her bed, drinking wine from the royal cellars and eating cheese and crackers. **MICHAEL FAGAN** was an unemployed builder who dared himself to break into the palace and succeeded. The Queen did not press charges against him.

The Festival of Britain

To cheer everyone up after the war the government dreamed up the idea of a great Festival of Britain as a 'tonic for the nation'. London was to host the festival on the South Bank near Waterloo station, and it opened in May 1951. There was a Dome of Discovery, then the largest dome in the world, and awe-inspiring exhibitions about the Living World, the Physical World, the Land, the Sky and Outer Space. An army Bailey bridge was put up over the river Thames to cope with the crowds crossing the river.

A rocket-shaped structure called the Skylon towered over the river bank. It was brightly lit at night, in dazzling contrast to the blackouts of the war. The first truly modern building, the Royal Festival Hall, opened with concerts with music by young British composers such as Benjamin Britten. The new Festival Hall was a striking emblem of the modern age and the festival showcased the latest urban design and architecture.

Poplar and South Kensington also hosted parts of the festival and there was a great fun fair at Battersea Park.

Sadly Prime Minister Winston Churchill hated the Skylon and had it scrapped in 1952.

London's Brutalist architecture

Post-war Britain needed new housing, shops and offices fast and cheaply. New methods of building were transforming the skyline in a new style called **BRUTALIST** architecture. The term was coined in 1953 from the French *beton brut*, which means **RAW CONCRETE**. The buildings are distinctive because their concrete surface is left exposed and rough looking.

BEST BRUTALIST BUILDINGS IN LONDON

The Festival Hall   THE HAYWARD GALLERY

The Barbican   Pimlico School

Trellick Tower   The Royal National Theatre

LONDON SMOG

London has always had a reputation for being a foggy place because of the terrible smogs that plagued the city at a time when everyone had raging coal fires in their hearths and there were still lots of factories in the capital. Sometimes the air was so thick with this smog that you couldn't see your own hand in front of your face. London fogs were nicknamed pea soupers.

One day in December 1952 the smog was worse than ever. It descended over the city like a blanket and clung on for four days. The air was horribly toxic, and Londoners had to cover their mouths with handkerchiefs whenever they went outside. London children were told to not to go to school in case they got lost on the way, cattle at Smithfield market suffocated and a shocking 4,000 people died as a result of this terrible air pollution. It became known as the Great Smog.

To prevent it ever happening again the Clean Air Act was passed in 1956 and Londoners were told only to burn smokeless fuel in their fires.

At Sadler's Wells Theatre a performance of the opera La Traviata had to be abandoned because the theatre was so full of smog the audience couldn't see the show.

LONDON PARTICULAR: A PEA SOUP

2kg/4½lb smoked gammon hocks
2 large celery sticks, chopped
1 leek, chopped
5 carrots, chopped
2 cloves of crushed garlic

450g/16oz yellow split peas
a large knob of butter
a splash of oil
1 onion, chopped
salt and ground black pepper

- Put the ham hocks and half the celery, carrots, leek and garlic into a big saucepan and cover with water. Simmer for 1 hour. Strain through a sieve, saving the stock in a jug. Strip the meat off the bone in small pieces.
- Rinse the split peas, put in a pan of water. Simmer until soft. Drain.
- Blend half the peas with a splash of the ham stock until smooth. Cook the chopped onion and vegetables in the oil and butter, until tender. Combine all the ingredients, season and add more ham stock to make a thick soup.

London's nickname is the Big Smoke

London spies

London is the spy capital of the world. Back in the 1400s, Thomas Cromwell ran secret agents from London to engage in foreign intelligence. Elizabeth I's private secretary had a network of 50 secret agents abroad. They intercepted messages and gathered information to use against their enemies.

At the start of the twentieth century, spying really took off and the two world-famous spy agencies were created: MI5 and MI6. The monolithic fortress-style building overlooking the river at Vauxhall is the HQ of MI6. This building is carefully protected against electronic espionage. The walls are impregnated with a mesh creating an electric field that blocks all transmissions both in and out. This clever device is called a Faraday cage after its inventor, London scientist Michael Faraday.

MI5 is the Security Service for the UK.
MI6 is the Secret Intelligence Service for foreign espionage.

The story of the cold war

London was a hotbed of espionage during the COLD WAR, the period of stand-off between the USA and the Soviet Union and their allies that began when the Iron Curtain came down between East and West after the Second World War. A battle of spies and spying was played out in Kensington's winding streets, with its public buildings and foreign embassies at the hub of this clandestine activity.

All sorts of covert operations went on under our very noses: Communist spies left secret messages behind pillars at the BROMPTON ORATORY and tucked MICROFILMS behind a statue of St Francis of Assisi in a flower bed at the next-door Holy Trinity Church. The CAMBRIDGE FIVE, a ring of British spies who betrayed their home country and became KGB moles, giving secrets to the Soviet Union, met regularly in a pub on the King's Road called the Markham Arms. For decades no one realized these men were double agents. One of them was Anthony Blunt, who worked for the Queen at Buckingham Palace.

Drop dead

- A Bulgarian journalist, Georgi Markov, who came to London as a dissident, was fatally stabbed with an umbrella impregnated with a lethal toxin called ricin while he innocently waited at a bus stop on Waterloo Bridge in 1978.
- An ex-KGB agent who fled to London from Russia for safety was suddenly taken ill after a meal in Piccadilly. He was found to have been poisoned with radioactive polonium-210 and died on 23rd November in 2006.

The modern London skyline

The Post Office Tower

In the late 1960s, the Post Office Tower, with its souvenir shop and Butlin's Top of the Tower restaurant on the top floor, dominated the London skyline. The restaurant revolved once every twenty-two minutes. Just off the Euston Road, the Post Office Tower was designed to carry communications equipment to support new television and telephone technology. Until 1993, the tower was officially a secret and it was not allowed to be marked on any maps, even though it stuck out like a sore thumb. The tower, no longer open to the public, is now called the BT Tower.

Lloyd's of London

The Lloyd's building at 1 Lime Street was designed by architect Richard Rogers. Londoners call it the Inside-out Building because all its services like staircases, lifts, pipes and electrics are on the outside of the building, leaving a vast uncluttered space inside. The Lloyds building has twelve glass lifts, which were the first of their kind in the UK.

The Gherkin

The Square Mile's most striking new building is at 30 St Mary Axe, known to Londoners as the Gherkin. It is forty floors high and is 180 metres/590 feet tall. It was designed by London architect Norman Foster. It is one of the most environmentally friendly glass skyscrapers, consuming half the energy of a similar-sized tower, trapping air and creating light shafts to save heat and light. Its other nickname is the Towering Innuendo.

One Canada Square

In 1991 when One Canada Square was built it was the tallest building in London at a towering 235 metres/770 feet. Nicknamed Canary Wharf, the glass and steel tower is fifty storeys high and is topped by a glass pyramid, which is so high up that it has a flashing aircraft warning light on it. The tower was designed by architect Cesar Pelli, who was inspired by the clock tower of Big Ben. It has 3,960 windows, which are cleaned by an automatic window-cleaning machine. It takes 2.6 seconds to clean each window and 1,936,634 litres/426,000 gallons of water to wash them all.

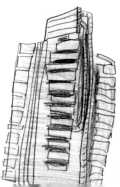

The Shard

This is the tallest building in London and the European Union. It is 310 metres/1,107 feet high and is nicknamed the Shard of Glass. It was designed by the Italian architect Renzo Piano and its construction rewrites the rules of how to build a skyscraper. Its seventy-two floors are entirely clad in glass. If the glass were laid out flat, there would be enough to cover eight full-size football pitches. No two panes of glass are the same, which will make the building shimmer in the sunlight. There is a public observation deck at the top.

The London Eye

The London Eye on the South Bank is the tallest ferris wheel in Europe and the third largest in the world. It is as high as sixty-four red telephone boxes piled on top of each other. The wheel and the egg-shaped capsules weigh 2,100 tonnes – as much as 1,272 black cabs. If each of the 32 capsules were completely full, there would be 800 people enjoying the view during the 30 minutes it takes to do one complete revolution. The London Eye was designed by London architects Julia Barfield and David Marks and is the most popular paid-for tourist attraction in Britain.

The Dome

The great tent-like structure in north Greenwich is the largest dome of its type in the world. Completed in 1999 to celebrate the Millennium, it was designed by London architect Richard Rogers and is now used as a venue for pop concerts and exhibitions. Its official name is the O2 Arena.

City Hall

City Hall on the south bank of the Thames, opposite the Tower of London, is the office of the Mayor of London. It is a round glass building that Londoners have nicknamed the Headlamp. Designed by Norman Foster and Partners, it is an eco building with 7300m² of triple glazing. Two bore holes from below London's water table provide water to cool it and flush the toilets. The sphere is 45m in diameter.

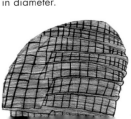

ROYAL LONDON

Where the Queen lives

Buckingham Palace is where the Queen and her family live when they are in London. But it has not always been the royal palace of choice. The royal family have lived in palaces all over London, with different kings and queens having favourites. Buckingham Palace used to be the private town house of the Duke of Buckingham. It was bought by George III in 1762 for £28,000 as a present for his wife, Charlotte, but they did not live there. Their son, George IV, had plans to turn the house into a sumptuous palace, with John Nash as his architect, but he died before it was finished. Queen Victoria was the first monarch to move in when she became queen in 1837 and she was shocked to discover that although the palace had had a complete makeover, it was a disappointment to live in. She complained that the lavatories were smelly, there were no sinks for the maids and many of the 1,000 windows would not open.

The palace is huge. It has 775 rooms, including 19 state rooms, 52 royal rooms, 52 royal and guest bedrooms, 188 staff bedrooms and 78 bathrooms. It costs a fortune to keep in good repair and to heat. The Queen is frugal and has reportedly asked her staff to refrain from walking down the middle of the corridors to stop the palace carpets wearing out. When the Queen is at home, the Royal Standard flag flies from the flagpole. Every morning while she has breakfast, a Scottish piper plays outside her window.

The Royal Mews

Alongside Buckingham Palace is the Royal Mews, a working stables where the Queen keeps her horses, the royal carriages and her cars. The three most important carriages are the Coronation Coach, the Glass Coach and the fairytale Gold State Coach.

RANDOM ROYAL MEWS FACTS

* Queen Victoria kept a cow at the Royal Mews to provide fresh milk for her family whenever they were in London. It is still known as 'the farm'.
* The Glass Coach is traditionally used by royal brides to travel to church on their wedding day.
* The fairytale Gold State Coach is the oldest royal carriage and was first used in November 1762.
* The Gold State coach has been used by every Monarch for their Coronation since George IV's in 1821. It weighs 4 tons and requires 8 horses to pull it.
* On the day of Queen Elizabeth II's Coronation in 1953, it was so cold that a copper hot-water bottle was strapped below the seat of the Gold State Coach to try to keep her warm.
* The horses that draw the Royal carriages are called Windsor Greys because they used to be kept at Windsor Castle.
* The Queen was given a new carriage by the Australians in 1988. They equipped it with central heating and electric windows.
* The Queen has her own horse-drawn post carriage which rides out from Buckingham Palace at 9.30am and 2.30 pm every day to deliver her letters.
* The Queen's carriages and cars are all painted a special colour called Royal Claret.
* The Queen's Rolls Royces bear no number plates.

Longest reigning British monarchs

* George III ruled for 59 years and 96 days.
* Queen Victoria is the longest serving monarch, ruling for 63 years and 216 days.
* If Queen Elizabeth remains on the throne till mid-September 2015 she will beat the record.

The soldiers of the Queen

The soldiers who guard Buckingham Palace are the Queen's foot soldiers, drawn usually from the Scots Guards, the Irish Guards, the Welsh Guards, the Grenadier Guards or the Coldstream Guards. The mounted soldiers at Horse Guards and Whitehall are the **HOUSEHOLD CAVALRY**. Founded to protect Charles II when he took back the throne in 1660, it is made up of two regiments: the Life Guards and the Blues and Royals. **THE LIFE GUARDS** were the soldiers who had travelled with Charles in exile and the **BLUES AND ROYALS** were what was left of Cromwell's army.

The helmets of the Household Cavalry are decorated with an **OAK LEAF**, the symbol of Charles II. The Blues and Royals have a helmet with a **STRAIGHT PLUME**, and the Life Guards have an onion-bulb shape at the top of the plume.

The colour of the horses the soldiers ride is important. Charles II instructed the Cavalry to ride **BLACK HORSES** to 'strike fear into the hearts of the enemy' should they charge in attack. The trumpeters ride grey horses and the drummers ride black, brown or white horses.

The Cavalry is inspected every morning at its barracks in **HYDE PARK**, Kensington, at ten o'clock before riding over to the Horse Guards.

Changing of the Guard

To see some of the finest soldiers in the world, head for Horse Guards Parade and follow them as they parade to Buckingham Palace for the Changing of the Guard. The ceremony starts at eleven o'clock (ten o'clock on Sundays) every day in summertime, every other day in the winter. Horses parade, bands play and soldiers march from Wellington Barracks to the Palace and on to St James's down the Mall. It's the best free entertainment in London.

On Her Majesty's Service

The Queen has special bodyguards who protect her when she is performing CEREMONIAL occasions like the State Opening of Parliament, royal garden parties, state visits and coronations. They are called by the very long title Her Majesty's Body Guard of the Honourable Corps of Gentlemen at Arms.

Created by Henry VIII in 1509 as his mounted escort in battles, the monarch's BODYGUARDS have not been on the front line since the English Civil War. In spite of this, they still wear a Cavalry sword and a long, ceremonial battleaxe. Their colourful costume is a red coat, white gloves and blue lapels, with facing embroidered with the Tudor royal badge of the portcullis. Splendid white swan PLUMES hang from their golden shiny helmets.

Trooping the colour

This colourful parade is how the monarch celebrates his or her official birthday on a Saturday in June each year. Dressed in all their finery, **1,400 OFFICERS** and soldiers march from Buckingham Palace to Whitehall and back again, flanked by **200 HORSES**. Rousing military music is played by **400 MUSICIANS**, drummers and pipers, who march along too. The monarch traditionally rides on horseback during the parade.

Trooping the Colour dates back to the early 16th century, when the colours – the brightly coloured flags of a battalion – were marched in full show, so that every soldier would easily recognize the flag of his own side in the fog and confusion of battle.

The Queen's favourite horse to ride in the Trooping the colour was a black mare named Burmese, a present from the Royal canadian Mounted police in 1969. She rode her sidesaddle every year until the horse retired in 1986. Since then, the Queen has ridden in a carriage as she did not want to replace her beloved horse.

Royal gun salutes

Several times a year, soldiers in full ceremonial dress perform royal gun salutes in London's parks, when 71 horses pull 6 guns, which fire 41 shots at Hyde Park and 62 shots at the Tower of London. As soon as the guns have fired they are hooked back up to the horses, who gallop away at high speed. The annual gun salutes are:

6 February: Accession Day
21 April: birthday of HM the Queen
2 June: birthday of HRH the Duke of Edinburgh
1st, 2nd or 3rd Saturday in June: the Queen's official birthday
1st day of the new paliamentary session, usually in
November: the State Opening of Parliament

SECRET SOLDIER STORIES

sshhh!

* Every afternoon at four o'clock, the troops are inspected again at Horse Guards, in a ceremony known as the Punishment Parade. The inspection dates back to 1894, when Queen Victoria walked in to discover the entire Guard drinking and gambling at four o'clock in the afternoon. Furious and shocked, she ordered a daily inspection at that time every day for the next 100 years. The Guard is still being punished today.

* The soldiers at Horse Guards Parade sometimes play tricks on each other by hiding an alarm clock in each other's bearskin helmets, set to go off when they are on duty.

LONDON'S ROYAL PALACES

St James's Palace was the main royal residence from 1702 to 1837. Although the royal family no longer live there, it is still London's most important royal palace because it is listed as the official palace residence of the sovereign. It is just off the Mall, round the corner from Buckingham Palace. Some of the original Tudor palace still survives, including the Chapel Royal, the gatehouse and a couple of Tudor rooms. We are not allowed to go in and see for ourselves, as it is used for official functions. A soldier stands outside in his sentry box to guard the palace.

Kensington Palace is a very grand but quite small palace in Kensington Gardens. William III suffered badly from asthma and found Whitehall Palace, on the river, far too damp. The village of Kensington, as it was then, was deemed to have 'good air', so William and his wife, Queen Mary, bought Nottingham House and commissioned the architect Sir Christopher Wren to do it up. They moved in at Christmas time 1689, and lived there until they died. Subsequent kings and queens came and went. Queen Victoria grew up here and her bedroom is on display. The King's Gallery is hung with the best paintings from the Royal Collection. Definitely a home fit for a king.

Kew Palace is an elegant palace loved by Queen Charlotte (wife of George II), who bought it from a rich merchant as a schoolhouse for her fifteen children. When George III became ill with one of his bouts of madness, he came here to get better. The family enjoyed country life at Kew and the King was nicknamed Farmer George. In the King's Breakfast Room is a dolls' house made by the princesses. It is decorated like the palace was when they lived there, with green wallpaper, cream paint and velvet bell pulls. The Queen built a little painted cottage in the woods at Kew, where she held tea parties and played at living like a peasant.

Hampton Court Palace was built by Cardinal Wolsey from 1514. It was so splendid and modern that Henry VIII was very jealous and wanted the house for himself. Being king, he got his way. He spent a further fortune (£62,000) on enlarging it. He added the Great Hall, the chapel, a grand dining room, sumptuous apartments, vast kitchens, a real tennis court, a bowling alley and a great house of easement – a giant lavatory for twenty-eight people. His son, Edward VI, was born here. His fifth wife, Katherine Howard, was dragged screaming from the gallery before she was tried and executed. Later, Charles I had his honeymoon at Hampton Court. William III and Mary, with the architect Sir Christopher Wren, upgraded the palace in 1689 in the latest Baroque style to create a palace that would rival Versailles in France.

London palaces: the odd ones out

Not only royal Londoners have palaces. In spite of the fact that they are called palaces, don't expect to find anyone coming and going from Lambeth or Fulham Palaces to be wearing crowns: they are not for kings and queens or princes and princesses. They were built for important people in the CHURCH.

FULHAM PALACE was the summer retreat for the bishops of London in the fields of Fulham on the banks of the river Thames. It dates back to the eleventh century. The medieval great hall was the scene of many sumptuous banquets and is supposed to be haunted.

For over 800 years, LAMBETH PALACE has been where the Archbishop of Canterbury stays when he comes to London. It looks across the river to the Houses of Parliament. Thomas More, Henry VIII's Lord Chancellor, lived here when he was just twelve years old in 1490. He worked here as a page.

On display in **LAMBETH PALACE** is the shell of a **TORTOISE** that belonged to an **ARCHBISHOP** in the 1600s. He kept it as a pet but it outlived him by 100 years. The unfortunate tortoise finally died at the grand age of 120, having been dug up out of winter **HIBERNATION** in the palace garden by a young gardener. He died of frost and **EXPOSURE** to cold.

Toilet trouble

Richmond Palace and Hampton court Palace were the first buildings to install flushing lavatories in Tudor times, one of which was invented by Sir John Harrington, Elizabeth I's godson.

The people's palaces

The CRYSTAL PALACE in south London and ALEXANDRA PALACE in north London were built by the Victorians for the people, to be places for entertainment and education. They had concert halls, art galleries, libraries, theatres and banqueting halls. The Crystal Palace burned down in 1936.

PUSSY CAT, PUSSY CAT

This is a nursery rhyme about a cat that used to roam one of the Queen's palaces. It is said that the cat belonged to one of Elizabeth I's ladies in waiting.

'Pussycat, pussycat, where have you been?'
'I've been up to London to visit the Queen.'
'Pussycat pussycat, what did you there?'
'I frightened a little mouse under her chair.'

ROYAL PALACES THAT NO LONGER EXIST

Palace of Westminster was once a splendid medieval palace on the banks of the Thames at Westminster and was built by Edward the Confessor in 1049, at the same time as he built Westminster Abbey. It was built on an island called Thorney Island, up river from the City of London. It became the home of all the medieval kings until 1530. The Great Hall, the largest in Europe at the time, was where all the affairs of state were conducted and was a bustling, crowded place. The coronation breakfast and banquets were served here at the King's high table. The early forms of English law were laid down in this hall. In 1365, Edward III added the Jewel Tower, in which to keep his treasures. It was guarded by a moat, filled with fish for the King's table. Tragically, the Palace of Westminster burned down in a terrible fire in 1834. The Houses of Parliament were built around its remains. The Great Hall and the Jewel Tower are all that survived.

Whitehall Palace was favoured by the kings and queens of Tudor London, who found the Palace of Westminster too shabby. Whitehall Palace was a sprawling series of buildings between Westminster and what is now Trafalgar Square, the King's stable yard in those days. The palace was well appointed with several real tennis courts, a tiltyard for jousting, a bowling green and a cockpit for bird fights. It grew to become the largest palace in Europe, with over 1,500 rooms. But in 1698, there was a fire that destroyed all but the Banqueting House. Where the palace once stood is still called Whitehall.

Richmond Palace was the royal residence on the Thames, 14 kilometres/9 miles west of the City. Henry VIII spent Christmas to Twelfth Night here with his first wife, Catherine of Aragon. His daughters, Mary and Elizabeth, both lived here at some point during their lives. Elizabeth loved it because of the nearby hunting on Richmond Hill. She died there in 1603. After Charles I's execution, Oliver Cromwell sold the palace for £13,000. It was demolished and the bricks were re-used. All that is left is the gatehouse, the Wardrobe and the Trumpeter's House. On Richmond Green, next door, is Maid's Row, traditionally where the unmarried princesses lived.

Greenwich Palace commanded the river to the east of London. It became important in Tudor times because of the growing importance of the navy in the nearby naval dockyards in Deptford and Woolwich. Elizabeth I signed the orders sending the British navy to fight the Spanish Armada at Greenwich. She held great feasts here to celebrate success at sea and launch parties for new explorations. Sir Francis Drake was knighted at Deptford after sailing round the world. Greenwich Palace was completely rebuilt by Sir Christopher Wren and became the Royal Hospital for Seamen.

The Tower of London

The Tower of London is the oldest surviving palace in London, made up of twenty-two towers and turrets built over centuries. William the Conqueror built the first tower, the **WHITE TOWER**, as a prison and fortress after he took the English throne in 1066. He built it to defend the City from attack from the Thames, and also to protect himself from the Saxon Londoners who were against him.

Never the main royal residence, this Norman castle was first and foremost a military base. The Tudor Henry III loved animals and expanded the **ROYAL MENAGERIE** to include elephants and a polar bear. Edward I established the Royal Mint, where coins were made, at the Tower of London and it stayed there until the nineteenth century. The Duke of Wellington drained the moat in 1845 as it was so smelly.

The Tower was used by royals as a prison for their enemies. It was also a place of imprisonment, torture and **ROYAL EXECUTION**. The Tower's most famous inmates include Lady Jane Grey, the Princes in the Tower, Guy Fawkes, Sir Walter Raleigh and Thomas More. During the Second World War, Hitler's deputy, Rudolf Hess, was kept prisoner here.

RANDOM TOWER FACTS

* The White Tower stood as the tallest structure in London until 1310.
* William the Conqueror built two other castles in London at the same time as the Tower: Baynard's Castle and the Tower of Montfichet. Both were destroyed long ago. There is a plaque marking the spot of Baynard's Castle on Upper Thames Street.

Spooky London

The ghost of Anne Boleyn, beheaded for treason in 1536, is said to haunt the Tower of London, walking around the White Tower and carrying her head under her arm.

Traitors to the crown were brought to the Tower on barges and entered through Traitors' Gate. When Elizabeth was accused of treason by her stepsister Mary I, she refused to enter the Tower through Traitors' Gate, denying she was a traitor.

Off with their heads!

- The Tower of London was the place where royals and nobles were executed. Most nobles were executed publicly on Tower Hill in front of large jeering mobs.
- A permanent scaffold was set up from 1485, and on the day of execution straw was strewn around the scaffold to soak up the blood and a basket was placed to catch the severed head.
- The first man to be beheaded at the Tower of London was Sir Simon Burley in the reign of Richard II.
- The last head to roll at Tower Hill was that of the eighty-year-old Lord Lovat in 1747, after the Jacobite rebellion.

Queen
Katherine
Howard

Royal executions

The privileged few were allowed to be beheaded in private behind the Tower's high walls on Tower Green, near the Chapel Royal. Seven nobles and queens have been spared the gawping crowds:

• Baron William Hastings, 1483 • Anne Boleyn, second wife of Henry III, 1536 • Margaret, Countess of Salisbury, 1541 • Queen Katherine Howard, fifth wife of Henry VIII, 1542 • Jane Boleyn, 1542 • Lady Jane Grey, Queen for nine days, 1554 • Robert Devereux, Earl of Essex 1601

DID YOU KNOW?

An expert swordsman from France was summoned for the execution of Anne Boleyn, in a kind gesture from the King, to make her death as swift and painless as possible. All others executed at Tower Green were beheaded by axe.

Wizard in the Tower

Henry Percy, 9th Earl of Northumberland, was imprisoned in the Martin Tower by James I for sixteen years. He had been involved in the Gunpowder Plot. His scientific experiments and alchemy earned him the nickname Wizard Earl. He made himself comfortable there and had a bowling alley installed.

Torture at the Tower

Underneath the Keep in the Tower of London is a series of **DUNGEONS** and torture chambers. The worst is called Little Ease. It is a 1.25 metre/4-foot square hole, so small a prisoner cannot sit, stand or lie down in it. The Tower also had instruments of **TORTURE** such as the rack, the scavenger's daughter, the **THUMB SCREW**, the breaks and the manacles.

Great escapes from the Tower

The first prisoner at the Tower was the unfortunate Bishop of Durham, **RANULF FLAMBARD**, in 1100. He was also the first prisoner to escape. He had a rope smuggled in to him and hosted a great banquet for his guards. When they had feasted and were drunk, he threw down the rope and climbed out of the Tower on to a waiting horse so that he could **GALLOP TO FREEDOM**.

The most daring escape from the Tower of London was that of William Maxwell, imprisoned in the Devereux Tower in 1715. His wife and a lady visited him the night before his intended execution and dressed him in identical clothes as the lady. **SOBBING DEEPLY**, with a handkerchief pressed to his face, he left the cell and escaped to safety in Rome.

Last executions at the Tower of London

- During the First World War, eleven **GERMAN SPIES** were tried and shot by firing squad at the Tower of London. They were shot at dawn.
- The last person to be executed at the Tower was German spy **JOSEF JAKOBS**, who was shot on 14 August 1941.

King Henry VIII

DID YOU KNOW?

When Queen Anne was crowned in 1702, she had such bad gout that she could not walk. She is the only English monarch to have been carried to her coronation throne.

The Ceremony of the Keys

The ancient Ceremony of the Keys takes place every night at ten o'clock at the Tower of London. It is performed with great formality and ceremony, just as it has been for the past 700 years. This is what happens.

At the great portcullis to the **BLOODY TOWER** four guardsmen, the chief Warder of the Tower and the duty sentries come to a halt. A challenger cries out: 'Halt. Who comes there?' Someone else replies: 'The keys.' 'Whose keys?' 'Queen Elizabeth's keys.' 'Advance Queen Elizabeth's keys. All's well.'

The Chief Warder raises his hat and calls out: 'God preserve Queen Elizabeth.' A final **BUGLE SOUNDS** and the tower is **LOCKED** for the night.

London landmark: Beefeaters

Beefeaters are one of the most instantly recognized symbols of London, proudly standing guard at the Tower of London in their bright red and gold ceremonial uniform with white ruff, red stockings and black patent shoes. They are really called Yeoman Warders but everyone calls them by their nickname, given to them because of their huge daily ration of meat. In 1813 thirty guards ate 24lb of beef, 18lb of mutton and 16lb of veal every day.

It is a very special honour to be become a Yeoman Warder and to qualify you must have served in the armed forces with a good record. In a ritual dating back to 1337, beefeaters are sworn in at a special ceremony. They must toast each other's health and drink from an old pewter punch bowl.

The Crown Jewels

The Crown Jewels are guarded in the Tower of London in their own Jewel Tower. The collection contains over 23,578 jewels.

The Crown Jewels are not just crowns but include sceptres, orbs, rings, swords, spurs, bracelets and robes. The **ST EDWARD'S CROWN** is worn for coronations. It is made of gold and studded with sapphires, tourmalines, amethysts, topazes and citrines. Wearing the crown must give you a headache because it weighs a substantial 2.23 kilograms/5 pounds, which is like having a large bag of sugar on your head. It was last used to crown Elizabeth II on 2 June 1953. This crown and the orb and sceptre are called the Coronation Regalia.

The **CORONATION REGALIA** is not as old as you might think. In a great act of vandalism, when Oliver Cromwell came to power he took the Coronation Regalia, plucked out the jewels and melted down the silver and gold and turned them into coins. When the King, Charles II, was restored to the throne in 1660 a whole new set of **CROWN JEWELS** had to be made for him before he could be crowned.

On the eve of a coronation, the Regalia leave the Tower of London, accompanied by watermen and lightermen from the City of London. They are taken to the Jerusalem Chamber in Westminster Abbey and watched over by the Yeomen of the Guard.

Little gems

- The smallest crown in the Crown Jewels is Queen Victoria's Diamond Crown. Just 9.5 centimetres/3.7 inches high, it weighs 145 grams/5.11 ounces. She used to wear it over her widow's cap.

- The Imperial Crown of India is the only crown that is allowed to leave the country. It was made for George V when he was crowned Emperor of India and is encrusted with more than 6,000 diamonds.

- The late Queen Mother's crown has set into it the Koh-i-Noor or Mountain of Light Diamond, which brings luck only to women.

The Star of Africa on the Royal Sceptre is the LARGEST cut diamond in the world.

fascinating facts

- The Imperial State Crown glistens with:

2,868 DIAMONDS   273 pearls   5 RUBIES
11 EMERALDS   **17 sapphires**

- The Queen wears the sparkling Imperial State Crown at the State Opening of Parliament.
- The sapphire in the Maltese cross on top of the crown came from a ring worn by Edward the Confessor and later removed from his grave.

- The ruby at the centre of the Imperial State Crown was worn by Richard III at the Battle of Bosworth Field in 1485. When he was killed, it rolled under a bush and was found by Lord Stanley and put on the head of the victorious Henry Tudor.

Two kings of Britain were never crowned: Edward V and Edward VIII.

A new monarch is crowned wearing the Edward crown but they only get to wear it for the service: for the journey home they pop on the Imperial State crown instead.

Stop thief!

There has only ever been one attempted robbery of the Crown Jewels. In 1671 Colonel Thomas Blood made friends with the Keeper of the Crown Jewels, Talbot Edwards, and knocked him on the head with a mallet. Blood flattened the crown, stuffed it down his trousers and ran out with it. He was caught and the Crown Jewels were returned. The King was charmed by Blood's bluster and decided not to punish him. No one has ever tried to steal the Crown Jewels since.

DID YOU KNOW?

Princess Diana's famous blue sapphire engagement ring was bought at Garrard & Co., 24 Albemarle Street, Mayfair, the jewellers who set the Imperial State Crown with the Koh-i-Noor diamond. The ring is now worn by Prince William's bride, Catherine, the Duchess of Cambridge.

The Undercroft Museum at Westminster Abbey has a complete set of imitation Coronation Regalia on display. These are used for practice runs before the big day.

Royal playgrounds

London has 5,000 acres of Royal Parks. They are largely a legacy of the kings and queens who kept them as private hunting grounds and royal chases for hundreds of years. As late as the mid-nineteenth century, ordinary Londoners were only allowed to play in many of them by royal decree.

The Green Park   GREENWICH PARK   Hyde Park

Kensington Gardens   The Regent's Park (and Primrose Hill)

RICHMOND PARK   ST JAMES'S PARK   BUSHY PARK

It is possible to walk 5 kilometres/3 miles in a straight line through the Royal Parks: St James's Park, Green Park, Hyde Park and Kensington Gardens without walking in London's streets.

By Royal Proclamation

All Royal Proclamations of royal births, deaths and marriages, the dissolution of Parliament and declarations of war are read out by the Lord Mayor of London's Sergeant at Arms, who stands on the steps of the Royal Exchange in the City and cries out the important news to all and sundry.

Knights and heralds

Kings and queens, and lords and ladies, have special heraldic coats of arms. The practice dates back to a time when the colours and symbols would identify them in battle. The College of Arms on Queen Victoria Street keeps records of all the coats of arms that have ever existed and gives out new ones.

ssshhh!

SECRET ROYAL LONDON

The College of Arms was founded in the reign of Richard III. In the entrance hall is a throne with the cushion that kings and queens sit on during their coronation.

BY APPOINTMENT TO HER MAJESTY THE QUEEN: WHERE THE QUEEN GOES SHOPPING

The Queen may not actually go to the shops much herself, but she does buy things. If she particularly likes a shop and it has supplied her for a minimum of five years, she might award it a special badge called a Royal Warrant. This practice goes back to 1155 in the reign of Henry II. These are some of the shops the Queen likes in London.

Shoes: Annello and Davide, Covent Garden

Theatrical shoemakers Annello and Davide make handmade shoes to match the Queen's outfits. They also made Dorothy's sparkly red shoes in the film *The Wizard of Oz*.

Wallpaper: Cole and Son, Chelsea Harbour

The Queen probably has a few Cole and Son hand-block-printed historic papers adorning the walls of Buckingham Palace.

Chocolate: Prestat, Prince's Arcade, Piccadilly

These delicious chocolate truffles were also a favourite of children's author Roald Dahl.

Paints: Papers and Paints, Chelsea

Papers and Paints, set up in 1960 by Patrick Baty, specializes in historic colours – perfect paints for a palace.

Perfume and toiletries: Floris, Jermyn Street

George IV gave Floris its first Royal Warrant in 1820 for its fine combs. Its exclusively mixed perfumes are made from flowers. James Bond, Ian Fleming's fictional spy, always wore Floris No. 89.

Rainwear: Burberry's, Knightsbridge

Burberry's trademark trench coat was commissioned by the War Office in 1914. It was an adaptation of an officer's coat to suit contemporary warfare conditions. After the war, the trench coat became popular with ordinary Londoners.

Cheese: Paxton and Whitfield, Jermyn Street

This is the oldest cheese shop in London. Wartime Prime Minister Winston Churchill commented that 'A gentleman only buys his cheese at Paxton and Whitfield.'

Groceries: Fortnum & Mason

Ex Royal Footman William Fortnum, opened this grocer's shop on Piccadilly in 1707. It is the poshest food shop in London.

Royal beasts

Royal beasts decorate London's important buildings. They are all taken from the heraldic arms of the Queen's ancestors.

- **THE LION OF ENGLAND** – From Henry I's coat of arms. The unicorn joined with the lion when the Scottish king James VI came to the English throne as James I.
- **RED DRAGON OF WALES** – Henry VII
- **GRIFFIN** – Edward III
- **WHITE GREYHOUND OF RICHMOND** – Henry VII
- **BLACK BULL OF CLARENCE** – Anne of Clarence, grandmother of Edward IV
- **WHITE HORSE OF HANOVER** – George I

The lion and the unicorn

The lion and the unicorn were fighting for the crown
The lion beat the unicorn all around the town.
Some gave them white bread, and some gave them brown;
Some gave them plum cake and drummed them out of town.

Royal emblems

Across London, pub signs, gates, stained-glass windows, soldiers' hats and carvings in important buildings still carry the royal emblems.

White hart – Richard II   FEATHERS – THE BLACK PRINCE

Red lion – John of Gaunt   AN OAK LEAF – CHARLES II

White and red rose - The Tudors

Royal cyphers

Every post box in London has the mark of the queen or king who reigned when it was put out on the street. This mark is called the **ROYAL CYPHER** and is usually the first initial followed by R for Rex or Regina, Latin words meaning king or queen. There were no **POST BOXES** before Queen Victoria's reign, so the earliest you can find is VR. The rarest one is Edward VIII's. He was on the throne for only a short time and abdicated in 1936. Londoners felt betrayed by him and vandalized lots of his post boxes.

Royal swans

Officially the Queen owns all the unmarked mute swans on the river Thames. Her ownership dates back to a time when eating swan was the preserve of the royal table. Every July all baby swans between London Bridge and Henley in Berkshire are caught and counted in a tradition called **SWAN UPPING**. The Vintners' and Dyers' livery companies share ownership of the swans with the monarch and have done since the fifteenth century. They all set off from London on the Thames in rowing **SKIFFS** for a five-day journey up the river. The Queen's Swan Marker wears a splendid scarlet coat and each boat flies a flag and pennant. The swans are counted but no longer eaten.

Royal boroughs

- The Royal Borough of **KINGSTON UPON THAMES** is the oldest borough in London and is royal by ancient title.
- The Royal Borough of **KENSINGTON AND CHELSEA** became royal in 1901, fulfilling Queen Victoria's wish to honour the place where she was born.
- The Royal Borough of **GREENWICH** was made royal in 2012 to celebrate Queen Elizabeth II's Diamond Jubilee.

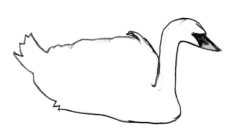

WHAT THE QUEEN SERVES AT HER GARDEN PARTIES AT BUCKINGHAM PALACE

27,000 cups of tea

20,000 sandwiches

20,000 SLICES OF CAKE

All from a 408 feet long buffet table

DID YOU KNOW?

The Queen Elizabeth Hall on the South Bank was named after the Queen when she came to the throne in 1952.
The Jubilee Tube line is named after Queen Elizabeth II's silver jubilee in 1977, celebrating 25 years on the throne.
The Queen Elizabeth Olympic Park is named after the Queen.

THE CITY OF LONDON

The City of London occupies just one square mile. This tiny core of London is known as the **CITY**. It is where London began and was once bounded by high walls. It has always been the **FINANCIAL** heart of London. Much of its wealth and culture derives from the rich medieval merchants and traders who built it. It is a city within a city and still has its own rules and regulations, its own police force, its own guildhall and its own mayor, the Lord Mayor of London.

The **CITY** is nicknamed the **SQUARE MILE**

Freedom of the city

In a ceremony at Guildhall dating back to 1237, you can be given the Freedom of the City if you have done something outstanding for the good of London. This gives you privileges that include:

- the right to drive sheep and cattle over London Bridge
- the right to be hung with a silken rope if you were ever to have the misfortune to be executed
- the right to carry a naked sword – one that is not in a sheath
- the right to be drunk and disorderly in the streets, without fear of arrest
- the right to be married in St Paul's Cathedral
- the right to be buried in the City of London
- freedom from being pressganged into the army or navy

City of London

The city's coat of arms

The symbol of the City of London is a white shield with a red cross, flanked by two heraldic dragons. These signs are peppered through the streets.

The city dragons

In 1963, two large stone dragons that had once guarded the Coal Exchange on Lower Thames Street were moved to Victoria Embankment to guard the entrance to the City of London. Copies were made of these statues and mark the City boundary at Aldersgate, Aldgate, Bishopsgate, Blackfriars Bridge, Holborn, Farringdon, London Bridge and Moorgate. Otherwise, the boundary is marked with a simple short black post stamped with the City's coat of arms.

The city guilds

The guilds of London date back to the **MIDDLE AGES**. They were created to protect the men and women who worked in every trade in the City. They were masters of their craft. They chose apprentices, decided how much everyone should be paid, set the prices goods were sold for at all London markets and set high standards of workmanship. The guilds were **VERY POWERFUL** and had almost total control of the City. It was not possible to work unless you belonged to the guild particular to your craft.

Most guilds had a great hall where all the members could meet. The richest guilds had the finest halls. Each guild had its own **UNIFORM**, called a **LIVERY**. There are still 107 guilds in the City.

The name guild comes from the Saxon word *gilde*, meaning payment.

HAHA! FUNNY NAMES – THE GUILDS OF LONDON

Haberdashers – People who sold threads and cottons
Tallow chandlers – Candle makers   Cordwainers – Shoemakers
Coopers – Barrel makers   Limners – Artists
Skinners – Leather makers   Ferrours – Ironworkers
Bowyers – Bow makers   Fletchers – Arrowmakers
Mercers – Cloth merchants   Chapemakers – Scabbard makers
Hurers – Hatters   Lateners – Brass workers
Girdlers – Pocket makers

High standards

The guilds judged the quality of each craftsman's work and had very high, strict standards. They inspected the markets to check everything was up to scratch. Punishment was severe if standards were found wanting: rotten meat would be burnt under your nose, bad wine would be poured over the seller's head, or if your loaves of bread were below weight you would be sent to the pillory with them hanging round your neck.

The apprentice

Boys who wanted to learn a trade started a seven-year apprenticeship to a guild at thirteen years old. An apprentice would live with his **MASTER** and his family, sleeping in the attic and working six days a week, without a break. Fortunately, there were lots of holidays: Christmas lasted thirteen days; saints' days and **FEAST** days were days off too. Celebrations were lavish and all the guilds took to the streets to join in candlelit processions. On **MAY DAY**, apprentices would dance around one of London's many maypoles. They would watch mystery plays full of slapstick comedy, elaborate costumes and special effects.

After many years of training an apprentice was allowed to craft his own piece of work to prove his **SKILLS**. When he had perfected it he would hope to be judged good enough to become a master himself – a great achievement.

★ LONDON LINGO ★

In 1516, the Lord Mayor ranked the City's guilds in order: number one on the list was the best. The Skinners and the Merchants were placed six and seven, but they argued bitterly over who deserved the higher ranking. Finally, they made a deal that every year they would swap places. This is how the expression at sixes and sevens was coined. It means confused and disorganized.

★ LONDON LINGO ★

On the return to Guildhall after the Lord Mayor's Show, the Lord Mayor and the guilds travelled down the river on decorated barges known as floats. These barges were the origin of the floats used in parades and processions today.

The Lord Mayor of London

The City of London has had its own Lord Mayor since the twelfth century. A new one is elected every year. The life of the Lord Mayor is full of pomp and ceremony. He (or she) has his own sword bearer, a common cryer, a sergeant at arms and a city marshal, all of whom attend him on important occasions. He works hard to promote the City of London. He makes 700 speeches a year and addresses 10,000 people a month.

London's first . . . LORD MAYOR of London was a man named Henry Fitz-Ailwin de Londonestone, elected in 1189.

The new Lord Mayor of London is the only person allowed to speak at his swearing in ceremony nicknamed the 'silent ceremony'.

The Lord Mayor's banquets

One of the great London feasts was always the grand banquet put on every year at Guildhall by the newly appointed Lord Mayor of London. Medieval mayors gorged on sea hogs, fat swans, conger eels and porpoises. There are stories about these fine feasts. In Elizabethan London, a great bowl of custard was wheeled into Guildhall while everyone was eating and the Lord Mayor's fool was made to jump into it, fully clothed, much to the entertainment of the guests. Over the centuries, the menus became more and more elaborate. Traditionally, every Lord Mayor's banquet since 1768 served turtle soup.

In the eighteenth century, a more modest Lord Mayor's banquet consisted of: partridges, quail, chickens, woodcock, snipe, leverets, crayfish, brawn, turtle, sweetbreads, veal, ham, two haunches of venison, a turkey roasted and creamed pippin tarts.

London landmark: the Mansion House

After the Great Fire of London in 1666, it was decided to build a house for the Lord Mayor of London so that he could entertain in style. A grand Georgian town palace, called the Mansion House, was finally completed in 1758. The Lord Mayor lives here during his term of office.

The Lord Mayor's Show

One of the oldest and most important occasions in the Lord Mayor's calendar is the Lord Mayor's Show, which dates back to 1215. The new Lord Mayor swears an oath of allegiance to the sovereign and shows himself to the people of London in a great parade through the streets, processing from Guildhall to the Royal Courts of Justice in Fleet Street.

Once upon a time this journey was made by horseback and the journey back was made on a barge along the Thames. But ever since one poor Lord Mayor fell off his horse and broke his leg, the Lord Mayor has travelled in a golden stagecoach. He is followed by the guilds of London, all dressed in their finest livery.

While the Mansion House was being built, the Lord Mayor was given a grand house in Groveland Court, off Bow Lane, to live in. It is now a pub called the Williamson's Tavern.

Lord mayors coach

DID YOU KNOW?

LONDON FACT • LONDON FACT • LONDON FACT

The Lord Mayor's coach is pulled by shire horses from the Whitbread brewery in the City.

The Lord Mayor's splendid gold coach was built in 1757 and cost a staggering £1,065 0s. 3d. It has been used in every Lord Mayor's Show since then and is kept safely on display in the window of the Museum of London.

London landmark: Guildhall

Guildhall is London's magnificent town hall. It was built by London's medieval guilds as a place to meet and do business. Their brightly coloured flags and pennants still hang from the hall's arched wooden ceiling.

The Lord Mayor hosts a grand banquet in the Great Hall every year, to which the Prime Minister is invited to give a speech.

The story of Dick Whittington:
Fable

The pantomime story goes that Dick Whittington is a poor boy who comes to London to make his fortune, thinking the streets are paved with gold. He works as a servant and falls in love with a rich merchant's beautiful daughter. Failing to make his fortune and win the girl, he decides to head back home. On the long journey with his cat, he stops on Highgate Hill for a rest and hears the bells of Bow Church chime. He imagines they are calling to him, saying:

> Turn again, Whittington,
> Lord Mayor of London,
> Turn again, Whittington,
> Thrice Lord Mayor of London.

He decides to return to the City, where he makes his fortune, becomes Lord Mayor of London and marries his sweetheart, Alice Fitzwarren.

Truth

The real Dick Whittington was the son of a wealthy nobleman who came to London to work in the Fitzwarren family business. He became a mercer – a dealer in fine cloth – and a hugely wealthy man. He was Lord Mayor of London not just three times but four.

Dick Whittington was a very generous man and built schools, almshouses and a library for the poor. His crowning glory was an enormous sixty-four-seat public lavatory, which Londoners nicknamed Whittington's Longhouse. He had no children and when he died he left all his money for the benefit of the City of London.

ssshhh!

SECRET LONDON

The Whittington stone at the foot of Highgate Hill marks the place where Dick Whittington is supposed to have turned around and gone back to London to make his fortune.

Giant grasshopper

On top of the Royal Exchange at Bank in the City is an 3.3-metre/11-foot-high grasshopper. It dates back to 1566 and was the inspiration of the man who built the Exchange for London, Sir Thomas Gresham. The grasshopper is a symbol on his family crest and shield. If you look around the streets of the City you will see lots of different signs and symbols hanging from its buildings.

Gruesome heads

The spikes on the top of Temple Bar, once on Fleet Street, were used to display the heads of traitors. The last heads displayed were of those of the unfortunate Towneley and Fletcher, rebels on the side of Bonnie Prince Charlie who were captured at the Siege of Carlisle in 1746.

Temple Bar

Temple Bar was a fine WOODEN GATEWAY through which you passed to enter the City on Fleet Street. It was one of the seven gateways to London. After the GREAT FIRE OF LONDON, when Temple Bar was destroyed, Sir Christopher Wren designed a new stone one. But it was too narrow for modern TRAFFIC and was taken down, stone by stone, in 1878 to widen the street. It was put into storage somewhere off Farringdon Road.

In 1880, Temple Bar was bought by the wealthy brewer SIR HENRY MEUX for his wife, a banjo-playing barmaid. The archway was re-erected as the gateway to their Hertfordshire mansion, THEOBALDS PARK. Years later it was found derelict and abandoned in a field.

In 2003, Temple Bar was bought for £1 and finally returned to the City of London. It was painstakingly rebuilt as the entrance to PATERNOSTER SQUARE near St Paul's Cathedral.

Temple Bar

The City's medieval ceremonies

The Loving Cup Ceremony

At every City banquet, a massive two-handled cup filled with hippocras – a mixture of wine and spices – is passed around from person to person to drink. Everyone takes it in turn to have a sip. While they are drinking, the person to their left stands up to guard them from attack, dating back to a time when everyone carried a sword.

Knolly's Rose Ceremony

Every year on 24 June a red rose is presented to the Lord Mayor at the Mansion House on an altar cushion from All Hallows by the Tower. This is a payment dating back to 1381, when Lady Knolly put up a small bridge on Seething Lane, without permission, so that she could reach her garden without getting her feet muddy. She was punished with a fine of giving one red rose from her garden every year.

Cart Marking Ceremony

A traditional cart marking ceremony takes place every year in Guildhall Yard. Only officially marked carts were allowed to ply for trade in the City streets from as early as the 14th century. These days, the Company of Cartmen bring their horse-drawn waggons, carriages, steamers and vintage vehicles to be branded with a red-hot iron. They all celebrate with a great feast.

Tales of the City bank

The author of *The Wind in the Willows*, Kenneth Grahame, had an important job at the Bank of England and retired in 1908, the same year his famous children's story was published. He wrote the stories for his son, Alistair, who was nicknamed Mouse. The headstrong character of Toad was inspired by his son.

RANDOM CITY FACTS

* The City of London has been paying an annual rent of six horseshoes and sixty-one nails to the Crown for land near Chancery Lane since 1118.
* The first underground public lavatory is near Bank in the City
* The National Anthem was sung for the first time at the Merchant Taylors' Hall in 1607.

At Hoare's private client bank on Fleet Street it was a tradition that one of the partners slept in the bank every night. This bank has been owned by the same family since 1672.

THE BANK OF ENGLAND

The Bank of England is one of the most important institutions in the City of London. It was set up in 1694 because the King, William III, needed to borrow money to pay for his war against France. In return for depositing money, the Bank gave its customers HANDWRITTEN bank notes with the promise to pay the bearer the sum of the note. These were the FIRST BANK NOTES on the London streets. They were issued only for sums of £50 or more, so, as ordinary people earned less than £20 a year, most Londoners never came into contact with them. The Bank of England was the world's first privately owned bank.

The story of the Old Lady of Threadneedle Street

The Bank of England is known as the Old Lady of Threadneedle Street. The old lady did exist. She was a woman called Sarah Whitehead whose brother had worked in the bank. He was hanged for forgery in 1811, but every day for the next twenty-five years Sarah came to the bank and asked to see him. She is buried in the churchyard that is now part of the Bank of England's garden. Her ghost has been seen on many occasions.

Not a bank robbery

In 1836, the directors of the Bank of England opened a strange letter from a man asking them to meet him in the gold bullion room. At the given time, they were astonished to see the man appear through a hole in the floor. He had come up through a drain that connected directly to the river Thames. The man wanted to show the bankers how easy it would be to rob them of all their gold. For his honesty, he was rewarded with a vast sum of money.

There is a real gold bar you can hold at the Bank of England Museum.

The BIGGEST bell in London

The biggest bell in London is called **GREAT TOM** and is at St Paul's Cathedral. Cast in the reign of Edward I, it once hung in **WESTMINSTER HALL**. Great Tom is tolled on the death of the Lord Mayor of London, the Archbishop of Canterbury, the Bishop of London, the Dean of **ST PAUL'S CATHEDRAL** or a member of the **ROYAL FAMILY**. The bell rings out over the City at one o'clock in the afternoon every day.

cockney bells

The Great Bells of St Mary-le-Bow Church are famously known as **BOW BELLS** and anyone born within the sound of them is considered a cockney. In the olden days the sound of the bells could be heard 9.5 kilometres/6 miles to the east, 8 kilometres/5 miles to the north, 5 kilometres/3 miles to the south and 6.5 kilometres/4 miles to the west of the City of London. London was then so small that almost everyone was a true **COCKNEY**.

The **BOW BELLS** were made at London's Whitechapel Bell Foundry. When the church was bombed in the war, the bells did not chime again for another twenty years. So, strictly speaking, no cockneys were born until the bells were replaced in 1961.

Oranges and Lemons is a nursery rhyme about the church bells of the city of London.

'Oranges and lemons' say the Bells of St Clements.
'You owe me five farthings' say the Bells of St Martin's.
'When will you pay me?' say the Bells of Old Bailey.
'When I grow rich' say the Bells of Shoreditch.
'When will that be?' say the Bells of Stepney.
'I do not know' say the Great Bells of Bow.
Here comes a Candle to light you to Bed,
And here comes a chopper to chop off your head.
Chip chop chip chop – the Last Man's Dead.

The story of the Lutine bell

The Lutine Bell is one of the few things recovered in 1858 from a ship that sank many years before, along with the ship's rudder, the captain's watch and some gold and silver bars. The bell was taken to Lloyd's of London, the company that insures the world's ships. The bell is traditionally rung once for bad news, such as the sinking of a ship, and twice for good news, such as that a boat thought to be lost is safe.

Fascinating facts

- There are no bells at London's Old Bailey. The bells mentioned in the nursery rhyme are the ones of the Church of St Sepulchre-without-Newgate next door. The words ' "When will you pay me?" say the Bells of Old Bailey' refer to the fact that Newgate was a prison for debtors.
- St Clements Eastcheap off Clement's Lane, the church of oranges and lemons, was close to the wharf where citrus fruit for London's markets were unloaded.
- The church of St Clement Danes also claims a connection to the nursery rhyme and holds an oranges and lemons service every year, at which local schoolchildren are each given an orange to take home.

Tower 42

City's tallest

- Heron Tower, also known as 110 Bishopsgate, is the **TALLEST** skyscraper in the square mile of the City of London, standing 230 metres high, including its 28 metre long mast. It opened in 2011.
- The second tallest building in the City of London is called **TOWER 42**. It is 183 metres/600 feet tall and when it was built in 1980 it was the tallest building in Europe. It was originally known as the Natwest Tower because it was built as offices for the National Westminster Bank. If you were to look down on the building from the sky, you would see that the top of the building is in the shape of the bank's logo.

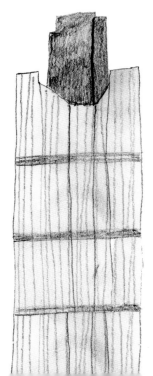

PARLIAMENT, POWER AND POLITICS

London landmark: The Houses of Parliament

The Houses of Parliament, on the river Thames, are built on the site of the old Palace of Westminster. This spot has been the centre of government since 1200, when the royal court moved here from the Tower of London. The magnificent building we see today is a Victorian replacement designed by architect Sir Charles Barry and his assistant, Augustus Pugin.

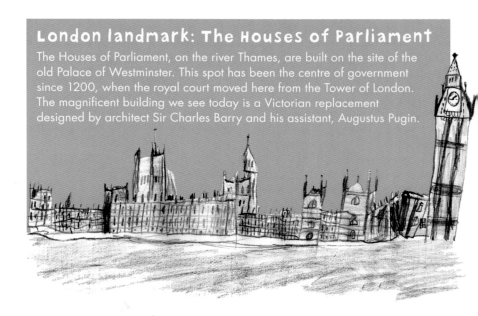

It is easy to get lost in the Houses of Parliament because it is vast: there are 1,200 rooms, 100 staircases and well over 3.2 kilometres/2 miles of passages. It is divided into two chambers. The House of Lords is for unelected members: earls, viscounts, lords and baronesses – some hereditary and some appointed. The House of Commons is for elected Members of Parliament, called MPs. Each House has its own separate entrance, at opposite ends of the building. These chambers are where the laws we live by are debated and agreed. A lantern in the clock tower burns brightly whenever Parliament is sitting for a debate at night.

The Queen has her own special entrance under a splendid arch. She is only allowed into the House of Lords. No king or queen has set foot inside the House of Commons since 1642, when Oliver Cromwell overthrew the King and took over the Palace of Westminster.

★ LONDON LINGO ★

★ The word exchequer is derived from the chessboard-squared table on which money was once counted at Westminster Hall. The minister in charge of the country's money is called the Chancellor of the Exchequer.

★ To lobby your MP means to try to persuade him or her to put forward your ideas in the House of Commons. The term comes from the room between the Lords and Commons, called the Central Lobby, where anyone can come to talk to their MP.

The best view of the Houses of Parliament is from the south side of the Thames at Lambeth Palace, looking across the river.

The Great Hall

The Great Hall of the Old Palace was once the most important room of all. It was where kings held banquets, matters of state were argued and trials were held. Bishops, nobles, ministers and lawyers all crowded in to take part in the action. It was crammed with shops and stalls selling wigs, pens and books.

Colour codes

- The chamber of the House of Commons has GREEN leather seats and the chamber of the House of Lords has RED leather seats.
- Westminster Bridge, close to the House of Commons, is painted GREEN. Lambeth Bridge, closer to the House of Lords, is painted RED.
- The striped awnings on the terraces of the Houses of Parliament are coloured coded too: the Lords sit under RED stripes, and the Commons sit under GREEN stripes.

The House of Lords is the second-largest parliamentary chamber in the world, second only to that of the Chinese National Party Congress.

House rules

Because this has been the seat of government for so many centuries there are lots of strange customs and funny rules that you have to know about if you are a member of the House of Commons or the House of Lords.

- You are not allowed to **EAT OR DRINK** in the House of Commons. The only exception is that when the Chancellor of the Exchequer is delivering the Budget he is allowed to have an alcoholic drink.
- **SMOKING** in the chambers has been banned since the seventeenth century, but you are allowed to sniff snuff. Even though no one takes snuff any more, the doorkeeper keeps a snuff box just in case.
- You are not allowed to put your hands in your **TROUSER POCKETS**.
- You are not allowed to wear a **SWORD** in the debating chambers, but you can hang one up on a special loop of ribbon in the cloakroom before you go in.
- You are not allowed to call another MP by his or her name when in the House of Commons. You must say either **'MY HONOURABLE FRIEND'** if they are a member of your own political party or 'the honourable gentleman/lady' for members from another party. When speaking to an MP who is a qualified lawyer you must call him or her 'my learned friend' whichever party they belong to.
- When the Lord Speaker of the House of Lords wants to speak, he has to sit on a giant red cushion called the **WOOLSACK**. This dates back to Edward III. The woolsack was stuffed with English wool to show the value and importance of wool to the wealth of the nation.

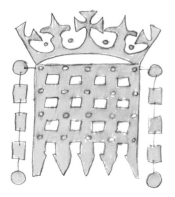

Portcullis: symbol of power

A crowned portcullis, the iron gate of a castle, is the symbol of the City of Westminster. The portcullis was once the heraldic badge of the Tudor kings. Used by Sir Charles Barry when he rebuilt the Houses of Parliament, it has become the symbol of British government and power. The new MPs' office building at Westminster is called Portcullis House.

Despite a history of terrible fires, London did not have a city-wide fire brigade until 1866.

The story of the terrible fire

When the deputy housekeeper arrived for work at the Palace of Westminster on 16 October 1834, the House of Lords was so full of smoke that she couldn't see the throne, but she was told not to worry. Workmen had been stoking the fires all day with 800 years' worth of wooden tallies – notched sticks that once recorded the accounts of England. But the fire grew too fierce and leapt out of control.

A fire brigade came to the rescue, but the water in the Thames was low and they couldn't put out the fire. Everyone volunteered to help, from ministers to labourers, rescuing precious documents, historic relics and paintings. The Deputy Sergeant at Arms climbed into a burning room to rescue the ceremonial mace, an important decorative staff carried in ceremonies, and escaped just in time. Thousands of people crowded on the bridges, in the streets and on the river to watch. The roof of Westminster Abbey was black with spectators. But nothing could save the palace and it was all but razed to the ground. New Houses of Parliament were ordered to be built.

The State Opening of Parliament

Once a year, the Queen leaves Buckingham Palace in her state carriage, wearing a splendid ermine-trimmed cape and escorted by her fancily dressed Household Cavalry, to open the new parliament. When she arrives, the King's Troop fires a gun salute in Hyde Park and at the Tower of London.

The Queen sits on a throne in the House of Lords. A ritual is enacted; Black Rod, a man who carries a large ceremonial stick, knocks on the doors of the House of Commons to demand they are opened. The door is ceremoniously slammed in his face, demonstrating the Commons' independence from the monarchy. Black Rod knocks again three times and this time the doors are opened and he brings the Prime Minister in to the House of Lords. All the Members of Parliament follow him and gather to listen as the Queen, wearing the Imperial State Crown, delivers a speech.

DID YOU KNOW?

The Imperial State Crown travels in its own carriage to the Houses of Parliament for the annual State Opening ceremony. It is placed on a crimson cushion and lit up so people can see it. It is guarded by the Royal Watermen in fine red and gold livery; this dates from the days when the crown would have travelled by barge.

BIG BEN, THE BIGGEST CLOCK IN THE WORLD

Big Ben is the nickname given to the bell of the clock of the Palace of Westminster and it is often used to refer to the clock or the clock tower as well. The clock is the largest four-faced chiming clock in the third-tallest freestanding clock tower in the world. Its official name is the Great Clock. It might look quite small from the ground but it's enormous. Each clock face is 6.9 metres/23 feet across. The minute hand is the length of a black cab and the hour hand is the same height as a telephone box.

Each of its four giant faces is made up of 312 pieces of milky-white glass. At the base of each clock face in gilt letters is an inscription in Latin that means 'O Lord, save our Queen Victoria the First'. The pendulum, which beats every 2 seconds, is enclosed in a windproof box. Piled on top of the pendulum is a stack of old penny coins, which are used to adjust the time. Adding or removing one penny changes the clock's speed by 0.4 seconds a day. Big Ben has been telling Londoners the time since 1859.

The Great Bell of Westminster

The bell we hear ring out over the rooftops of London is actually the second bell made for the job. The first bell cracked while undergoing tests before it was even installed and was melted down to make a new one. The second bell was cast at Whitechapel Bell Foundry in the East End of London on 11 April 1858. It is 2.3 metres/7 feet 9 inches tall, and 2.28 metres/7 feet 6 inches wide, and the largest bell the foundry has ever cast.

A huge fanfare accompanied the great bell on its journey to the Houses of Parliament. The streets were decorated and scores of people lined the way to watch the incredibly heavy bell being pulled on a trolley by sixteen very strong horses. It took eighteen hours for the bell to be hauled to the clock tower's belfry and it finally rang for the first time on 31 May 1859. Then disaster struck: the second bell cracked.

London was silent again for three years until it was fixed; people say the bell has never sounded the same since.

Fascinating facts

- The clock tower has leaned slightly to one side ever since the tunnels for the Jubilee line were dug out beneath it.
- Big Ben is not the tallest tower at the Houses of Parliament: that honour goes to the Victoria Tower.
- There is a 9-metre/30-foot model of Big Ben on a traffic island outside Victoria train station. It is known as Little Big Ben.

New Prime ministers were expected to bring all their own bedding, crockery, furniture and servants to No. 10 Downing Street. Because the house was so big, Gladstone spent £1,555 on new furniture when he moved in in 1880 because he didn't have enough stuff to fill the rooms.

London landmark: 10 Downing Street

No. 10 Downing Street has been the home of the British Prime Minister ever since Sir Robert Walpole moved in on 23 September 1735. It was conveniently close to Parliament, but it was very run down and costly to run and whoever was prime minister often preferred to live in his own house. Benjamin Disraeli was the first prime minister to make it his home when he moved there in 1877.

No. 10 looks like a modest terrace house but behind the front door is a grand mansion that overlooks a garden and Horse Guards Parade. The Prime Minister's next-door neighbour is the Chancellor of the Exchequer, who lives at No. 11.

The most important room at No. 10 is a room called the Cabinet, where the Prime Minister meets all his senior ministers. They all sit at a long curved table specially designed so that everyone can see each other without leaning forward. This was the idea of a former prime minister, Harold Macmillan. The ministers of government are called the Cabinet.

The famous black front door with its white-painted number ten has a black lion's-head door knocker and a letter box inscribed with the words 'First Lord of the Treasury'. The old wooden door has been replaced with a blastproof steel one.

A gas lamp hangs outside, topped with a crown. A hooded chair, with a drawer for hot coals underneath to keep a guarding policeman warm, is now kept inside the front door.

Speakers' corner

A corner of Hyde Park close to Marble Arch is known as SPEAKERS' CORNER, as it is a place where people make open-air public and political speeches. It is said to be a tradition that is connected to the nearby TYBURN GALLOWS, where a condemned man was allowed to make a final speech before the noose was placed around his neck. Famous political activists who spoke at Speakers' Corner include Karl Marx, Vladimir Lenin, George Orwell, Marcus Garvey and William Morris.

Assassination of the Prime Minister

Spencer Perceval is the only British prime minister ever to have been ASSASSINATED. On 11 May 1812, he walked through the lobby of the House of Commons and was confronted and shot by a man called John Bellingham, who felt betrayed by the British government, as he had been wrongly imprisoned in Russia. An inquest was held at the Cat and Bagpipes pub on the corner of Downing Street and Bellingham was hanged a week later. His descendant Henry Bellingham is an MP today.

The Whitebait Dinners

The Whitebait Dinners were started by MP Robert Preston at the end of the eighteenth century, when he invited the Prime Minister, Pitt the Younger, and friends to dine at his fishing cottage in Dagenham. This became an annual event, which moved to the TRAFALGAR TAVERN on the river at Greenwich and was enjoyed by London's MPs, who would travel down the Thames to Greenwich to feast on whitebait. Prime Minister Gladstone dropped the tradition in the 1880s.

DID YOU KNOW? · LONDON FACT ·

* A London company called Barrow and Gale makes the famous red briefcase that is waved by the Chancellor of the Exchequer on Budget Day.
* Winston Churchill often dictated speeches, memos and letters to his secretary while lying propped up in bed, cigar in hand, at No. 10.
* While he was Prime Minister, the Earl of Rosebery rode around London at night in a primrose-coloured carriage because he found it hard to get to sleep and he thought it might help.
* The Prime Minister who lived longest at Downing Street was William Pitt the Younger. He resided at No. 10 for twenty years.

PRIME MINISTERS

Fifty-two men and one woman have lived at No. 10 as Prime Minister:

1721–42	Sir Robert Walpole
1742–3	Spencer Compton, Earl of Wilmington
1743–54	Henry Pelham
1754–6 and 1757–62 Thomas Pelham-Holles, Duke of Newcastle
1756–7	William Cavendish, Duke of Devonshire
1762–3	John Stuart, Earl of Bute
1763–5	George Grenville
1765–6 and 1782 Charles Wentworth, Marquess of Rockingham
1766–8	The Earl of Chatham, William Pitt 'The Elder'
1768–70	Augustus Henry Fitzroy, Duke of Grafton,
1770–82	Lord North
1782–3	William Petty, Earl of Shelburne
1783 and 1807–9 William Bentinck, Duke of Portland
1783–1801 and 1804–6 William Pitt 'The Younger'
1801–4	Henry Addington
1806–7	William Wyndham Grenville, Lord Grenville
1809–12	Spencer Perceval
1812–27	Robert Banks Jenkinson, Earl of Liverpool
1827	George Canning
1827–8	Frederick Robinson, Viscount Goderich
1828–30	Arthur Wellesley, Duke of Wellington
1830–34	Earl Grey
1834 and 1835–41 William Lamb, Viscount Melbourne
1834–5 and 1841–6 Sir Robert Peel

1846–51 and 1865–6 Earl Russell
1852, 1858–9 and 1866–8 The Earl of Derby
1852–5	Earl of Aberdeen
1855–8 and 1859–65 Viscount Palmerston
1868 and 1874–80 Benjamin Disraeli
1868–74, 1880–85, 1886 and 1892–94 William Ewart Gladstone
1885–6, 1886–92 and 1895–1902 Robert Gascoyne-Cecil, Marquess of Salisbury
1894–5	The Earl of Rosebery, Liberal
1902–5	Arthur James Balfour
1905–8	Henry Campbell-Bannerman
1908–16	Herbert Henry Asquith
1916–22	David Lloyd George
1922–3	Andrew Bonar Law
1923, 1924–9 and 1935–7 Stanley Baldwin
1924 and 1929–35 James Ramsay MacDonald
1937–40	Arthur Neville Chamberlain
1940–5 and 1951–5 Sir Winston Leonard Spencer Churchill
1945–51	Clement Richard Attlee
1955–7	Anthony Eden
1957–63	Harold Macmillan
1963–4	Sir Alec Douglas-Home
1964–70 and 1974–6 Harold Wilson
1970–4	Edward Heath
1976–9	James Callaghan
1979–90	Margaret Thatcher
1990–97	John Major
1997–2007 Tony Blair
2007–10	Gordon Brown
2010 to date David Cameron

The River Thames

The River Thames is even older than London. It was here first. London was founded on its banks and flourished largely because the river nourished the city: it gave London a good water source, a plentiful supply of fish to eat, and an excellent route in and out of the city and the heart of England, while also being close enough to the sea for Londoners to forge great trade links and embark on voyages of exploration across the globe.

Over the centuries the Thames has worked hard for the city as a source of water, food, transport, trade and entertainment. It has had a crucial and important part to play in London's history.

The Thames is the most ancient name recorded in England, apart from the place name Kent.

Tides on the Thames

The stretch of the river that runs from Teddington Lock all the way out to the coast, and includes the Pool of London, the Thames Gateway and the Thames Estuary, is called the Tideway because it has tides, just as the sea does. The tide ebbs and flows twice each day, and it is easy to see whether it is in or out: at low tide, stones, shells, mud and even sandy beaches appear at the edges of the water. The Thames used to be tidal all the way to Staines until the lock at Teddington was built. This is marked by the London Stone, erected in Staines in 1285.

At London Bridge there is a 7-metre/23-foot difference in the height of water at high tide.

vital statistics

- The Thames is 346 kilometres/**215 MILES** long.
- Thames means '**THE POURING OUT OF WATERS**' in Celtic.
- The Thames is nicknamed **OLD FATHER THAMES**.
- The Thames is the **LONGEST RIVER** in England.
- The Thames flows **EAST** into the North Sea.
- The Thames is now the **CLEANEST** river flowing through a city in Europe.
- Both **SEA WATER AND FRESH WATER** mix in the river Thames in London.
- The **THAMES PATH** is a national footpath that starts at the river's source in Gloucestershire and ends at the Thames Barrier, a distance of 296 kilometres/184 miles.
- There is a **SPEED LIMIT** of 8 knots/15kmh on the Thames in London.
- Rubbish munchers trap floating debris in the Thames, each one trapping **20 TONNES** a year.

Islands in the Thames

There are eighty islands in the Thames.
Some of them are in London:

OLIVER'S ISLAND, KEW   ISLEWORTH AIT

Chiswick Eyot

Corporation Island, Richmond   Glover's Island, Twickenham

Isle of Dogs

Swan Island, Twickenham   EEL PIE ISLAND, TWICKENHAM

The story of the whale in the Thames

On 20 January 2006 a northern bottle-nosed whale 5 metres/16–18 feet long was spotted in the Thames and was seen as far upstream as Chelsea. This was extremely unusual because this type of whale is generally found in deep sea waters. Crowds gathered along the riverbanks to witness the extraordinary spectacle. A rescue attempt was made but the sick whale died in the process. Its body was rescued and donated to the Natural History Museum.

* In the 1930s and the 1950s, London families sunbathed, swam and built sand castles on an official beach on the shore at Tower Bridge.

* Charles Dickens described the Thames as 'a dank, stinking sludge, the scene of murders and crime'.

* The Thames has narrowed since the building of the Victoria Embankment – so much so that the watergate that once led from the grand York House to the river is now stranded in the middle of Embankment Gardens, nowhere near the water's edge.

* More than 100 fish species have been recorded in the Thames Estuary since the river was cleaned up, including chub, roach, bream, perch, gudgeon, barbell, bass, bream, eel, flounder, carp, pike, perch and trout.

* The watermen would often take a rest on south bank of the Thames near the Globe Theatre. A stone ferryman's seat is still there on Bankside in the wall.

Man overboard

There are four lifeboat stations on the river, set up after the pleasure boat the *Marchioness* sank in 1989 and 51 people lost their lives. The stations are at Teddington, Chiswick, Victoria Embankment and Gravesend.

On average one dead body a week is retrieved from the river Thames.

The story of the sinking of the *Princess Alice*

The *Princess Alice*, owned by the London Steamboat Company, was a large passenger steamship which made regular trips up and down the river. On 3 September 1878 it was involved in the worst British river disaster on record. At about eight o' clock in the evening, just as the *Princess Alice* was approaching Woolwich Pier on its way back from Gravesend, the ship was struck by a coal boat, called the *Bywell Castle*. The impact practically sliced the *Princess Alice* in half, causing it to sink in a matter of minutes. More than 600 people lost their lives. An inquiry concluded that the captain of the *Princess Alice* had been at fault.

Frost fairs

From time to time in London's history the river THAMES would freeze into solid ice, creating a spectacular WINTER WONDERLAND on which people could play. Londoners would celebrate by putting on magnificent frost fairs.

The first known fair was in 1608 and the last in 1814, when the river froze for four days. This time the ice was strong enough to allow an ELEPHANT to be led across it at Blackfriars Bridge. During the Great Freeze of 1683–4 the Thames froze for two whole months and the ice was 28 centimetres/11 inches thick.

Frost fairs were carnivals on ice and THOUSANDS OF PEOPLE came. In 1607, a great tented city was set up on the frozen river. Great hogs were roasted on spits over fires; families ice skated; children played on boat swings and merry-go-rounds, took PONY-DRAWN RIDES and watched puppet shows; boats and coaches were turned into sledges; toy makers came to sell their wares; ICE BOWLING alleys opened; and even barber shops, coffee houses and taverns moved on to the river. There was music and dancing and feasting, and BEAR BAITING and bull baiting to entertain.

More often the freezes lasted only a matter of days. Thaws came quickly and revellers and stall holders had to run fast to avoid being washed away in the icy meltwater.

In January 1789, a ship anchored to a pub on the riverside was dragged so fiercely by the MELTING ice water that the whole building came down with it, killing five people.

The knocking down of the old London Bridge, the embankments built by the Victorians and milder winters have meant that London's Thames no longer freezes solid.

Fascinating facts

- The watermen, boatmen and fishermen who could not work when the river was frozen paraded through the City streets dressed in mourning.
- In 1483 a fox was chased by a hunt on the frozen Thames.
- In the winter of 1536, Henry VIII travelled to his palace in Greenwich by sleigh on the river.
- Elizabeth I would practise her archery skills on the ice.

LONDON BRIDGE

London Bridge was the only roadway across the Thames for hundreds of years. No other bridges were built until 1750.

The first London Bridge was a simple WOODEN bridge built over the Thames by the Romans, and then the Saxons. Then, in 1176, a man called PETER DE COLECHURCH decided to replace it with a strong, STURDY STONE bridge. Over the years, this became the longest, inhabited bridge ever built, stretching for 183 metres/900 feet across the Thames. It had nineteen arches and a DRAWBRIDGE.

On top were scores of SHOPS and a chapel dedicated to St Thomas Becket, a Londoner who had become the Archbishop of Canterbury. Heads of traitors were gruesomely displayed on spikes above the bridge. The arches under the bridge were so narrow that they acted as a dam against the river. Water piled up against them and gushed through like high-speed RAPIDS, falling in terrifying eddies and whirlpools. Travelling under it was fraught with danger: fifty watermen a year DROWNED while trying to shoot the rapids. Risk-averse passengers would get off the boats at the Three Cranes on Upper Thames Street, and get on again, after the rapids, at Billingsgate, avoiding the perils of London Bridge altogether.

By the 1750s, the narrow bridge was so CROWDED with people, horses, carts and carriages that it could take over an hour to cross. The houses and shops were pulled down to make more room for traffic to pass, but this did not solve the problem. It was reluctantly decided that the old bridge would have to be pulled down and REBUILT. Londoners, deeply fond of London Bridge, were upset to hear the news. Many of them were terrified that the Thames would run dry if the bridge was removed, as so much of the water was dammed behind it.

But in 1831, the new London Bridge was officially opened, with great ceremony. The King, William IV, came by barge from Somerset House. A great pavilion stretched across it, tables were laid for 500 GUESTS, 100 bands played music and artillery salutes sounded throughout the day. The caterers ordered 840 dozen bottles of the best wine, 300 TURTLES and chickens, 150 hams and tongues, 40 sirloins of beef and 350lb of pineapple (then still an exotic treat) for the feast.

But the new bridge was not to last as long as the old: its heavy piers began to sink into the soft silt of the Thames. By 1968, this London Bridge had been dismantled and sold to an American businessman. A new, stronger, bridge was built, more practical than charming, which is the one you see today.

ssshhh!

SECRET LONDON BRIDGE FACTS

* The arched entrance to St Magnus the Martyr Church, on Lower Thames Street, is the original route to the old London Bridge. Inside the church is a model of the old London Bridge, complete with houses and shops as it would have been in the olden days.
* Two stone alcoves from the old London Bridge have ended up in Victoria Park in Hackney, for no particular reason. They were used by people walking on the narrow bridge as protection from the traffic.
* Traffic congestion was so bad on the old London Bridge that in 1722 the Lord Mayor of London decreed that everyone coming from Southwark to the City had to keep to the west side of the bridge, clearing the east side for those leaving the City. This is possibly the origin of driving on the left in England.
* Freemen of the City of London had an ancient right that allowed them to drive a herd of sheep across London Bridge.

LONDON BRIDGE DITTY

Upon Paul's steeple stands a tree
As full of apples as may be,
The little boys of London town
They run with hooks to pull them down;
And then they run from hedge to hedge
Until they come to London Bridge.

Anon.

London's last wooden bridge

The last wooden bridge across the Thames was the former TOLLBRIDGE at Battersea, built in 1771. It was supposed to be stone, but there was no money to pay for it, so a cheaper wooden one was put up instead. Unfortunately, it was badly designed, dangerous and always being knocked into by passing ships. It was finally pulled down in 1885. Victorian ARTISTS J.M.W. Turner and James McNeill Whistler painted it because it was so unusual looking.

London landmark: Tower Bridge

Tower Bridge is the most photographed bridge in London and is such a symbol of the city that lots of people think it is London Bridge. A public competition was held to find a design for a bridge that wouldn't interfere with the many sailing ships bringing cargo up the Thames. The solution was a bridge that opened and closed, allowing tall ships to continue on their way to the Pool of London. It took eight years to build and was opened on 30 June 1894. The bridge is 244 metres/800 feet long and the two towers are 65 metres/213 feet high. Connecting the towers is a high-level walkway, once open to the public. It was closed in 1910, because people rarely bothered to climb the stairs and avoided it as it was a haunt for pickpockets.

The river was busy with boats and when it was first built Tower Bridge would open and close several times a day. Semaphore signals and bells were used to warn people when the bridge was going to open. At night, green lights were displayed when it was open, and red when it was closed. In foggy weather a gong sounded.

In December 1952, the watchman forgot to ring the warning bell and a No. 78 double-decker bus was already crossing Tower bridge when it started to open. The driver accelerated across the gap and, amazingly, managed to get to the other side just in time, and in one piece.

Vauxhall Bridge is decorated with vast 2-ton sculptures that can only be seen from the river. They are giant figures representing Agriculture, Architecture, Engineering and Pottery on one side and Science, Fine Arts, Local Government and Education on the other. Architecture is clutching a miniature model of St Paul's Cathedral.

Bridges across the Thames

In the days before 1750 when there was only one bridge across the Thames, if you were in a hurry, ferrymen and wherry boats could take you across the river for a penny. The last **FOOT FERRY** in London is at Ham, near Richmond. Today, the river is crisscrossed with bridges for cars, trains and pedestrians. The bridges you might walk or drive across in London are:

Tower Bridge, 1894   London Bridge, 1973   Southwark Bridge, 1921

MILLENNIUM BRIDGE, 2002   Blackfriars Bridge, 1869

WATERLOO BRIDGE, 1945   WESTMINSTER BRIDGE, 1862

Hungerford footbridges, officially the Golden Jubilee Bridges, 2002

Lambeth Bridge, 1932   Vauxhall Bridge, 1906   CHELSEA BRIDGE, 1937

Albert Bridge, 1873   Battersea Bridge, 1890   Wandsworth Bridge, 1938

PUTNEY BRIDGE, 1886   Hammersmith Bridge, 1887

Chiswick Bridge, 1933   KEW BRIDGE, 1903   TWICKENHAM BRIDGE, 1933

Richmond Lock and Footbridge, 1894   Richmond Bridge, 1777

KINGSTON BRIDGE, 1828   Hampton Court Bridge, 1933

DID YOU KNOW?

* The Millennium Bridge, called the Blade of Light by its architect Norman Foster, has been nicknamed the Wobbly Bridge because it shook so much when the first people tried to cross it when it opened in 2000.
* Blackfriars Bridge is named after the Black Friars whose monastery was on the north bank of the Thames.
* Waterloo Bridge is named after the British victory at the Battle of Waterloo.
* Chelsea Bridge changed its name from Victoria Bridge to save the royal family from embarrassment when it was thought it might fall down.
* Albert Bridge is nicknamed the Trembling Lady because it vibrates if too many people cross it at one time. Signs warn soldiers from the nearby Chelsea Barracks to break step when crossing.
* Putney Bridge is the start line for the annual Oxford and Cambridge Boat Race.
* Twickenham Bridge has special hinges in the concrete so that it can move with temperature changes without cracking.
* Richmond Bridge is the oldest surviving bridge in London.

The old horse ferry across the Thames at Vauxhall was famous for capsizing and once tipped Oliver Cromwell into the river, much to his annoyance.

Lost rivers of London

You'd be forgiven for thinking there was only one river in London, the Thames, but right under our feet are the buried rivers of London. Here are some of them.

THE FLEET is the largest underground river in London. It flows from Hampstead Heath to Fleet Street. If you put your ear to a grating in Ray Street in Farringdon you will be able to hear it rushing past.

THE TYBURN runs underground from Hampstead to Vauxhall. It flows underneath St James's Park and Buckingham Palace. The Tyburn still springs up in the basement of Grays Antiques Market in Davies Street. When the building was done up, the trickle was made into a water feature, complete with goldfish.

THE WESTBOURNE flows from Hampstead and runs into the Thames at Chelsea. Queen Caroline had the river dammed in 1730 to create the Serpentine Lake in Hyde Park. At Sloane Square Tube station there is a giant overhead pipe that carries the Westbourne River out to the Thames.

THE WALBROOK now flows completely underground from London Wall to Bucklersbury. The street called Walbrook is where it once ran above ground.

THE EFFRA rises at Crystal Palace and flows through Herne Hill, Brixton and Kennington, and then into the Thames just beside Vauxhall Bridge: you can see it from the bridge if you look south. Elizabeth I would go by boat on the Effra to visit Sir Walter Raleigh at his Brixton home.

London's drinking water

Londoners relied on the Thames for their drinking water, even though the river was dangerously **POLLUTED** with sewage and waste from the city. Water was drawn from the Thames and carted in wagons from house to house, and then carried inside in buckets. In 1581, a Dutchman was given a lease for 500 years to pump water from a **WATERWHEEL** on London Bridge from Thames Street to Eastcheap. Fresh water was also piped from springs in the nearby countryside at:

Sadler's Wells   MUSWELL HILL   Spa Fields

HAMPSTEAD   clerkenwell   Camberwell

More water, please!

In spite of efforts to get Londoners fresh drinking water, there was not enough water to serve the city's growing population. Something had to be done. The solution was provided by a wealthy man called Hugh Myddleton, who had made his fortune as a goldsmith in the City. He backed a plan to dig a canal all the way from springs in Hertfordshire, bringing new water to London. It took many years of labour, but by 1613 the New River had arrived in Hornsey, Newington, Holloway and Clerkenwell. A reservoir was built to store the spring water, called New River Head. From here, the water was piped to any Londoner who wanted to pay for it. It was carried across the city in hollow elm trunks clasped together with iron bands. The London guild who had previously made a living delivering tankards of fresh drinking water around the city were furious at finding themselves losing business.

RANDOM WATER FACTS

* Dick Whittington paid for the first drinking fountain in London.
* There were once little wells and springs across the city. Water still bubbles up at Holywell underneath Australia House on the Strand.
* In the eighteenth century, spas were set up at the London springs. The fashionable flocked to drink the spring waters. Some spas claimed the waters had medicinal and health-giving properties. Theatres and pleasure gardens grew up around these spas, complete with music, dancing, promenading, eating, drinking and socializing.
* The first mechanically pumped public water supply was near the junction of Cornhill and Leadenhall Street, constructed in 1582. It was called the London Standard.
* In Victorian London, wealthy families had hot water pumped into their houses, but the poor had to stand and queue at water pumps on street corners and carry their water home.
* There is a fine water pump, complete with a lamp, on Jockey Fields, near Gray's Inn.
* Cattle and horse troughs were dotted round the city to provide drinking water for London's animals.
* The well at Clerkenwell can be seen through an office window in Farringdon Lane, near Well Court.

GREENWICH AND THE ROYAL OBSERVATORY

Situated on the Thames to the east, Greenwich has long been the sea-faring heart of London. The nearby naval docks at Deptford and Woolwich, founded by Henry VIII, were an important place for building **WAR SHIPS** and where many great sea voyages began and ended.

Greenwich's connection with ships and global exploration made it a centre for the study of navigation, **STAR GAZING** and map making and it was the site of the Royal Observatory, founded in 1675.

London was the largest producer of scientific instruments in the world in the mid-eighteenth century. At the time of Capain Cook, it was said that 'no people ever went to sea better fitted out for the purpose of natural history nor more elegantly.'

Greenwich now houses the **NATIONAL MARITIME MUSEUM**, keeping the tradition of the connection of London and the Thames to the sea.

London's first public time signal

High on the top of Flamsteed House at the Royal Observatory is one of the earliest public time signals, dating back to 1833, and built so that it could be seen by boats, and Londoners, on the river.

A giant, bright **RED BALL** rises halfway up a mast on top of Flamsteed House at 12.55 p.m. It steadily rises over the next three minutes, reaching the very top. At precisely 1.00 p.m. it plummets to the bottom of the mast. In the days before most people had watches, it was a very good way of communicating the exact time.

DID YOU KNOW?

Sir Francis Drake was hailed as the first English man to sail all the way around the world in 1580. His adventures on the high seas were legendary and the spanish saw him as a dangerous thieving pirate. They called him 'El Draque'.

When Captain Cook set off to explore the South Seas and the Pacific, his ship, HMS *Endeavour*, was altered for the three-year voyage at Deptford, given new deck, masts, yards and sails. The ship was loaded with 6,000 pieces of pork, 4,000 of beef, 9 tons of bread, 5 tons of flour, 3 tons of sauerkraut, 1 ton of raisins, sundry quantities of cheese, salt, peas, sugar and oatmeal, 250 barrels of beer, 44 barrels of brandy and 17 barrels of rum.

Greenwich and the beginning of time

The Greenwich **MERIDIAN LINE**, at the Royal Observatory, also known as 0° longitude, is the Prime Meridian of the world, the point from which every measurement east or west around the world is made. If you stand with one foot on each side of the line you will have one foot in the **WESTERN HEMISPHERE** and one foot in the **EASTERN HEMISPHERE**. The Prime Meridian passes through a giant and very special **TELESCOPE** in the Observatory Meridian Building. At night a **GREEN LASER** projects the Prime Meridian Line spectacularly across the London sky.

The Prime Meridian is also the official starting point of every new day, year and millennium. We call the time at this meridian **GREENWICH MEAN TIME** (GMT), which provides a standard time for the world.

The need for a standard time became important in the 1850s with the expansion of the railway networks and the need for accurate train **TIMETABLES**. Before that, everyone organized their own clocks and time keeping, and every town was different. World leaders met in Washington in 1884 and decided that **GREENWICH** should be centre of world time because most of the trading ships already used maps that placed Greenwich as the Prime Meridian.

The length of one day was worked out by averaging a year's worth of natural days. GMT is a **SCIENTIFIC** timescale used no matter which time zone you happen to be in.

Cutty Sark

Funeral processions on the Thames

ELIZABETH I died at her favourite palace in Richmond on 28 April 1603. Her body was brought to Westminster in a black royal barge. Her coffin was draped with purple velvet, the colour of royalty. William Campden, a poet, described the scene:

The Queen was brought by water to Whitehall
At every stroke of oars did tears fall.

Thousands of Londoners lined the streets for the procession to Westminster Abbey. The coffin was drawn by four horses draped in black livery and covered by a canopy carried by six knights of the realm. On top was a giant effigy of the Queen, dressed in her finest clothes, which was so lifelike that it terrified the people who saw it. The effigy is kept at Westminster Abbey Undercroft Museum.

Lord Nelson

ADMIRAL LORD NELSON lay in state in the Painted Hall at Greenwich after his death at the Battle of Trafalgar in 1805. He was carried from there on a funeral barge shrouded in black velvet and decorated with black ostrich feathers. The City livery companies, the Lord Mayor and the Prince of Wales accompanied the procession in their own ceremonial barges. The grand procession travelled up the river Thames to Whitehall Stairs, Westminster, and Nelson's gold-encrusted coffin was set to rest at the Admiralty for the night. The next morning, the funeral cortège set off to the City of London, accompanied by 32 admirals, 100 captains and 10,000 soldiers in reverent silence. Nelson was buried in an ornate tomb in the crypt beneath the dome of St Paul's Cathedral.

WINSTON CHURCHILL'S body was taken up the Thames from Tower Gate to Waterloo Pier after his funeral at St Paul's Cathedral on 29 January 1965. From there it was taken on a train to his home town for burial.

Thirteen Royal Navy ships have been called
HMS London since 1636.

All Aboard! Ships on the Thames

The Cutty Sark is at Greenwich, in a dry dock by the Thames. It was the fastest clipper of the nineteenth century and is the only one of its kind left in the world. She voyaged from London to Shanghai in 1870, filled with wine, spirits and beer, and brought home 1,450 tons of tea. When the invention of the steam ship put the tea clipper out of business, the *Cutty Sark* made her living moving coal from Nagasaki, jute from Manila and wool from Australia. She was sent back to London in 1951 as an exhibit in the Festival of Britain.

The Golden Hinde, a perfect replica of Sir Francis Drake's Tudor warship, is dry docked on the South Bank. Sir Francis Drake set sail in 1577, with Elizabeth I's blessing and some money, on an expedition to South America. He captured a Spanish galleon and the largest hoard of treasure ever taken. The Queen was so pleased that she came aboard his ship at Deptford and knighted him there and then. Her share of the booty was £160,000, enough to clear all her foreign debt and have some left over. Over time the original ship rotted, but a ceremonial cupboard in London's Middle Temple Hall is said to have been made with wooden hatch covers from the original *Golden Hinde*.

HMS Belfast is a twentieth-century steel, 6-inch-gun warship, once active in the Second World War. It was the first ship to be preserved by the nation since Nelson's ship, the *Victory*. It is one of the most powerful large light cruisers ever built and was fast enough to attack and destroy the enemy. The ship dominates the Thames, opposite the Tower of London.

The story of a ship called *The London*

In 1866, a ship called *HMS London* set sail from London carrying passengers bound for a new life in Australia. The ship was heavily laden and in poor shape. As she sailed up the Thames at Purfleet, she was sinking very low in the water. Onlookers predicted that, like many 'coffin ships' before her, she'd never make it to the other side of the globe. They were right. The *London* got as far as the Bay of Biscay and then sank. Only nineteen people survived. As a result, a man called Samuel Plimsoll campaigned in Parliament to stop such a disaster happening again, devising the Plimsoll line, the waterline that is drawn around the hull of a boat to mark a ship's load limit in the water.

Fascinating facts: London's secret waterways

- The first London canal was cut in 1766, joining the river Lee to the Thames, and was called the Limehouse Cut. It was a great success and plans were made to cut a canal through the heart of London and link the docks to a network of canals being built across the country.

- The Regent's Canal runs through the centre of London and is named after the Prince Regent, the future George IV. It was completed in 1820.

- The Regent's canal is 14.5 kilometres/9 miles long and runs from Limehouse in the east to Little Venice in the west, passing through Islington, Camden and Regent's Park on its way.

- The longest tunnel on the Regent's Canal is in Islington and is 886 metres/960 yards in length. Too narrow to take horses, children would lead them overhead while the men and women moved the barge through the tunnel by legging – lying on their backs with their legs pushing on the tunnel walls – to drive it along.

- The Regent's Canal connects up with the Grand Junction Canal at Paddington Basin, which was once London's thriving inland port. The Grand Union Canal then stretches from London to Birmingham.

canal boat

Little tunnels under the Thames

TOWER SUBWAY Just by the Tower of London is a small round building – the entrance to a long-forgotten tunnel that goes under the river Thames. Built in 1870 by James Greathead, this was the first ever train tunnel, with a cable car that shuttled a dozen people back and forth, in each direction. After just a few months it was deemed too expensive to run. It became a foot tunnel, which proved a highly popular way to cross the river until Tower Bridge was built just down river. It closed in 1894. It is now used to transport water mains.

GREENWICH FOOT TUNNEL On the banks of the Thames at Greenwich is the entrance to the Greenwich Foot Tunnel, which allows you to walk under the Thames to the Isle of Dogs and back. The elegant circular entrance, opened in 1902, houses a very smart wood-panelled lift.

WOOLWICH FOOT TUNNEL
Further downstream is the Woolwich Foot Tunnel. This was built to help people who worked in London's docks to get from one side of the river to the other.

★ LONDON LINGO ★

Wet docks = For unloading ships
Dry docks = For ship repairs
Dockyards = For ship building
A dolphin = A mooring point
Lightermen = Carried loads between ships and quays aboard
small barges called lighters
Deal porters = Carried timber and were famous for their
acrobatic skills
Wharfingers = Wharf owners
A hogshead = A large barrel normally used for liquid cargo.
Tobacco was transported from America in hogsheads.
Customs = Tax paid on goods
Legal quays = Customs inspection point

London is sinking by 30 centimetres/12 inches
every 100 years.

The busiest port in the world

In the eighteenth and nineteenth centuries the Pool of London was the largest and busiest port in the world. The Upper Pool runs between Tower Bridge and London Bridge. The Lower Pool runs east to Rotherhithe.

The dock workers formed tight-knit local communities with their own distinctive cultures and slang. In 1920 the residents of the Isle of Dogs, where Canary Wharf is now, blocked the roads and declared their independence from London.

The Port of London today handles over 50 million tonnes of a wide range of cargoes every year, including cars, grain, paper, oil and sugar.

DID YOU KNOW? · LONDON FACT · LONDON FACT · LONDON FACT ·

King George V Dock has become London's City Airport.
Factories were set up just behind the docks to process the cargoes. In 1939 the Tate and Lyle sugar cane refinery which dominated the river was the largest in the world. It produced 14,000 tons of sugar per week.

Ships and cargoes

Each London dock specialized in different goods from different places. Most were built from the 1800s onwards and were designed to accommodate sailing ships.

WEST INDIA DOCK	Goods from the West Indies such as tea, sugar, molasses and rum
THE LONDON DOCK	Ivory, spices, coffee, cocoa, wine and wool
EAST INDIA DOCK	Spices, indigo, silk, Persian carpets. This was the first private dock in London and was owned by the East India Company, who had the only rights to import tea into London from China. They were very rich.
SURREY DOCKS	Timber, hemp, flax, tar, grain, salt, fruit, cheese, bacon and coal
ST KATHARINE'S DOCK	Wool, sugar and rubber
ROYAL VICTORIA DOCK	The first London dock to be designed for large steam ships and the first to be connected to the national railway network
MILLWALL DOCKS	Grain and timber
ROYAL ALBERT DOCK	Hogsheads of tobacco
TILBURY DOCKS	Madeira, sausage skins packed in brine, Indian chutney
KING GEORGE V DOCK	Fruit and vegetables

Treasure hunting

Modern day mudlarks **RUMMAGE** on the muddy banks of the Thames at low tide to scavenge for treasures from London's past. Old coins, fragments of pilgrim's badges, pottery, tudor bricks, roman sandals, medieval pins, 17th century trader's tokens, discarded oyster shells, bones and pre-fire of London roof tiles secretly await discovery by the **EAGLE EYED**. Most prolific of all are the fragments of disposable clay pipes, smoked by Londoner's ever since Sir Francis Drake brought

TOBACCO back from the Americas in Elizabethan times. They come in all shapes and sizes and are sometimes elaborately moulded or stamped with the maker's mark such as a fleur de Lys or a wheel.

London's only lighthouse at Trinity Buoy Wharf was built in 1866. It was never used for guiding ships, but was a place where scientists like **MICHAEL FARADAY**, whose laboratory was across the river, conducted experiments and tested new kinds of lighthouse lamps.

Landmarks to spot on the River Thames

Hampton Court Palace   BATTERSEA POWER STATION   London Eye

Houses of Parliament   The Festival Hall

TOWER OF LONDON   Tate Modern at Bankside   canary wharf

ROYAL GREENWICH   Millennium Dome

London at risk

From time to time the Thames overflowed its banks and flooded London. There is an account from 1236 of gentlemen rowing in wherry boats through the halls of the Palace of Westminster. In January 1928 a sudden thaw caused the volume of water in the Thames to double and flooded the city. When the tide turned, the force of water washed over the Thames Embankment and caused the Chelsea embankment to collapse. Local people had to swim for their lives and 14 were unable to escape and drowned. In 1953 another great wave of water surged up the Thames, causing terrifying flooding, with water lapping the walls of the Houses of Parliament. 24,000 houses were deluged and the streets of West Ham were turned into rivers. 34,000 people had to be evacuated and 300 people died. Something had to be done and plans were made to build a barrier across the Thames to hold back the flood waters.

The Thames Barrier has been raised to save London from flooding one hundred times.

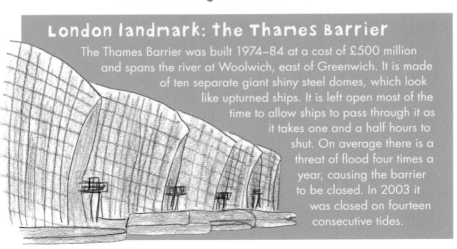

London landmark: the Thames Barrier

The Thames Barrier was built 1974–84 at a cost of £500 million and spans the river at Woolwich, east of Greenwich. It is made of ten separate giant shiny steel domes, which look like upturned ships. It is left open most of the time to allow ships to pass through it as it takes one and a half hours to shut. On average there is a threat of flood four times a year, causing the barrier to be closed. In 2003 it was closed on fourteen consecutive tides.

PIRATES

The eighteenth century was the golden age of piracy.

British pirates were brought to justice in front of the **HIGH COURT OF ADMIRALTY** in London. Any pirates captured on the high seas were sent to London and locked up in Newgate Prison or the Marshalsea **PRISON**.

Once convicted, a condemned pirate was thrown into an open cart and driven through London's streets to **EXECUTION DOCK** at Wapping. There the pirate was strung up on a short rope and hung across the Thames below the tide line until three tides had passed and he was **DROWNED**. A pirate's body was left to hang for all to see, coated in **SHIP'S TAR** to preserve it and to stop it being pecked to pieces by hungry birds. The pirates who had committed the most heinous crimes were taken to **GRAVES POINT** at the mouth of the Thames and hung in an iron cage as a deterrent for others.

Notwithstanding their cruelty and terrible crimes, pirates fascinated the public and the most **DARING** were celebrated. In 1724, a book called *A General History of the Most Notorious Pyrates* by a Captain Johnson was a runaway best-seller. No one ever knew who the author was, as it was written under a pseudonym. Robert Louis Stevenson used it for pirate research when writing *Treasure Island*.

London's most villainous pirates

Pirate captain William Kidd was a cruel and ruthless pirate who was tried and convicted of piracy and murder, and executed in 1701. The rope snapped while he was hanging, so the poor man had to be hanged twice. His body was left gibbeted in an iron cage on the river for twenty years. There is a pub in Wapping named after him, called the Captain Kidd.

Pirate John Gow was a pirate who plundered the high seas in his ship, the *Revenge*. Once captured, he was tortured repeatedly before he would confess his heinous crimes at sea. Prison guards bound his thumbs together and squeezed them with whipcord to make him talk. His body was stretched on a rack and his body weighted with heavy stones and iron. Eventually he broke his silence and confessed all. He was sent to the gallows on 11 June 1725.

Pirate Mary Read was one of the greatest women pirates. Brought up in the slums of London, at thirteen she ran away, dressed as a boy, to make a life at sea. Her ship was captured by pirates and she was forced to join them. In 1720, she hooked up with two pirates called Calico Jack and Anne Bonny. Together they became the toughest and most ruthless pirates on the high seas. After capture, she 'pleaded the belly', as she was pregnant, and bought herself a stay of execution. She died in prison in 1721.

★ LONDON LINGO ★

★ Hanging at Execution Dock was called doing the Marshal's dance,
as a pirate's legs would jiggle as he died.
★ To 'gibbet' a criminal was to hang his body on
public display after death.

Smugglers

London's ports, pubs and wharves were thick with smugglers in the eighteenth century. Everyone wanted the BRANDY, LACE AND TOBACCO being brought up the Thames but taxes were steep and prices were sky high. Smuggling was rife but fraught with DANGER. Customs officials patrolled the river and had the right to search all boats heading towards London once they were past Gravesend.

Smugglers worked under the cover of night to get past the PROWLING customs officials. They used ILLEGAL quays to unload their cargoes or risked unloading it on to smaller boats at the estuary mouth. Some customs officers turned a blind eye if they were paid enough. A warren of SECRET TUNNELS ran from the quaysides into the City to get the goods to market. If a smuggler was caught, he could be HANGED and his booty was confiscated. Much to everyone's displeasure it would be burnt in one of two special ovens at the docks. These were known as the QUEEN'S PIPES.

The Prospect of Whitby pub on the Thames at Wapping is London's most famous smugglers' haunt. It was once called the Devil's Tavern.

Tea Smuggling

Tea was an expensive commodity in the seventeenth century. It took months to travel all the way from China. It was also heavily taxed and tea and coffee houses had to pay for a licence to serve London's most fashionable drink. A thriving tea-smuggling trade soon began. By the eighteenth century, just as many pounds of tea were being smuggled into London as were arriving through the official channels. This illegal trade flourished until a new Act in 1784 dropped the tax on tea from 119 per cent to 12.5 per cent, making tea more affordable.

The Olde Wine Shades in the City - the oldest wine bar in London - reputedly has smugglers' tunnels underneath it that run all the way to the river.

THE SMUGGLER'S SONG

If you wake at midnight, and hear a horse's feet,
Don't go drawing back the blind, or looking in the street,
Them that ask no questions isn't told a lie.
Watch the wall, my darling, while the Gentlemen go by.

Five and twenty ponies,
Trotting through the dark –
Brandy for the Parson, 'Baccy for the Clerk.
Laces for a lady; letters for a spy,
Watch the wall, my darling, while the Gentlemen go by!

Running round the woodlump if you chance to find
Little barrels, roped and tarred, all full of brandy-wine,
Don't you shout to come and look, nor use 'em for your play.
Put the brushwood back again – and they'll be gone next day!

If you see the stable-door setting open wide;
If you see a tired horse lying down inside;
If your mother mends a coat cut about and tore;
If the lining's wet and warm – don't you ask no more!

If you meet King George's men, dressed in blue and red,
You be careful what you say, and mindful what is said.
If they call you 'pretty maid', and chuck you 'neath the chin,
Don't you tell where no one is, nor yet where no one's been!

Knocks and footsteps round the house – whistles after dark –
You've no call for running out till the house-dogs bark.
Trusty's here, and Pincher's here, and see how dumb they lie –
They don't fret to follow when the Gentlemen go by!

If you do as you've been told, 'likely there's a chance,
You'll be give a dainty doll, all the way from France,
With a cap of Valenciennes, and a velvet hood –
A present from the Gentlemen, along 'o being good!

Five and twenty ponies,
Trotting through the dark –
Brandy for the Parson, 'Baccy for the Clerk.
Them that asks no questions isn't told a lie –
Watch the wall, my darling, while the Gentlemen go by.

Rudyard Kipling, 1906

Crime and punishment

Londoners were punished severely for their crimes. The courts gave out the death penalty, known as **CAPITAL PUNISHMENT**, for any number of serious or minor crimes. In 1723, an act was passed in the House of Commons called the Waltham Black Act, where fifty crimes, from theft of a few shillings to poaching, were made punishable by death. Nobility were beheaded at the Tower of London. Most ordinary people were condemned to hang at Tyburn.

Hangings at Tyburn

Tyburn was the most famous public place of execution in London. The execution spot was close to Marble Arch at the top of the Edgware Road. There were so many people to hang that a permanent **GALLOWS** was erected in 1571. It was called the Tyburn Tree, a triangular design with a gibbet that could hang at least twenty-four people at the same time, eight on each side. Children as young as eight years old could legally be hanged, though few actually were. **EXECUTIONS** took place at Tyburn every six weeks.

Hanging day

A hanging day was a public holiday for everyone: it was supposed to be a lesson for the masses. Everyone – **ORANGE SELLERS**, ballad sellers, pickpockets and footmen – jostled for good seats: it was seen as a great entertainment and a social event. Crowds of 80,000 were common, with the wealthier spectators buying tickets for the raised seating of **MOTHER PROCTOR'S PEWS**.

Those condemned to death were taken from Newgate Prison to Tyburn on the back of an open cart, sitting beside their own coffins. The journey down Tyburn Road, now Oxford Street, could take as long as three hours, as thousands gathered to watch them pass by. Friends gave the condemned flowers in exchange for their coats.

Before hanging, a doomed man or woman was expected to speak to the crowd. Copies of final speeches were sold afterwards. When the moment came, the prisoner would climb a ladder with a rope around their neck and the ladder would be pushed away. But there was no quick **SNAP** of the neck: hanging was a slow and agonizing death – it could take up to thirty minutes to die. Relatives and friends would pull on the prisoner's legs to speed up the process. Pieces of the rope that hanged the most **NOTORIOUS** criminals were sold as souvenirs.

★ LONDON LINGO ★

★ Before they were executed, prisoners on their way to Tyburn were allowed one last drink in a pub, probably the Mason's Arms in Seymour Place or the Bowl Inn at St Giles. This last drink was known as 'one for the road'.

★ Once back on the cart, a prisoner was not allowed any more drinks. If anyone offered him one, the guard would shout, 'No, he's on the wagon.'

★ We still use both these expressions today.

★ To 'dance the Tyburn jig' was to be hanged.

Newgate

Newgate took over from Tyburn after 1783 as the home of London's gallows, to save prisoners the long journey across London. The OLD BAILEY Criminal Court now marks the site of this long-gone prison and execution place. All that is left is the street called Newgate. Throughout the nineteenth century men and women were hanged here in front of crowds of 80,000 Londoners. They would gather to pelt the criminals with ROTTEN FRUIT and the rich would watch from the overlooking windows of nearby pubs such as the Magpie and Stump, while feasting on a hanging breakfast. It is said there is a secret tunnel that connected the prison and the church across the road, so that a priest could visit the CONDEMNED without having to push through the crowds.

Military executions took place by firing squad in Hyde Park. This was also a popular spot for duels to the death.

Lucky escapes

JOHN 'HALF-HANGED' SMITH was strung up at Tyburn on 24 December 1705 for robbery. Halfway through the hanging, the judge came along with a reprieve and ordered him to be cut down. Still alive, he was set free.

In 1819, a woman called MARY GREEN, who had been found guilty of using forged banknotes, was sentenced to death by hanging and taken to a scaffold in front of Newgate Prison. As she was cut down, her family noticed that she was still alive. She was allowed to go FREE and made a new life in Halifax, Nova Scotia.

London's last . . .

Ruth Ellis was the last woman to be given the **DEATH PENALTY** in Britain. She was hanged in Holloway Prison on 13 July 1955.

High treason

Until 1870, the law stated that if you were convicted of high treason you should be punished by being 'drawn on a hurdle to the place of execution where you shall be hanged by the neck and being alive cut down, your privy members shall be cut off and your bowels taken out and burned before you, your head severed from your body and your body divided into four quarters to be disposed of at the King's pleasure.'

Only men were hanged, drawn and quartered; women convicted of treason were mostly burned at the stake.

Smithfield: hanged, drawn and quartered

For many years, hanging, drawing and quartering for high treason took place at the open field at Smithfield. Famously, the Scottish rebel William Wallace was hanged, drawn and quartered here in 1305. Smithfield was also the best place to see a heretic or dissenter being burned at the stake. It was where 200 Protestants were burned to death by the Catholic Tudor Queen Mary I.

RANDOM TYBURN FACTS

* The first recorded execution at Tyburn was of William Fitz Osbern, a populist leader, in 1196.
* On 23 June 1649, twenty-three men and one woman were hanged at Tyburn for burglary and robbery. This was London's largest single execution.
* The highwayman John Austin was the last person to be hanged at Tyburn in 1783.
* The last fully public hanging in England was in 1868, when Michael Barrett was hanged at Newgate for setting off a bomb in Clerkenwell, killing seven people. From then on executions took place in private, away from the jeering crowds.
* Ingenious thief Tom Gerrard taught his dog to pickpocket; he was sent to hang at Tyburn in 1711 for the animal's crimes.
* A brass plaque marks the spot where the Tyburn Tree once stood, close to Marble Arch.

Heads on Spikes

The first head to be placed on a spike on London Bridge was that of Sir William Wallace, the Scottish rebel leader in 1305. Londoners were so delighted to see him on display that from then on, all severed heads of traitors were stuck up on spiked poles on the Bridge. A cauldron of tar was kept at one end for the chopped heads to be dipped in to preserve them. A horrified German visitor wrote how he saw more than thirty heads on display at the same time. This practice lasted until the Restoration in 1660.

The most ham-fisted of all executioners was a man called Jack Ketch (1663-86). On one bungled job, he took eight chops to cut off the Duke of Monmouth's head.

Doing time: London's old prisons

Dark, dank, smelly and overcrowded, for many centuries London's prisons were a scary place to be. Torture was commonplace, and was even legal in cases of treason until 1640. Prisoners were treated cruelly and disease was rife. More prisoners died of gaol fever than were hung.

If a mother was sent to prison, her children were sent too. Visitors and family came and went as they pleased. They were relied on to bring all meals, clothing and everything a prisoner needed to survive. Otherwise, you had to pay the guards to do this for you, or bribe them at every turn.

London's oldest . . .

The Clink was a **PRISON** in Southwark, close to the river. It dated back to 1144 and was built on the lands of a monastery. At the Clink, if you had no money and no family, you were thrown into a dungeon called the Hole, and scraps of food were thrown down to you in the crowded darkness. The Clink Prison Museum is on the site of the old prison in Clink Street.

★ LONDON LINGO ★

The term 'the clink' has come to mean prison.

Fleet Prison was London's first purpose-built prison in 1197.

Marshalsea Prison

From 1329 to 1842, Marshalsea was a prison for those who had committed **CRIMES AT SEA**, built on what is now Borough High Street in Southwark. It was also the place where people who **OWED MONEY** were sent: London's debtor's prison. Debtors would be locked away with their families until they had paid up. Children and relatives who lived at the prison were sent out to work to earn the money to **PAY THE DEBTS**. Charles Dickens's father was thrown into the Marshalsea and he describes prison life in his book *Little Dorrit*. Demolished in the 1870s, there is nothing left of the Marshalsea Prison except a high brick wall that marked its boundary.

Newgate Prison

Newgate was overcrowded with the **WORST CRIMINALS** in London, most kept here while waiting for execution. **TERRIBLE TORTURE** took place in a chamber called **LIMBO**, described by one prisoner as 'a place underground, full of horrors, without light and swarming with vermin and creeping things'. There was also the **WATERMAN'S HOLD**, a 'terrible dark and stinking' place reserved for women, and the **STONE HOLD**, where those who could not pay for their food or keep were thrown and abandoned. The first prison at Newgate opened in 1188, and the last prison built on the site was finally demolished in 1904.

LONDON'S PRISONS TODAY

WORMWOOD SCRUBS   BRIXTON   Pentonville

Wandsworth   Belmarsh   Holloway (for women)

The Victorians oversaw the building of more prisons than at any other time in London's history: fifty-two new prisons were built to house newly arrested criminals. The first prison they built was at Pentonville, Islington.

The story of Elizabeth Fry

Elizabeth Fry (1780–1845) was the child of the wealthy Barclay banking family. As a good deed, she would visit poor women in prison, and she was horrified by what she saw. At Newgate Prison, she was confronted by 'a swarm of drunken, half naked, starving women, living more like beasts than humans'. Even the governor of the prison was too scared to see them. Elizabeth resolved to campaign for prison reform. She set up a school for prison children, taught women prisoners to sew and to read, and brought them food and clothing. She also set up the Elizabeth Fry Refuge in Hackney for London's homeless. Her picture is on the back of the five-pound note.

Elizabeth Fry

convict ships

Convicted criminals could escape the death penalty or prison by being transported to distant COLONIES by ship, embarking from Hungerford Stairs on the river at Charing Cross. Until the American War of Independence, this was mostly to North America. From 1788, convicts were sent to Australia. TRANSPORTATION began in the reign of Elizabeth I and the last fleet to Western Australia sailed in 1867.

London's floating prisons: the incredible hulks

To ease overcrowding in London's prisons, in 1776 Paliament decreed that old merchant ships and naval vessels were to be converted into floating prisons. These were known as the HULKS, and kept on the River Thames. The first hulks were moored off the deserted marshes at Woolwich alongside a network of warehouses, barracks, firing ranges and foundries. Soon hulk after hulk lined the river, the boats hanging with ROTTING RIGGING. The prisoners were put to work for long hours on the river, dredging channels, digging out canals and building the Arsenal and neighbouring docks.

Conditions were worse than in any prison. The hulks were cramped and filthy. Prisoners slept with chains around their waists and ankles and were often flogged or thrown into a tiny cell nicknamed the 'BLACK HOLE' as a punishment. Meals were thin and mean, with pea soups and biscuits that were so mouldy they were green on both sides. When the beer ran out convicts drank water drawn from the river. Many of the prisoners on the hulks were awaiting their fate of being sent to the colonies of America and Australia. But many of them never left the hulks: between 1776 and 1795, 2000 out of 6000 prisoners died before their sentences were over. Originally a temporary measure, these terrible hulks remained as FLOATING PRISONS for eighty years.

The law in London

The centre of London law has been at the Inns of Court near Fleet Street since the middle Ages. All barristers must belong to one of the four Inns of Court:

Gray's Inn   LINCOLN'S INN   Inner Temple   MIDDLE TEMPLE

The Royal Courts of Justice, a grand gothic palace on the Strand dating back to Victorian times, is the Court of Appeal and the High Court for England of Wales, where some of the most important cases are tried. The building is vast with 1000 rooms, 88 courtrooms, a labyrinth of halls and corridors over 3 miles long, and a secret passage nicknamed the Chicken Run.

clever crooks used to make their escape from the Royal court by slipping out of a trapdoor hidden under some old lino, through a tunnel into a nearby shop and freedom. The secret escape route was only discovered in 1928.

The Old Bailey

The Old Bailey is London's most famous criminal courthouse. This is where trials are held for London's most serious crimes, including murder. Dating back to 1539, it takes its name from the Roman fortified wall called a bailey and has been rebuilt over the years. This Old Bailey was built using the stones of Old Newgate Prison.

In 1902, a gold statue of a woman, a sword in one hand and scales in the other, was placed high up on top of the dome of the Old Bailey to represent justice.

In the dock

For centuries, London court cases were conducted almost entirely in **LATIN**, so ordinary people could not understand what was happening. Barristers were not brought in to defend an accused man or woman until the end of the 1700s. Trials were short and cases were usually dismissed in a matter of minutes. Being tried must have been a terrifying experience.

The accused would stand in the **DOCK** with a mirror reflecting light from the window above so that those in the dingy courtroom could clearly see the expression on his (or her) face through the **TRIAL**. A wooden board was put above his head to amplify his voice.

SWEET HERBS and flowers were scattered on the benches of the courtrooms of the Old Bailey and judges were given nosegays of flowers to carry to protect themselves against gaol fever, a sickness that killed thousands of prisoners.

To catch a thief

Before the seventeenth century, there was no police force: London relied on individuals and part-time officials to catch criminals.

As the city grew, CRIME levels escalated in London. 'Violence and plunder are no longer confined to the highways . . . the streets of the city are now the places of danger,' lamented one Londoner in 1731. The government set up a system of substantial rewards for catching and convicting criminals guilty of specific serious crimes such as HIGHWAY ROBBERY and coining. People who caught a criminal and brought him to justice were called THIEF-TAKERS. Cries of 'stop thief!' or 'murder' would draw the attention of crowds of Londoners, who competed to catch the criminal. REWARDS were also offered by the victims of crime for the return of stolen goods. A criminal was taken to a constable or justice of the peace for arrest. By the 1730s, a more formal system was beginning to emerge and MAGISTRATES paid salaries to thief-takers.

The streets at night were patrolled by the NIGHT WATCHMEN from the evening until sunrise. They were expected to examine any suspicious characters out and about in the dark and would cry out the time as they paraded. They were nicknamed 'CHARLEYS' after Charles II, who introduced them.

The City of London had its own special MARSHALS AND BEADLES who patrolled the streets in the daytime as well.

Bow Street Runners: London's first police

In 1749, novelist and magistrate Henry Fielding, working with his half-brother John Fielding, set up London's first professional police force, with power to arrest criminals. Wearing red waistcoats, they reported to the court in Bow Street in Covent Garden, where Henry and later John were magistrates, and became known as the Bow Street Runners. At first there were only eight of them in the entire city but within two years there were eighty. The Bow Street group continued until 1839.

DID YOU KNOW?

* The Thames Police Force was set up in the 1800s to stop the smuggling, piracy and theft of cargo that were rife on the Thames.
* Policemen were nicknamed bobbies and peelers after Sir Robert (Bobby) Peel, who set up the Metropolitan Police Force in 1829.
* Today the streets of London are pounded by two police forces: the Metropolitan Police and the City of London Police. The Metropolitan Police wear silver badges on the front of their helmets and the City of London Police have a black and gold helmet plate.

The story of thief-taker Jonathan Wild

Jonathan Wild was a notorious figure in the London criminal underworld of the eighteenth century. Befriending both thieves and magistrates, and charming the courts and the lawyers into thinking he was honest, he worked for both sides, playing them off against each other. He ran scores of criminal gangs across London, setting up grand heists, burglaries and skulduggery. But at the same time he was a thief-taker, and as soon as a thief had outlived his usefulness to him, he would sell him to the courts and pocket the money.

He was paid £40 for each highwayman, coiner (someone who makes counterfeit coins) or burglar he turned over to the law. There was a bonus of £100 if the crime was committed within 5 miles of Charing Cross. This was more than an ordinary man could earn in four years. Wild was lauded as a great hero by the people of London and praised for his phenomenal success at bringing London's criminals to trial and making the streets a safer place.

Eventually, his trickery was uncovered and Wild was exposed as betraying trust on both sides of the law. When he was finally arrested for the trifling matter of stealing 50 yards of lace, the true story of his duplicitous crimes unfolded and he was sentenced to death at the Old Bailey. Londoners were furious with him. Angry crowds pelted him with faeces and shouted at him on his journey to Tyburn. The number of people attending his execution was one of the highest ever. The authorities were so concerned his body would be ripped apart by the mob that he was buried in secret in the night. Even so, his body went missing, reappearing at the Royal College of Surgeons for dissection. His skeleton is on display at the Hunterian Museum in Lincoln's Inn Fields.

Scotland Yard

It was not until 1829 that Sir Robert Peel created a police force for the whole of London, based at 4 Whitehall Place, which backed on to a courtyard once owned by the kings of Scotland, known as Scotland Yard. A policeman carried a truncheon, a whistle and a lantern for night duties. The first detective department of London's Metropolitan Police was set up in 1842, created to solve murders and other heinous crimes in the city.

Policeman's helmet

Sherlock Holmes

Arthur Conan Doyle's pipe-smoking, deer-stalker-wearing **DETECTIVE** Sherlock Holmes is one of the most famous fictional Londoners. One of a new kind of detective established in the late nineteenth century, especially to solve **MURDERS** using all the latest **SCIENTIFIC** techniques, he investigated his first crimes in a Christmas annual in 1887 and was the hero of a number of subsequent short stories and novels. He lived at 221b Baker Street and had a sidekick called **DR WATSON**. The Sherlock Holmes Museum in Baker Street was the first museum in the world to be dedicated to a fictional character.

London's highwaymen

From Elizabethan times, **DASTARDLY** highwaymen haunted the dark, wooded roads in and out of London, **AMBUSHING** unsuspecting ladies and gentlemen as they rode by in their carriages or on horseback. London's most notorious and dangerous places to travel through were Hampstead Heath, Hounslow Heath, Shooter's Hill and Finchley Common. Terrifying as these raids were, the highwayman was a **DASHING** figure who captured the hearts of Londoners, and was the stuff of legends and stories.

Even the centre of London was dangerous. **STAGECOACHES** were frequently held up in High Holborn, Pall Mall, Soho and Whitechapel. Hyde Park was just as unsafe: at dusk highwaymen were so **BRAZEN** that they tied their horses to the railings and sallied forth on foot to rob passers-by and people in their sedan chairs and carriages.

In Kensington Gardens a bell was rung every night at dusk to warn those going home to gather together in large groups to defend themselves against attack. Horace Walpole, son of Prime Minister Sir Robert Walpole, who narrowly escaped death from a highwayman's bullet in Hyde Park, said, 'one is forced to travel, even at noon, as if one were going into battle.'

Dick Turpin and Black Bess

Probably the most dastardly highwayman of all was Dick Turpin, who robbed anyone who passed his hideout at Loughton Camp in **EPPING FOREST**. He became so notorious that the *London Evening Post* regularly reported his exploits and in 1735 **THE KING** offered a reward of £50 for his capture, but by the skin of his teeth he managed to escape from the hands of the law. Pubs across London still lay claim to stabling his beautiful black horse, Bess.

Dick Turpin often hid out at the Spaniard's Inn at Hampstead Heath, ambushing unsuspecting travellers on the road to London. His horse Black Bess is said to haunt the nearby lanes.

Stand and deliver, please!

Eighteenth-century highwaymen **JAMES MACLAINE** and his accomplice **WILLIAM PLUNKETT** lived like gentlemen by day in St James's, one of London's smartest addresses, but by night carried out outrageous hold-ups in Hyde Park. They covered their faces with **VENETIAN MASKS** as if they were off to a ball and were terribly polite, which is how they got their nickname, 'the gentlemen highwaymen'. Their **LIFE OF CRIME** was short-lived. After only twenty heists in six months MacLaine was arrested trying to pawn a particularly distinctive coat that he'd stolen during a hold-up on Hounslow Heath. He was thrown into **PRISON** at Newgate. Three thousand people flocked to see him and witness his trial at the Old Bailey. He was **HANGED** at Tyburn in 1750. His lucky accomplice Plunkett got away with his money and his life.

Jack Sheppard

Jack Sheppard, one of London's most **NOTORIOUS** thieves, was born in Spitalfields in 1702. He was as famous for his crimes as for his daring escapes: he was imprisoned five times and **ESCAPED** four times even though he was often manacled in irons stapled to the stone floor. He used all the tricks in the book including filing through bars, scaling down the wall of New prison in Clerkenwell on a string of knotted bed sheets and once **DISGUISED** in women's clothing. He was so popular and **HEROIC** a figure that when he was finally hanged at Tyburn in 1724, more than 200,000 people to watch the spectacle. His friends collected his dead body and took it to the Barley Mow Tavern in Long Acre. He was buried the next day at St Martin-in-the-Fields. He was such a celebrity that he was **IMMORTALIZED** in the stories and songs of the time. The character of **MACHEATH** in John Gay's *The Beggar's Opera* is based on Jack Sheppard.

★ LONDON LINGO ★

Scotland Yard, the London street where the first police force was based, is the name everyone still uses for the HQ of the Metropolitan Police Force, even though it has now moved.

Jack the Ripper: murder most horrid

Jack the Ripper is the most notorious **MURDERER** ever to stalk the dark alleys and streets of London. He cruelly **SLASHED** the throats of his victims, killing five, possibly six, women in the slums of Whitechapel in the **EAST END** in 1888. More than **600 POLICEMEN** worked day and night on the case; detectives conducted house-to-house enquiries and examined evidence using the latest forensic techniques. More than 2,000 people were interviewed and eighty people detained. A group of volunteer citizens called the Whitechapel Vigilance Committee patrolled the streets looking for suspicious characters. In spite of all this, he was **NEVER CAUGHT**.

The Jack the Ripper case was the first to cause a worldwide **MEDIA FRENZY** and some good came out of this. The press coverage drew attention to the overcrowded, unsanitary living conditions in London's East End and the slums were eventually cleared. Some of the Ripper's victims used to go the **TEN BELLS PUB** in Commercial Street.

The demon barber of Fleet Street

Sweeney Todd is London's most famous Victorian fictional murderer. In the story of the Demon Barber of Fleet Street, Sweeney Todd, slit the throats of unsuspecting wealthy customers who came to his shop. Still sitting in the barber's chair, they were dispatched through a revolving trapdoor into the basement, where he robbed them, cut them up and made them into meat pies. His friend Mrs Lovett sold the pies in her shop in Bell Yard, connected to the barber's by a secret underground passage.

Some say that the story of Sweeney Todd was based on the true exploits of a gruesome London murderer, graphically told in the popular penny dreadful newspapers of the day.

London first . . .

The Commissioner for Police in London in 1901 was a man called Sir Edward Henry. While an inspector in Bengal, India, he noticed that Indian workers who could not write collected their pay with a thumbprint, as every thumbprint is unique. Back in London, he set up a Central **FINGERPRINT** Branch to catch criminals and by 1902 it had 2,000 fingerprints on file and had caught a murderer by tracing his fingerprints. It was a revolution in crime detection.

The Krays: East End gangsters

The East End has always had its fair share of criminal gangs, of whom the most famous in its recent history are the twin brothers Reggie and Ronnie **KRAY**. They masterminded armed robberies, arson and protection rackets in the 1950s and 1960s from their headquarters in Bethnal Green. Infighting in the underworld led to the murder of **JACK 'THE HAT'** McVitie in a basement in Hackney, and the shooting of George Cornell at the Blind Beggar pub in Whitechapel.

The Krays presented a front as nightclub owners, mixing with celebrities such as Diana Dors, Frank Sinatra and Judy Garland and even being photographed by the cult 1960s photographer **DAVID BAILEY**. They were finally arrested on 9 May 1968 by Detective Superintendent Leonard 'Nipper' Read, who had made their capture his life's work. They were sentenced to 30 years in prison.

The Great Train Robbery

A London gang, inspired by the train robberies of the Wild West, carried out a daring heist on the Glasgow-to-London mail train on 8 August 1963. The gang stole a record-breaking £2.6 million in used bank notes. This is the largest robbery in British history. Detective Chief Superintendent Jack Slipper of the Metropolitan Police, nicknamed Slipper of the Yard, was put in charge. In six months twelve of the gang had been sentenced to gaol terms totalling more than 300 years.

One of the train robbers, Ronnie Biggs, escaped from Wandsworth prison by scaling a wall with a rope ladder and jumping into a waiting furniture van. He had plastic surgery and lived abroad as a fugitive for thirty-six years. He gave himself up when he was a sick old man and was finally sent to Belmarsh Prison.

Another train robber, Ronald 'Buster' Edwards, fled to Mexico for three years but missed home so much he gave himself up. After doing time, he set up a flower stall at Waterloo station.

PLAGUE, PESTILENCE AND DISEASE

Healing London's sick

The first hospitals in London were monasteries. They gave shelter to travellers and the blind, the lame, elderly and mentally ill, as well as looking after the sick. There were no doctors. It was the monks who cared for the ill. There was little medicine and no real cures: prayers, holy water, magic and **HERBAL REMEDIES** were all they had. Monastery gardens were used to grow medicinal herbs.

Only the poor went to hospital; the rich were visited by a doctor at home. In spite of hospitals opening across London, most people who became sick simply died. The Priory of St Bartholomew opened in 1123, founded by a former courtier of Henry I. In 1197 a priory hospital called St Mary's Spital opened just outside Bishopsgate. It became the largest and most important hospital in Europe. By 1500, **SPECIALIST** hospitals were springing up across the city: one for the blind, another for lepers.

Until Victorian times, there were no doctors as we know them today, just **APOTHECARIES** and herbalists. Apothecaries were medically trained men who knew all about pharmacy and remedies.

London's oldest hospital is St Bartholomew's in Smithfield.

Secret garden

In 1673, the **WORSHIPFUL SOCIETY OF APOTHECARIES** created the Chelsea Physic Garden to teach students about plants and to grow herbs to make medicines for poorly Londoners. Close to the river, it had a unique warm microclimate and was the perfect environment to grow the new and interesting herbs and plants that were being brought to London from all over the world. Hidden behind a high wall the plants are still growing strong and it is **LONDON'S OLDEST** botanic garden.

The most famous professor of herbology was **NICHOLAS CULPEPER** (1616–54), who concocted great potions and remedies made from herbs to treat his patients. Keen for the poor as well as the rich to have access to his special treatments, he set up a free clinic in Spitalfields where he could examine patients in person. His remedies were so effective he was accused of **WITCHCRAFT** by the Society of Apothecaries, who were jealous of his success. He put all his secret recipes together in a famous book called **THE COMPLETE HERBAL** in 1653.

★ LONDON LINGO ★
Londoners nicknamed Bethlem Hospital 'Bedlam'. We still use the word
bedlam today to mean 'a noisy uproar, chaos and confusion'.

It's Bedlam in here!

In 1247, Bethlem, the first London hospital for the mentally ill, was opened.
Although its intentions were good, little was known about mental illness and
treatment was harsh. Violent and dangerous patients were MANACLED and
chained in their cells to the stone floor. The more able were allowed to beg in the
streets of London during the day. Bethlem was called a MADHOUSE and it was
fashionable entertainment to peer at the inmates. Tickets cost two pennies a visit in
1676. In 1814, 96,000 people came to Bedlam to gawp.

St Thomas's Hospital operating theatre

The first ever operating theatre in London was at London Bridge in the roof space of
an old church in 1822. It backed on to the wards of St Thomas's Hospital next door.

The operating theatre was used to perform AMPUTATIONS. This was
a dangerous, painful and scary experience. Surgeons worked quickly to shorten
the HORROR of surgery: there were no painkillers or anaesthetics. A slug of
alcohol was the only way to help dull the pain. The patient was held down on the
operating table by strong men. A good surgeon could perform an amputation in a
minute or less.

DRIPPING BLOOD was collected in a box of sawdust under the operating table.
If you did not die from shock, you might well die from disease, as the operating
conditions were FILTHY. The galleried theatre was crowded with apprentices,
which compounded the already unhygienic conditions. The surgeon was no more
likely to wash his hands after than before the operation, and his frock coat would
be 'stiff and STINKING WITH PUS and blood'. Fresh from an amputation, the
surgeon would walk through to the next-door maternity wards to examine women
and their new-born babies. Scores of women died of TERRIBLE INFECTIONS
caused by the filthy hands of these surgeons.

The story of the Royal Free Hospital

One day a doctor called William Marsden found a poor young girl dying
of cold in the churchyard at St Andrew's in Holborn. He couldn't find a
hospital that would take her in and she died in his arms. He was so distressed
by this episode that in 1828 he founded the Royal Free Hospital in the
Gray's Inn Road, where the poor would be treated free.

The World's first children's hospital

GREAT ORMOND STREET Hospital was founded in 1852 by Dr Charles West. Children from the nearby slums of Clerkenwell, Holborn and St Pancras were its first patients. Before this CHILDREN were not allowed to be treated in hospitals. It was tiny: there was only one ward with ten beds. Open fires kept the children warm. Families were NOT ALLOWED to visit and everyone had to go to church on Sundays.

The hospital only performed a few operations: tracheotomy, the removal of kidney stones and the repair of a CLEFT LIP and palate. These operations were only carried out on children over fifteen because the patient needed to be awake to help the surgeon. No one younger could stand the PAIN. Great Ormond Street is now one of the most famous children's hospitals in the world.

> The writer J.M. Barrie left the rights of his famous book, *Peter Pan*, to Great Ormond Street Hospital to help it raise money.

The Lady with the Lamp: Florence Nightingale

One of the reasons we wash our hands after going to the lavatory is because of the Victorian nurse Florence Nightingale, or the Lady with the Lamp, as she was called by the soldiers she nursed in the Crimean War of 1854–6. It was here that she made her breakthrough about the importance of cleanliness in preventing DISEASE. By cleaning the filthy wards and keeping wounds clean, she ensured that many more soldiers survived.

Florence nightingale

Florence Nightingale started London's first nursing school at London's new St Thomas' Hospital. The entire hospital was rebuilt in line with her insistence on free CIRCULATION of air and keeping patients apart from one another. It opened in 1871, with 588 beds for patients, across the Thames from the Houses of Parliament. It had two lifts, one for patients and one for food and medicines. Every ward had its own bathrooms, lavatories and cupboards. The walls were coated with smooth cement that could be kept clean.

Florence lived in Chelsea and, as an old lady, she would receive guests lying down, as she would not get out of bed.

Spooky London

Wealthy philanthropist Jeremy Bentham left all his money to the newly founded London University when he died in 1832. He also left it his dead body. He asked in his will for his body to be studied and dissected, and when this was finished, for his skeleton to be dressed in his finest clothes and put on display. His remains still sit in University College behind a glass-fronted case with a new waxwork head. His mummified head is kept in a basket.

clever cures: the world's first vaccination

Smallpox was a terrifying disease with nasty symptoms of a rash and painful blisters. Catching it often ended in blindness and horrific scarring. There was no cure and 80 per cent of children who caught it died.

In 1786, Dr Edward Jenner in his lab at St George's Hospital Medical School in Tooting set about finding a way to stop this disease in its tracks. He noticed that dairymaids rarely caught smallpox. He took the fluid from a cowpox pustule on a dairymaid's hand and injected it into an eight-year-old boy called James Phipps. Six weeks later, he deliberately put the boy to the test, exposing him to smallpox. James did not catch the disease because he had developed an immunity to smallpox. Jenner's plan had worked. This was the first ever vaccine in the whole world.

Jenner coined the term vaccine from the Latin word vacca, which means cow.

DID YOU KNOW?

* The cow responsible for the dairymaid's cowpox infection was called Blossom and her hide hangs on the wall of the library of St George's Medical School.
* The orphans at Thomas Coram's Foundling Hospital were some of the first children to benefit from the new smallpox vaccine.
* Smallpox has now been completely eradicated from the world. Hurrah.

London's oldest medical specimens are kept in rows and rows of jars in all shapes and sizes at the Hunterian Museum in Lincoln's Inn Fields.

Killer cholera

Cholera was once rife in London. The potentially **FATAL SICKNESS** starts with violent vomiting and diarrhoea, causing the victim to dehydrate rapidly. No one knew how to treat it or what caused it to spread. Some doctors thought cholera was transmitted in **BAD AIR**. Then, in 1854, there was a sudden outbreak in Soho. A doctor called John Snow noticed that many of those who died of cholera had been drinking water from a public **PUMP** in Broad Street.

Dr Snow had a theory that cholera was spread through water. To put it to the test, he took away the handle of the pump so that no one could draw water from the well any more. The epidemic ended immediately.

It was discovered that a **SEWER**, contaminated with the diarrhoea of cholera victims, had been leaking straight into the well. Snow had proved that cholera was spread through infected water and his discovery saved many millions of lives across the world. A pump has been put up in Broad Street to remember his work.

Penicillin: the first antibiotic

In the summer of 1928 a bacteriologist called **ALEXANDER FLEMING** left his laboratory at St Mary's Hospital to go on holiday with his family. When he came back, he noticed something that changed medical science for ever. Being an untidy scientist, he had left a stack of **DIRTY PETRI DISHES** piled up beside his workbench. He noticed that one dish was contaminated with mould, and that the straphylococci bugs around it had completely disappeared. He had accidentally discovered a new bacteria-killing substance – **PENICILLIN**. This was the world's first antibiotic, and its discovery revolutionized medicine. Alexander Fleming's old laboratory is still there and is open to the public.

Barber Pole

Bloody barber

The stripy red-and-white candy cane poles that hang outside barber shops are a legacy of a time when barbers were the only surgeons and dentists that London had to offer. They performed tooth extractions, wound surgery and the gruesome practice of bloodletting, where patients grasped a pole until their veins showed, were cut open and bled until they fainted. The red and white of the barber pole represent the bloodstained bandages of the patients that were hung out to dry.

The story of the Elephant Man

A man called Joseph Merrick (1862–90) suffered from a crippling disease that deformed his body so much that he was nicknamed the Elephant Man. Freak shows were popular entertainment in those days. He was cruelly put on display at 259 Whitechapel Road until a doctor took pity on him and took him to the London Hospital, where he looked after him away from peering eyes.

Bodysnatchers

With medical science growing and hospitals opening, young doctors needed HUMAN BODIES to cut up and study. Legally, the bodies of convicted criminals and people who had died in hospital and poor houses could be DISSECTED for research. But there weren't enough bodies to go round. People were paid handsomely for bringing doctors FRESH CORPSES. Few questions were asked about where they came from and so an underworld trade in BODYSNATCHING began in London's graveyards.

Grave-digging thieves known as RESURRECTION MEN would steal corpses from churchyards in the dead of night. London graves were typically shallow and it was easy to dig down to the coffin. A rope would be tied around the neck of the corpse and the body DRAGGED out.

To stop this happening, rich people buried their dead in impenetrable IRON COFFINS or covered the grave with iron railings. Otherwise, friends and relatives would guard a grave until the body had decomposed. Churches built WATCHTOWERS for watching over the graves. Although it was a crime to steal bodies, the punishment was not severe enough to stop the lucrative trade. Stealing the jewellery or clothes of a dead person was much more heavily punished, however, so these were always left behind.

Some criminals went even further than snatching the bodies of the dead: the LONDON BURKERS were a ruthless band who murdered people to sell to medical students. They lured their victims, usually the very poor, to their hideouts in Bethnal Green and Shoreditch, where they would DRUG them and kill them.

★ LONDON LINGO ★

Houndsditch, a big road just outside the old City of London walls, was where Londoners used to dump the bodies of their dead dogs.

Dead and buried

London was so crowded that only the lucky dead could be buried in churchyards. Three hundred years ago, most Londoners were buried in COMMUNAL GRAVES, where coffins were piled one on top of the other, sometimes up to seven coffins deep. The graves were left open until they were completely full, and the stench of the ROTTING BODIES was often so unbearable that at funerals the preacher and mourners would have to stand some distance away.

As the population of London doubled in the nineteenth century, the need for more cemeteries became desperate. Churchyards were bursting at the seams; graves were not only piled high with bodies but rotting into the new sewers. To cope, a special railway line was built in 1854 from Waterloo to Brookwood Cemetery in Surrey to carry the dead out of the city. It was called the NECROPOLIS RAILWAY and even the dead had to have a ticket. The funeral trains ran until 1941, when the station was bombed in the war.

Dissenters Londoners who disagreed with commonly held beliefs were buried in Bunhill Fields, Finsbury. This graveyard is the last resting place of the poet WILLIAM BLAKE, Daniel Defoe, author of *Robinson Crusoe*, John Bunyan, author of *Pilgrim's Progress*, and Eleanor Coade, who created Coade stone, which was used in so many London buildings.

RANDOM GRAVE FACTS

✳ There is a watchtower at the churchyard opposite St Bartholomew's Hospital, a graveyard that was popular with and convenient for bodysnatchers hoping to sell bodies to the doctors across the road.

✳ The crypt of St Bride's Church, Fleet Street, has some metal coffins built to protect the dead from bodysnatchers.

✳ Until the nineteenth century, people were buried in the crypt of St Clement Danes in the Strand. The chain hanging on the crypt wall was used to secure the coffin lids against bodysnatchers.

✳ Captain Bligh, famous for the mutiny on board his ship HMS Bounty, is buried in the churchyard behind the Museum of Garden History by Lambeth Palace.

The magnificent seven

Between 1832 and 1841, seven new cemeteries were built. Railings were kept high to keep out body snatchers. Grand gateways and elegant tombs, lined with avenues of statues, were built. They became known as the Magnificent Seven:

Highgate cemetery

BROMPTON CEMETERY

Abney Park Cemetery

Nunhead Cemetery

Kensal Green Cemetery

WEST NORWOOD CEMETERY

Tower Hamlets Cemetery

Highgate cemetery

Highgate Cemetery is perhaps the most famous and interesting cemetery in London. Built by the Victorians and rich with grand **MAUSOLEUMS**, catacombs, stucco-faced vaults, obelisks, crumbling sculptures and statues, it was described as **THE CREEPIEST PLACE IN LONDON**. Famous Victorians buried here include the poet Christina Rossetti, the novelist George Eliot, six Lord Mayors of London and the father of the Communist movement, Karl Marx.

Spooky London
The Highgate Vampire

In the 1960s and 1970s, there were reports of a tall, red-eyed man in a black cloak and top hat who drifted near the gate of Highgate's Western Cemetery at dusk. The cemetery had been badly neglected: tombs were cracked and broken, and the graveyard was overgrown with wild plants and brambles. The mysterious figure was nicknamed the Highgate Vampire and Londoners flocked to Highgate in hopes of catching a glimpse of him.

The Streets of London

. . . .

The story of London can be told through its streets.
Many of the streets are named after the goods that
were sold there . . .

FISH STREET HILL Bread Street HONEY LANE Milk Street

Poultry Shoulder of Mutton Alley POTTERY LANE

Haymarket HOG LANE Duck Lane GOOSE LANE Floral Street

. . . or after things that went on there . . .

PUDDING LANE	Named after the butcher's offal thrown into the street
HOUNDSDITCH	Where dead dogs were thrown over the London wall
SCALDING ALLEY	Where feathers were burnt off chickens to prepare them
FRIDAY STREET	Where fish was sold on Fridays
BLEEDING HEART YARD	Where Lady Elizabeth Hatton was murdered. Legend has it that her still-beating heart was ripped from her body.
BIRDCAGE WALK	Where James I once had an aviary for birds near St James's Park
ADDLE STREET	From the Old English *adela*, meaning 'stinking urine'
COCKPIT STEPS	Where cockfights were held
CLOTH FAIR	The site of a medieval fair where merchants from across Europe came to sell cloth
MAYFAIR	Where a fair was held on 1 May every year in the seventeenth and eighteenth centuries. It lasted for fifteen days
MILLBANK	Where the Abbot of Westminster had a mill
HORSEFERRY ROAD	Where the horse ferry crossed the Thames at Vauxhall.
PETTICOAT LANE	Petticoat Lane Market near Spitalfields is named after the French lace and underwear that used to be sold here.
SMITHFIELD	Smooth Field, as it was an open field for horse trading, tournaments and archery
BYWARD STREET	From a secret Beefeater password

... or after the jobs that people did there ...

THREADNEEDLE STREET	Named after tailors
VINE STREET	The site of a vineyard
CARMELITE STREET	The site of a monastery
LOMBARD STREET	Named after gold sellers from Lombardy, Italy

Sometimes they are named after the history of the place ...

BARBICAN	Roman tower
OLD JEWRY	The Jewish quarter
GARRICK STREET	Named after a famous actor, David Garrick
SOHO	The sound of the battle cry of the Duke of Monmouth

Many of the streets around Covent Garden's theatres are named after the famous actors who performed there over the centuries: Betterton, Macklin, Kemble and Kean.

The names of the streets in London's Docklands tell us about the cargoes that were unloaded there:

Gun Wharf WEST INDIA DOCKS Tobacco Wharf Sugar Loaf Walk

canary Wharf - For goods from the canary Islands

The seven gates into old London

Aldersgate ALDGATE BISHOPSGATE cripplegate

Ludgate MOORGATE NEWGATE

Long ago the seven gates to the City of London would be shut at nine o'clock at night (or dusk depending which came first) when the Bells of St Mary-le-Bow and other city churches chimed the CURFEW.

After the Restoration of the monarchy in 1660, the gates of London were taken down and their PORTCULLISES were wedged open. They were finally demolished in the 1760s to allow traffic to flow more smoothly.

HAHA!

HOW MANY?
QUESTION: HOW MANY ROADS ARE THERE
IN THE CITY OF LONDON?
ANSWER: NONE! THEY ARE ALL STREETS AND LANES.

Fascinating facts

- London has an estimated 85,000 streets.
- The road that leads to the Savoy Hotel, off the Strand, is the only road in London where you must drive on the right.
- Watling Street in the City, London's oldest street, was the high street of Roman London.
- The prudish Victorians changed the name of Petticoat Lane to Middlesex Street because they did not think it was polite to talk about women's underclothes.
- Just opposite Apsley House at Hyde Park Corner is the grand Wellington Arch, which rather surprisingly doesn't have a statue of Wellington on top. Instead there is a fierce winged lady riding in a four-horse chariot called a quadriga. It is the largest bronze sculpture in Europe. You can take a lift to the top and get a great view.
- No. 1 Strand was the first house in London to be given a house number.
- Wooden paving was a popular surface for roads as it deadened the clip-clop of horses' hoofs and the noise of metal-rimmed cartwheels. Chequer Street in the City is the only remaining Victorian wooden-cobbled street in London.
- There are green-painted sheds perched on the kerbsides of London streets which date back to the nineteenth century. These are cabmen's shelters, specially built to give cabbies a quick, good-value hot meal. Only 13 of the original 200 are still standing.

cannon fodder

The first London bollards were upturned French cannons captured at the **BATTLE OF TRAFALGAR** in 1805. They were placed on street corners to stop cart wheels from damaging London's kerbs. Once all the cannons had been used up, new bollards were manufactured to look just the same as the old ones. There are **ORIGINAL** French cannon bollards all over London, including on the South Bank near the Globe Theatre.

TALES OF A STREET

Piccadilly

Once called Portugal Street, it became known as Piccadilly, named after 'pickadils', the ruche ruffs that the fashionable upper classes of the sixteenth and seventeenth centuries wore around their necks. They were made by a young tailor called Robert Baker, who lived here. Piccadilly never has the word 'road' or 'street' after its name.

The Mall and Pall Mall

The Mall, which leads from Trafalgar Square to Buckingham Palace, and Pall Mall, are where a game a bit like croquet, called pall-mall, or *pallemaille*, was played in the seventeenth century, with mallets and balls. Samuel Pepys wrote about the game in his diary and it appears in Samuel Johnson's dictionary as 'a play in which the ball is struck with a mallet through an iron ring'.

Rotten Row

Now just a broad track on the south side of Hyde Park, Rotten Row was created by William III after he moved to Kensington Palace. It was called the Route de Roi, the King's Road, but the name was corrupted over the years to Rotten Row.

King's Road

This was once the King's private road to Kew Palace, which only the King and his friends were allowed to use. It was not opened to the public until 1830.

High Holborn

Once the main road from the old City of London to Westminster, High Holborn is named after the stream that runs below it, Hole Bourne. The word bourne means stream.

Strand

The street that runs from Trafalgar Square to Fleet Street is known as Strand. It was once right on the water's edge and in Old English *strand* means bank or shore.

★ LONDON LINGO ★

The expression 'to be on tenter hooks' comes from an open space near Spitalfields where textile workers stretched out fabrics on wooden frames to dry to stop them shrinking. It means 'to be in a state of anxiety, stretched and nervous'. The street is still called Tenter Ground.

London circuses

A circus is a round point where several roads meet and comes from the Latin meaning circle. There are several in London:

OXFORD CIRCUS   Ludgate Circus   Finsbury circus

ARNOLD CIRCUS   Cambridge Circus

Holborn Circus   PERCY CIRCUS   Piccadilly Circus

Piccadilly circus

Piccadilly Circus was built in 1819 to connect the newly opened Regent Street to Piccadilly. The bright neon advertisements above the circus shine night and day and have only been switched off in exceptional circumstances, such as the deaths of Winston Churchill (1965) and Princess Diana (1997).

PICCADILLY
-CIRCUS W1-
CITY OF WESTMINSTER

★ LONDON LINGO ★

Piccadilly Circus is always crowded with people and traffic, and the phrase 'Piccadilly Circus' has come to mean 'busy and bustling'. It was also used during the Second World War as the code name for the place in the English Channel where 7,000 boats met before the Allies' D-Day landings on the Normandy beaches.

London landmark: the statue of Eros

The famous statue at Piccadilly Circus of a Greek god firing his bow was erected as a tribute to Anthony Cooper, the 7th Earl of Shaftesbury, who helped to improve life for the poor of London in the nineteenth century. It is actually a sculpture of Eros' brother, Anteros, also (wrongly) sometimes called the Angel of Christian Charity. It was sculpted by Alfred Gilbert in 1885. The statue was removed temporarily during the Second World War and hidden away. Londoners were delighted when it was put back.

London signs

London streets were once crowded with huge, heavy signboards framed in iron, some as large as paving stones, hanging outside every shop to advertise their wares. These signs were extremely **DANGEROUS** for anybody passing by, as they were often badly fixed and it was quite common for them to fall down. Once in Birde Lane a shop sign killed four people when it crashed to the ground, causing the entire shopfront to collapse. These signboards were banned from London at the end of the eighteenth century.

As well as signboards, London shops had **LARGE MODELS** made of wrought iron or carved wood hanging on the street. Different shops had different symbols:

Three golden balls – Pawnbroker • Three sugar loaves – Grocer
Three tents – Upholsterer • Three hats – Hatter

HAHA!

FUNNY STREET NAMES

Pardon Street • Quaggy Walk • Crutched Friars • Knobs Hill Road •
Scout Approach • Bird-in-bush Road • Petty France • George and Catherine
Wheel Alley • The Pigs Lane • Eureka Road • Cyclops Mews • Elf Row •
Dog Kennel Hill • Lamb's Passage • Cock Lane • Amen Court • Little Britain •
Knightrider Street • Wardrobe Terrace • Plumbers Row •
Hanging Sword Alley • Ha Ha Road • Tweezers Alley

World's oldest: London's blue plaques

- The idea of putting up blue plaques to remember famous people and places in London was first thought of in 1866. It is the **OLDEST** scheme of its kind in the world.
- In 1867, the first blue plaque was put on the house where the poet **LORD BYRON** was born in Holles Street, Marylebone. Unfortunately, the house was knocked down and the plaque has never been replaced.
- The longest surviving blue plaque is that for Napoleon III on a house in King Street, St James's, erected in 1867.
- There are more than 850 blue plaques in London and the number is constantly growing.
- Not all blue plaques are blue. Some are green, brown, white or terracotta. When the plaques were first being made it was difficult and expensive to produce the vibrant blue colour. They also vary in design.
- A standard colour and design was agreed after the Second World War. The plaques are now always round and **DARK BLUE**.
- The City of London has its own separate blue plaque scheme. These plaques mark places of historical interest as well as famous people and are usually square.

London landmark: No. 1 London

The Duke of Wellington lived at Apsley House, with the best address in town of No. 1 London. His home was the first house at the turnpike into London at what is now Hyde Park Corner.

A great military leader, Wellington commanded the allied army that defeated Napoleon at the Battle of Waterloo in 1815. The government gave him Apsley House as a reward for his victory. He was nicknamed the Iron Duke, because of the metal shutters he had fitted on the windows of Apsley House to protect him from rioting mobs.

He would ride his horses around London, and there is a special mounting block outside his club, the Athenaeum, in Waterloo Place, put there to allow the duke to dismount and mount elegantly.

The Duke of Wellington's boots

Wellington wore specially made, waterproof leather boots with a low heel. Hard wearing enough for battle but also smart enough to wear for dinner, these soon became all the rage among London society and so the Wellington boot was born.

The smallest house in London

The smallest house in London is 10 Hyde Park Place, Marble Arch. Built in 1805, the TYBURN CONVENT is 1.06 metres/3 feet 6 inches wide and consists of an alley way and has a bathroom. It is thought to have been built as a watch house, as it overlooked the old St George's graveyard – extremely popular with body snatchers in the eighteenth century.

London's oldest . . .

- The oldest HOUSES in the City of London are 41–42 Cloth Fair. They survived the Great Fire of 1666 because they were enclosed by the priory of St Bartholomew's Church at Smithfield. Occupied since 1614, the house has a Tudor well in the basement.
- The oldest BRICK TERRACE house in London is at 52–55 Newington Green in Islington, dating back to 1658.
- Bloomsbury Square is the oldest GARDEN SQUARE in London.

Thatched roofs have been banned in London since the Great Fire of 1666. The only one allowed is on the Globe Theatre on Bankside.

STATUE SECRETS

* Whenever you see a statue of a man on horseback, have a look at the horses' legs: the position tells a story. If all four hoofs are on the ground, the person died of old age; if the two front legs are in the air, the rider died in battle; if one front leg is raised, the person died of battle wounds.
* The horse that William III is riding in his statue on St James's Square has his back hoof resting on a molehill, because the king died when his horse slipped on one.
* In the middle of Leicester Square there is a statue of Shakespeare which stands on a plinth inscribed with someone else's name. It was once mounted with the statue of a man called Albert Grant, who bought Leicester Square and gave it to London. After he was involved in a financial scandal his statue was torn down and replaced with that of Shakespeare. No one bothered to change the name plaque.

London's first . . .

* The first artificially **LIT ROADWAY** in Britain was Rotten Row, running through Hyde Park. William III thought the road was too dangerous to travel down after dark from St James's, so, in 1690, he had 300 oil lamps lit to light the way.
* The first street to be lit by **GAS LAMPS** was Pall Mall in 1807.
* Behind the grand Savoy Hotel was one of the first gas lamps in London to be powered by a new technology that used **METHANE** gas from the toilets and sewers. It was called a Webb Sewer Gas Lamp and the original lamp is still there on Carting Lane, which has been nicknamed **FARTING LANE!**
* The first electric street lighting in London was along the Thames Embankment. It caused a **SENSATION** in 1879 when the beautiful lamps beside the river were switched on. They fast became a tourist attraction. The lamp-posts are very elaborate and the giant sturgeons entwined around them are often thought to be dolphins.

London's last . . .

On many of the roads coming into London you had to pay a fee at a **TOLLGATE**. The last remaining tollgate in London is in **DULWICH VILLAGE**. It costs £1 for a car to drive through the tollgate. Passers-by on foot are free.

The story of the London plane tree

London plane trees line the city's streets and squares and are its most common and successful tree. It is a cross between an American plane and an oriental plane. The London plane grows happily in our damp grey climate and in a polluted city, as it sloughs its bark from time to time, ridding itself of any urban grime. It is called the London plane because London was one of the first cities to grow it in such numbers.

The first London plane trees were planted in Berkeley Square in 1789 and they are still there. The Berkeley plane tree has a circumference of 6 feet/1.8 metres and is Britain's most valuable tree, priced in 2008 at a staggering £750,000.

London's oldest . . .

- There is an ancient yew tree in St Andrew's Churchyard, Totteridge, that is thought to be 2,000 years old, the OLDEST TREE in London.
- Climbing the walls of the Griffin Brewery, Chiswick, is the oldest WISTERIA in London, brought over from China in 1616.
- The Great Vine at Hampton Court is the largest and oldest VINE in the world, planted by landscape gardener 'Capability' Brown in about 1768. The sweet black grapes have always been eaten by the royal family for dessert. George V sent bunches of the grapes to the patients at London hospitals.
- The holm OAK TREE at Fulham Palace is 500 years old and was planted when the palace was built. It is possibly one of the oldest in Britain.

The Marylebone Elm somehow escaped the ravages of Dutch elm disease that swept across England in the 1970s and is the last elm tree in Westminster.

A big mistake: Marble Arch

Designed by John Nash in 1827 as the magnificent, marble gateway to Buckingham Palace, Marble Arch was not kept there for long as, reputedly, the archway was thought to be TOO NARROW for the Queen's coaches; so, in 1851, it was moved to north-east of Hyde Park, where it is now, marooned on a traffic island at the top of Park Lane. Traditionally, only the royal family and the King's Troop Royal Horse Artillery are allowed to pass through it. Three tiny rooms above the arch have served as a police station.

London landmark: Admiralty Arch

Standing guard at the top of the Mall since 1912 is Admiralty Arch, commissioned by Edward VII in memory of his mother, Queen Victoria.

If you look closely on the inside wall of the northernmost arch, you will find a small nose-like protrusion, which if you were riding through the arch on horseback would be at nose height. No one quite knows why it is there but it is rumoured to honour the great soldier the Duke of Wellington, who had a particularly large nose. Any royal soldier riding through was supposed to rub 'Wellington's' nose for good luck. The rooms in the arch are used for government offices.

London street games

Children have always played on the streets and alleyways of London. The Victorians tried to ban children from the streets and in 1860 a twelve-year-old boy called George Dunn was sent to prison for playing **ROUNDERS**.

In 1931, a man called Norman Douglas published a book of all the games children played, called *London Street Games*. Girls played clapping and skipping games, singing rhymes like 'Mother I'm Over the Water', 'Turning Mother's Wringer' and 'Charlie Chaplin':

> *Charlie Chaplin meek and mild*
> *Stole a sixpence from a child*
> *When the child began to cry*
> *Charlie Chaplin said goodbye.*

Boys played marbles on the drain covers. Children played hopping games on chalked pavements or kick the can on car-free streets. In the evenings, brave children played a game called **NICHO MIDNIGHT** in the dark alleyways. In the 1950s, there were 700 play streets in London, set aside especially for children to play in between early morning and sunset. These have long gone.

There is a game of tag called Feet Off London, in which you cannot be caught if your feet are not touching the ground.

TRAFALGAR SQUARE

Trafalgar Square is the CENTRE of London. Every distance in and out of London is measured from a brass plaque by the statue of Charles I at the top of Whitehall. It is where Londoners meet to celebrate, protest and just hang out. It is one of the most famous squares in the world.

But it hasn't always been as it is today. It used to be the King's stable yard and it was full of HORSES, as the old Whitehall Palace was just next door. Then in 1812 London architect Sir John Nash was given the task of creating fine new streets and elegant squares by the King. He built Regent Street, transformed St James's Park and came up with the idea of a central square for the people of London to gather in for cultural events and mass CELEBRATIONS. A site was chosen that was easy for all Londoners to get to. The rich would drive in from the West in their smart carriages, yet it was not too far for ordinary Londoners to walk to from their homes in the East End. It was named Trafalgar Square in 1830 after NELSON'S victorious battle at Trafalgar.

The only building left after the site was cleared for construction was the Church of St Martin in the Fields, built in 1726, and it still stands at the eastern edge of the square. The NATIONAL GALLERY opened its doors in 1838, with free admission for all, putting the King's private paintings on display for the first time. The architect William Wilkin, who designed it, wanted it to be imposing, but the columns he designed weren't big enough, so to make it seem more impressive it was built on a raised terrace.

The architect of the Houses of Parliament, Sir Charles Barry, is responsible for the grand staircase down from the gallery to the central square, the fabulous FOUNTAINS (the mermaids, dolphins and tritons or male mermaids were added later) and the area around Nelson's Column.

Weights and measures

To check the exact length of old-fashioned measurements such as a perch, pole or chain, look for the brass measures embedded in granite near the National Gallery.

The Landseer lions

The four famous huge blackened bronze lions guarding Nelson's Column that everyone loves to climb were designed by Queen Victoria's favourite artist, Sir Edwin Landseer, who was known for his beautiful animal paintings. He used the cast of a dead lion that had belonged to the King of Sardinia as a model for his sculptures. Londoners were so appreciative of his efforts that they draped the lions with wreaths the day Landseer's funeral cortège passed by.

London landmark: Nelson's column

One of London's most famous landmarks, Nelson's Column towers 46 metres/151 feet above Trafalgar Square. It was built to remember the great naval hero Admiral Horatio Nelson. He triumphantly led the British to victory at the Battle of Trafalgar in the Napoleonic Wars against the French in 1805. The column was not completed for another forty years.

The statue of Nelson, which looks tiny from the ground, is a staggering 5.5 metres/18 feet high. The decorations at the top of the column are made from the cannons of HMS *Royal George*, the sister ship of Nelson's *Victory*. The brass panels at the bottom are made from melted-down guns captured from the French. Nelson looks out across the square to the Admiralty, the navy's London headquarters. All the lamp posts from Trafalgar Square to Buckingham Palace are topped with miniature versions of every ship in Nelson's fleet at the Battle of Trafalgar.

Police Station

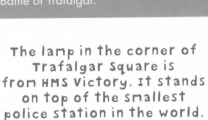

The lamp in the corner of Trafalgar Square is from HMS Victory. It stands on top of the smallest police station in the world.

There are other Nelson's columns in Dublin and Great Yarmouth.

Fourteen stonemasons enjoyed a delicious dinner on the plinth at the top of the column before the statue was put in place on 23 October 1843.

THE WORLD IN LONDON

L ondon is the most ethnically diverse city in the world. For centuries people have flocked here from across the globe. The twentieth century has brought some of the most dramatic change to the city's **CULTURAL** landscape. Some people have come because they were forced to leave their homelands to escape war, persecution, natural disaster and poverty. Others have come because their work has brought them to London. Some have come just to make a better life.

Some parts of London have become synonymous with the nationalities that have settled there.

chinatown

Chinese people have lived in London since the seventeenth century, working as sailors and living in the Docklands at **LIMEHOUSE**. This was London's original Chinatown. Badly bombed in the war, the area was abandoned and the inhabitants moved to **SOHO** and the streets around Leicester Square.

Little Italy

Italian bankers and moneylenders came to London from **LOMBARDY** in the thirteenth century. Lombard Street in the City is named after the place where they worked.

More Italians came to **CLERKENWELL** and King's Cross, an area called Little Italy, in the nineteenth century, working as skilled craftsmen, street entertainers, knife grinders, **ICE-CREAM** sellers, musicians, artists and decorators.

Londoners speak more than 300 different languages - more than any other city in the world

Top twenty languages spoken by London schoolchildren

English   Bengali and Sylheti   Punjabi   GUJARATI
HINDI/URDU   TURKISH   Arabic   Creoles   Somali
CANTONESE   Greek   Ashanti   PORTUGESE   FRENCH
Spanish   Tamil   Farsi   Italian   VIETNAMESE

★ LONDON LINGO ★

Mush = Romany for friend or mate
Intelligentsia = Russian for social elite
Chav = Mate – Romany for child
Clan = Irish for family
Pundit = Hindi for learned man
Schmooze = Yiddish for gossip
Wonga = Money, from the Romany word for coal
Nicker = Nickel from the USA

East Enders

Spitalfields in the East End has been the first home of many of London's immigrants. On the very edge of the old City, it was once one of London's poorest places. Over the centuries a succession of different people have moved in and brought their families to live and work here, each leaving a distinct cultural flavour on its streets.

- The **FRENCH HUGUENOTS** were Protestants who came to live here when they were forced out of Catholic France in the seventeenth and eighteenth centuries. Many of them built beautiful large shuttered houses for themselves where they lived and worked as weavers.
- **IRISH WEAVERS** came to the East End in the nineteenth century after the terrible Potato Famine of 1845–52 and moved in alongside the Huguenot weavers.
- **ASHKENAZI JEWS**, escaping from Russian persecution in the late nineteenth and early twentieth centuries, also headed first for the cheap accommodation in Spitalfields. They brought the bagel to London.
- **BANGLADESHI** people settled here after the partitioning of India in 1947. London is home to the largest number of people of Bangladeshi origin outside Bangladesh. People in Bangladesh call British Bangladeshis **LONDONIS**.

London's oldest Jewish synagogue is Bevis Marks, near Houndsditch in the city, built in 1702.

Ssshhh!

SECRET LONDON

There is a mosque on the corner of Brick Lane and Fournier Street that captures the history of immigration to the East End. It began life as La Neuve Eglise in 1742, a Huguenot chapel. By 1809 it was known as the Jews' chapel, with the task of promoting Christianity to Jews. By 1898, it had become the Spitalfields Great Synagogue and finally, in 1976, it became the Brick Lane Jamme Masjid Mosque.

250,000 Londoners are of Jamaican origin

The Windrush years

After losing so many men in the Second World War, England was desperately short of labour and turned to its colonies for help. A battered old troop carrier called the SS *Empire Windrush* arrived at Tilbury docks on the Thames on 22 June 1948. On board there were 490 men and 2 women, all English speakers, nurses, engineers and war veterans from the West Indies. Its arrival marked the start of mass immigration to Britain. This period of history is known as the WINDRUSH YEARS.

WEST INDIANS had been promised great opportunities if they came to London, but life was hard. Accommodation was rough. New arrivals were put up in a Tube station at Clapham Common, which had been used in the war as a bomb shelter. Nearby Brixton became one of the places where they settled in London. London Transport led the recruitment drive from the Caribbean, and by 1958 125,000 people had come to work on the tubes and buses. Women were later encouraged to come to train as nurses for London's hospitals.

After a decade of the West Indians suffering cold weather, lack of decent jobs, poor housing and an unfriendly white population, the situation erupted in violent RACE RIOTS in 1958.

The King of calypso, Trinidadian singer Lord Kitchener, sang a song about how great London was as he disembarked from the Windrush.

LONDON FIRSTS

- 1593 The first record of an African in London. His name was Cornelius.
- 1892 London's first Asian MP, Dadabhai Naoroji, was elected.
- 1913 London's first black mayor, John Archer, was elected in Battersea.
- 1931 Dr Harold Moody founded London's first black pressure group, the League of Coloured People.
- 1959 The first Notting Hill Carnival was set up by journalist Claudia Jones.
- 1973 Trevor McDonald was London's first black newsreader.
- 1987 Diane Abbott was elected Britain's first black women MP.
- 2004 Linda Dobbs QC was the first black person to be appointed a High Court judge.

★ LONDON LINGO ★

'Jafaican' is a new kind of London slang used by
inner city kids rather than cockney rhyming slang. It is a
mixture of Jamaican English, Asian and West African speech
made popular in Grime rap music. Now everyone's using it

Peak = got one over on someone else
Wagwan = a man who's good with the ladies
Safe = a cool person or used to signify something is good
Skeen = noticed and understood   Sick = cool
Alie = I'm not lying   Wavey = swaggerific and cool
Long = annoying   Bare = an excessive amount
Wallad = idiot   Badman = gangster

There is a black trumpeter painted on the Westminster
Tournament Roll of 1511. African musicians came to London
as part of Katherine of Aragon's entourage from Spain.

India in London

There are about half a million British Indians people living in London and most of
them are Hindu. London has had a close relationship with India since the days
of Empire. A man called Sake Dean Mahomet, a captain of the British East India
Company, set up London's first Indian restaurant in 1810. He is also famous for
introducing shampoo and massage to Londoners. Victorian London was thronged
with Indian students, soldiers and diplomats.

The LARGEST HINDU TEMPLE outside India is the Baps Shri
Swaminarayan Mandir Temple in Neasden, north London.

RANDOM WORLD FACTS

* The original passenger list from the SS *Empire Windrush*
is kept at the National Archive in Kew.
* Peckham is known as Little Lagos and is home to one of the
largest overseas Nigerian communities in the world.
* Southall in West London is nicknamed Little India.
* Vauxhall in Lambeth is nicknamed Little Portugal.

London has 40 Hindu temples, 25 Sikh temples and about 150 mosques.

Muslim London

The first Muslim settlers in London were Turkish galley slaves freed from Spanish ships by English pirates. In 1627 there were 40 Turkish Muslims living in London. They were working as tailors, shoemakers and button-makers – and they were among the first people in London to drink coffee. Much later, in the nineteenth century, Somali and Yemeni sailors headed to London following the opening of the Suez Canal. After the Second World War many Muslims came to London from former British colonies including Pakistan, Gujarat in India and Bangladesh.

Islam is London's largest religion after christianity.

The Baitul Futuh Mosque in Morden is the largest mosque in Western Europe.

London's first purpose-built mosque was the ornate Fazi Mosque in Southfields opened in 1926.

Fasting, Feasts and Festivals

CHINESE	Festival to welcome in the New Year
HINDU	Diwali, the festival of light
JEWISH	Pesach, passover feast
SIKH	Vaisakhi, harvest festival
CHRISTIAN	Christmas, celebration of the birth of Jesus
MUSLIM	Ramadan, a month of fasting ending with Eid

DID YOU KNOW?

Some words have come into London slang from the days of the Empire. Any market trader will tell you that £500 is a 'monkey' and £25 is a 'pony'. They probably don't realize that these names come from the animal pictures painted on the back of old Indian rupee notes.

STARS AND STRIPES

London has had a special connection with America ever since the Pilgrim Fathers left England to establish a colony in Massachusetts in 1620.

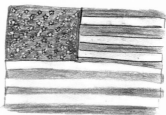

Pocahontas (1595-1617), the Virginian Indian chief's daughter, married an English settler called John Rolf and came to live in London for a year. As she was setting sail to travel back home, she caught smallpox and died on the Thames at Gravesend.

Benjamin Franklin (1706-90), signatory to the American Constitution, lived and worked at 36 Craven Street, close to Trafalgar Square, for several years. His house was the first US embassy and is now a museum, Benjamin Franklin House.

John Quincy Adams (1767-1848), the sixth US President, was married at All Hallows by the Tower Church in 1797. He is the only US president to have a foreign-born First Lady.

George Peabody (1795-1869) was a London-based American banker who built homes for the London poor through the Peabody Trust, and is known as the 'father of philanthropy' for his good works. He was the first American to be given the Freedom of the City of London. He made his fortune building the railroads in the Wild West.

Nancy Astor (1879-1964) was a wealthy American heiress who was the first woman to take a seat in the Houses of Parliament in 1919. Women had had the right to vote for only a year (and only if they were over thirty years old). She was married to Waldorf Astor and owned a grand London house at 4 St James's Square. Over 100 wealthy American heiresses married into the British aristocracy in the nineteenth and early twentieth centuries.

Gordon Selfridge (1864-1947) was an American retail magnate who wanted to show Londoners how to shop. He opened his dazzling Selfridges store on Oxford Street in 1909. Gordon Selfridge is said to have created the saying 'the customer is always right'. The great man sadly lost his fortune in the economic depression of the 1930s and died in relative poverty in Putney in 1947.

5.1% of Kensington and Chelsea's population is American.

RANDOM AMERICAN FACTS

* The Mayflower left Rotherhithe to collect the Pilgrim Fathers from Plymouth to start a new life in America on 6 September 1620. It sailed with 102 passengers plus a crew of 25 to 30. It was bound for the Hudson River, where New York City is today, but went off course on the journey and ended up at Cape Cod Bay. Only 53 passengers and about half the crew survived the voyage and the first disease-ridden winter in America.

* The captain of the *Mayflower* was called Christopher Jones and he is buried at St Mary's Church, Rotherhithe.

* Londoner William Penn left his home to sail to the New World of America, founding Pennsylvania in 1682.

* The Piccadilly line on the London Underground is the legacy of the American entrepreneur Charles Tyson Yerkes, who invested in the construction of railway lines across London. Sadly, he died in 1905 before the Tube line opened.

* An American actor, Sam Wanamaker, was the energy behind the reconstruction of Shakespeare's Globe Theatre on the South Bank, completed in 1997.

Americans in London

Franklin D. Roosevelt memorial: Grosvenor Square • Dwight D. Eisenhower statue: Grosvenor Square • Abraham Lincoln statue: Parliament Square • George Washington bust: St Paul's Cathedral crypt • George Washington statue: outside the National Gallery, Trafalgar Square • John F. Kennedy bust: Euston Road • Martin Luther King statue: doorway above Westminster Abbey • Benjamin Franklin's house: 36 Craven Street, Westminster • Jimi Hendrix's house: 23 Brook Street, Mayfair • Paul Robeson's house: The Chestnuts, 1 Branch Hill, Hampstead • Mark Twain's house: 23 Tedworth Square, Chelsea

★ LONDON LINGO ★

Americans call their shopping centres malls after the Mall in London, which was a fashionable place to promenade and meet friends. Malls are shopping streets without any cars.

DID YOU KNOW?

* The American Bar at the Savoy Hotel was the first place in Europe to serve cocktails.
* Before it became part of the United States, Texas had its own embassy in London, from 1836 to 1845, in a passageway off St James's Street, in the same building as the premises of the wine merchant Berry Bros & Rudd. A sign marks the spot today.
* At the east end of St Paul's Cathedral is the American Memorial Chapel, to commemorate members of the US forces based in Britain who died during the Second World War. There are 28,000 names on the American Roll of Honour.

Dr Crippen, an American living in London, was hanged in Pentonville Prison for the murder of his wife, Cora, in 1910. Her body was buried under the floor at 39 Hilldrop Crescent, Camden. Crippen, a doctor, had meticulously disposed of her in the stove and was dissolving what remained in an ACID BATH. A gallstone in her body was not dissolved by the acid and was critical evidence in his conviction. The house at Hilldrop Crescent was destroyed by a German bomb during the Second World War.

Where to find London in America

* The Wren church St Mary Aldermanbury was moved to the US in 1965 and rebuilt in the grounds of Westminster College, Fulton, Missouri. Wartime Prime Minister Winston CHURCHILL had made a famous speech at Westminster College in 1946, describing the post-war problems in Europe, saying 'an iron curtain has descended across the Continent'. The phrase IRON CURTAIN became shorthand for the political divide between East and West.
* The 1831 LONDON BRIDGE was sold off in 1968 and rebuilt stone by stone in the middle of nowhere in ARIZONA. The buyer was a rich oil tycoon called Robert McCulloch, who had founded a new town called Lake Havasu on the border with California. He bought the bridge as a tourist attraction to draw visitors to his new city. Some say he bought it by mistake, thinking he had paid for the famous TOWER BRIDGE.
* LIBERTY BELL, the symbol of American Independence that hangs in Philadelphia, was cast at London's WHITECHAPEL Foundry in 1752, the same bell maker who made Big Ben.
* There are several RED LONDON telephone boxes in the United States, including one in the University of Oklahoma and another outside the British Embassy in WASHINGTON DC.

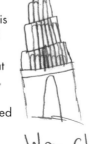

Wren Church

London's Animals

. . . .

Horses

Before the bus, car and taxi, Londoners got around by horse power. In 1900, there were over **50,000 HORSES** in London. They pulled carriages, cabs, canal boats and even buses and were an essential part of life, vital for the city's success. They were also very messy, creating over 1,000 tonnes of **SMELLY MANURE** on London's streets every single day. Today there are very few horses in London and many of the mews and stables that once housed them have been turned into homes for people.

Foxes

Most Londoners have caught a glimpse of the bold, red fox that pads quietly through our streets. More than **10,000 FOXES** now live in London: that's sixteen foxes in every square mile. The bushy-tailed creature sought refuge in the city after the **SECOND WORLD WAR**. Rummaging through Londoner's bins is an easier life than surviving in the wild.

Foxes have been found in the garden of **10 DOWNING STREET** and have killed the Queen's pink flamingos at Buckingham Palace.

A fox was found living on the seventy-second floor of the half-built Shard building, surviving on the left-over sandwiches of the workmen and builders.

Grey squirrels

The grey squirrel is London's most commonly seen form of wildlife. It thrives in London parks, gardens and woods, munching garden bulbs, birdseed, **CATKINS**, flowers, fungi, eggs and even young birds. Grey squirrels have big **BUSHY TAILS** to keep them warm at night and help them balance in the trees. They have four **FINGERS** and five toes and can be right or left handed.

Deer

Red deer and fallow deer in London are a
legacy of the days when kings and queens
went hunting and kept herds of deer for
their entertainment. The direct descendants
of the deer introduced by Henry VIII still live
in **HAMPTON COURT PARK**. Greenwich is the
OLDEST deer park in London and Richmond Park
has a healthy deer herd.

These days there is a new kind of deer on the streets
of London: wild **MUNTJAC** are creeping in from the
countryside to the capital. These Chinese deer escaped
from **WOBURN PARK** in Bedfordshire in the 1920s
and have started to colonize London woods, commons and even gardens,
living on brambles, roses, ivy, honeysuckle, clematis and bluebells.

The rat

The rat is as successful in London as the human being. There are thought
to be about 10 million of them in the city. Rats thrive in our sewers,
under our houses and in our rubbish bins. For centuries, the **FLEAS**
that fed on them gave us terrible diseases like the **BLACK DEATH** and
the Great Plague.

The English brown rat, which loved to live cheek by jowl with us in
our homes, slowly became dominated by the Norwegian brown rat in
the early eighteenth century. Fortunately for us, the Norwegian brown
much prefers the sewers and the docks to houses, so the risk of **NASTY
DISEASES** from rats has diminished. In other words, the rats have moved
out, but not gone away. They breed fast: a female Norwegian brown rat
can produce about fifty babies a year.

**When David Cameron became
Prime Minister a rat was
seen scuttling past the
front door of 10 Downing
Street. The Prime Minister
quickly got himself a cat.**

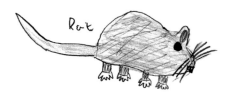

Rat

Battersea Dogs and Cats Home

The home for stray and unwanted dogs and cats in Battersea has become world famous. Formerly the 'Temporary Home for Lost and STARVING DOGS', it was set up by Mrs Mary Tealby in 1860 in Holloway. It aims never to turn away an animal in need of help. The singer Elton John adopted a dog from Battersea.

Dog Show

Charles Cruft was born in Bloomsbury in 1846 and stated his working life selling dog food in James Spratt's shop in Holborn. He set up the 'First Great Terrier Show' in 1886, followed by the CRUFT'S GREATEST DOG SHOW in 1891, the first dog show to be named after him, at the Royal Agricultural Hall in Islington. All breeds of dogs were invited to compete. It has become one of the most famous dog shows in the world.

Kaspar, the cat at the Savoy

The Savoy Hotel on the Strand keeps a 1-metre/39-inch-high lucky, black wooden cat for seating at tables when there are an UNLUCKY THIRTEEN guests. The cat, called KASPAR, is given its own chair and is served all courses of the dinner. Why? The Savoy has been superstitious about the number thirteen ever since a table of thirteen guests sat down to eat there 100 years ago. One of the diners who scoffed at the idea that it was unlucky to be thirteen was shot dead a few weeks later in his office in South Africa. THE SAVOY vowed never to serve a table of thirteen again. Kaspar is brought out whenever the need arises.

Spooky London

There is a doggy gravestone at 9 Carlton Terrace, once the home of the German Ambassador to London. It reads 'Giro: ein treuer Begleiter: Giro: a true friend'. The beloved Alsatian belonged to the German Ambassador in the pre-war 1930s and had died chewing an electric cable.

Near Hyde Park's Victoria Gate is a graveyard of tiny gravestones, for London's pets. It started with a dog called Cherry, the beloved Maltese terrier of the Duke of Cambridge, who died in 1880. By the time it closed, over 300 animals were buried here, from cats and dogs to birds and monkeys. The writer George Orwell described it as 'perhaps the most horrible spectacle in Britain'.

SOME FAMOUS LONDON CATS

DICK WHITTINGTON'S CAT

Hodge, Samuel Johnson's cat

Cats, the musical

Humphrey, a Downing Street cat

Tiddles, the cat at Paddington station

The Prime Minister's cats

LARRY the tabby cat, a former resident of Battersea Dogs and Cats Home, has recently taken up residence at 10 Downing Street. It was hoped he would be a good rat catcher but he seems to prefer snoozing.

There has been a long line of cats at Downing Street, each known there as CHIEF MOUSER to the Cabinet Office. One predecessor called WILBERFORCE served no fewer than four prime ministers and it is said that Margaret Thatcher once fed him on tins of Russian sardines brought back from Moscow. In the 1920s, Prime Minister Ramsay MacDonald had a cat called RUFUS OF ENGLAND, nicknamed Treasury Bill. In the 1930s and 1940s, under Neville Chamberlain and Winston Churchill, the Downing Street cat was called the MUNICH MOUSER

London landmark: the coade stone lion

The magnificent stone lion guarding the south end of Westminster Bridge was once painted red and was the icon of the Red Lion Brewery on the south bank of the Thames. The French writer Emile Zola wrote about it in 1893. When the brewery was demolished to make way for the Festival of Britain in 1951, the lion was rescued and moved.

It is made of Coade stone, a durable, artificial stone perfected by an eighteenth-century businesswoman, Eleanor Coade, whose fashionable showroom was once near Westminster Bridge. When she died, she took the secret recipe for Coade stone to her grave.

Elephant stories

Elephants were kept in the Tower of London Menagerie by medieval kings. Then, in 1679, the scientist Robert Hooke recorded seeing a **PERFORMING ELEPHANT** in London in his diary.

From 1773, **EXOTIC** animals arrived at London's ports from all over the world and were put on display for a curious public in iron cages and cramped rooms. Pidcock's Exhibition of **WILD BEASTS** in the upper rooms of the Exeter Exchange on the corner of the Wellington Street and the Strand was one of London's most celebrated menageries.

In 1826, one of the old Indian elephants from the menagerie was taking his usual stroll through the streets to draw the crowds, when he bolted in anger. A keeper was killed in the **STAMPEDE** and, later, soldiers from Somerset House were summoned to shoot the raging beast. The elephant refused to die until a keeper eventually **SPEARED** him to death. 152 bullets were found inside it. Hundreds of Londoners flocked to see the dead animal. Medical students dissected the **CARCASS** and the meat was sold off. The elephant **SKELETON** was put on display at the Royal College of Surgeons in Lincoln's Inn Fields.

Two elephants from a Parisian circus performed at the City of London theatre in 1846.

Bears

Animals were brought to London for entertainment and sport, and performing bears could often be seen on the streets. London had a **BEAR GARDEN** from the reign of Henry II. Bear baiting was hugely popular and was a particular favourite of Elizabeth I. The sport was cruel: the bear's teeth and claws were removed, and it was kept chained up. Dogs were sent in to attack it to see how it would defend itself. **BEAR BAITING** was finally banned in 1835.

Royal menagerie

- Kings and queens may have collected exotic animals long before, but in 1235 it is recorded that Henry III was given three **LEOPARDS** by the Holy Roman Emperor Frederick II.
- In 1252, the King of Norway gave England a **POLAR BEAR**.
- All manner of animals were collected and kept in the Royal Menagerie at the Tower of London. King John kept **ALLIGATORS** in the moat and lions in cages below the entrance gates to intimidate visitors.
- In the nineteenth century, the wild animals were moved out of the Tower of London and taken to a new home at **LONDON ZOO**.
- The Queen is often given animals as presents, among them jaguars and **SLOTHS** from Brazil and two black beavers from Canada. She places her more unusual animals in the care of London Zoo.

London Zoo

London Zoo is the world's oldest scientific zoo and was established in 1828 for the scientific study of animals, thanks to the efforts of Sir Stamford Raffles. It opened to the public to exhibit strange and wonderful creatures, including the first hippopotamus seen in England since the Roman occupation and two creatures now sadly extinct: the quagga (a kind of half-striped zebra) and a thylacine (a kind of marsupial wolf, known as the Tasmanian tiger).

Stories from London Zoo

The Wombat House at London Zoo was the Victorian artist Dante Gabriel Rossetti's favourite place to meet his friends. He was obsessed with curious creatures and at his home in Chelsea he kept two pet wombats, who entertained his guests at dinner by sleeping in a bowl in the centre of the table. Rossetti also had a pet llama and a toucan. The bird was taught to ride on the llama's back and trot round the table at dinnertime.

In 1914, an American black bear called Winnipeg Bear was given to the zoo. Alan Alexander Milne would visit the zoo with his young son, Christopher Robin. Seeing the bear was one of the highlights of their visits and inspired the Winnie-the-Pooh stories A.A. Milne went on to write.

The story of the Bengal tiger

The *Boys' Own Paper* of 1879 tells the story of a Bengal tiger who escaped from an importer of zoo and circus animals in London's East End. Wild animals from across the world were, from time to time, unloaded to be sold at the docks. On this occasion, the tiger escaped from his cage and took off down the Commercial Road. Londoners fled in panic, all except for a young boy who walked right up to the tiger and reached out to stroke him. The tiger cuffed him and knocked him to the ground, picking him up in his jaw and taking him away down an alley to eat in private. The animal importer, a Mr Charles Jamrach, bravely came to the rescue and followed them down the alley, snatching the boy from the tiger's mouth. The child was remarkably unscathed. The story spread through London and the now famous tiger was sold for the high price of £300 to the owner of Wombwell's Menagerie. He exhibited him as the tiger who swallowed the boy, and made a fortune. There is a statue in Tobacco Dock that marks the incident.

LONDON BIRDS

Blackbird

BLUE TIT

JAY

Magpie

Robin

Thrush

Pigeons

Trafalgar Square, in the centre of London, was once full of pigeons. The flock, estimated to be over **35,000** birds, drew tourists from across the world who came to have their photographs taken with pigeons on their heads. But these 'rats with wings' are **FERAL** and carry diseases, so in 2000 the Mayor of London decided to ban the feeding of pigeons and to phase them out. A pair of **HARRIS HAWKS** hovers in the skies of London to keep the streets clear of pigeons and their acidic droppings.

Cockney Sparrows

The little brown sparrow was once so commonplace in London it was nicknamed the cockney sparrow. Drawn to the bugs that live on horses and spilt grain, when the horses left the number of sparrows started to decline. The bird has now all but disappeared from London's skies.

Pelicans

There are five pelicans living in **ST JAMES'S PARK** near Buckingham Palace, descendants of the first Pelican who came to London in 1664 as a present from the Russian Ambassador to Charles II. They are fed 5.4 kilograms/12 pounds of fish every afternoon by the park keepers. One pelican was spotted by tourists swallowing an entire pigeon whole.

Good luck charms

The most famous birds in London are the **RAVENS** at
the **TOWER OF LONDON**. They date back to the time
when the Tower was a place of execution. Ravens,
who are meat eaters, would gather at the gallows
in search of juicy scraps. Legend has it that if the
ravens were ever to leave the Tower, the kingdom will

PERISH. Suffice to say, no one wants to take that kind of risk, so the ravens are
well looked after. Six ravens are on duty and four are kept in reserve, just in case.
They are so important that one beefeater is given the task of looking after them
and rearing them by hand. Their costs are paid for by the British government.
During the Second World War, the fall of the kingdom got close: there was only
one raven left. His name was **GRIP**.

Pretty Polly

The skies of London rather incongruously throng with
10,000 brightly coloured **GREEN PARAKEETS**. It is
said that they are descendants of some that escaped
during filming from the set of Humphrey Bogart and
Katharine Hepburn's *The African Queen* at Shepperton
Film Studios in the 1950s.

There are five pairs of breeding peregrine falcons in
London. One of a pair can often be seen on top of the big
chimney at the Tate Modern.

Hawks are used at Tube stations to control the pests.

A famous parrot who lived in the Olde Cheshire Cheese pub
in Fleet Street knew such an extensive range of rude words that
people would come to London just to hear it swear. The parrot
became so famous that when it died in 1926, obituaries
appeared in newspapers across the world.

Charles Darwin called his London house in Gower Street Macaw
Cottage because the furniture in the drawing room combined all the colours
of the macaw in hideous disorder.

Sport in London

Football fanatics

Kicking a ball on the streets of London is as old as the city itself. The first football game to be written about was in the twelfth century. It was a completely lawless activity: there were no rules. Because it was such a free-for-all it was looked on as a sport for **RUFFIANS**. Apprentice boys were banned from playing and in 1409 Henry IV outlawed football in London. If you were caught playing football, you were sent to prison. But football never disappeared entirely and the Elizabethan headmaster of St Paul's School argued in its favour, saying it had health and educational benefits and all it needed was a **FEW RULES**, a referee and a fixed number of players. But the game was not brought into order for another 300 years.

The London Rules

On 26 October 1863, twelve London football clubs met in a pub called the Freemason's Tavern near **LINCOLN'S INN FIELDS** to write the laws of football. Though football had been played for hundreds of years, every team played to a different set of rules, ensuring chaos and trouble on the pitch. The meeting had been called by Ebenezer Cobb Morley, who lived in Barnes. The meeting led to the founding of the Football Association and it was he who drafted the rules of football, known as the **LONDON RULES**. No running with the ball in hand, no nails sticking out of the ends of your boots – that sort of thing. After the **FIRST MATCH** with the new FA rules, a toast was given – 'Success to football, irrespective of class or creed' – and the FA Cup was established.

DID YOU KNOW?

* The oldest football club in London is Fulham, set up in 1879 by a group of Sunday School boys.
* London hosted the football World Cup at Wembley in 1966. This is the one and only time England has ever won it.
* Arsenal Football Club is the only London football club to have an Underground station named after it.
* Women were banned from playing on London's Football League pitches by the FA in 1921. The ban was finally lifted in 1971. Women's football had a golden age in the 1920s when some matches had over 50,000 spectators.
* Arsenal Ladies Football Club, founded in 1987, is the most successful club in English women's football.

The FA Cup is the longest-running football competition in the world

cup finals

There have been only five all-London-club FA Cup finals:

1967	Tottenham Hotspur v. Chelsea (2–1)
1975	West Ham v. Fulham (2–0)
1980	West Ham v. Arsenal (1–0)
1982	Tottenham Hotspur v. Queen's Park Rangers (1–1 after extra time)
2002	Arsenal v. Chelsea (2–0)

Wembley first . . .

From 1923 to 2000, the FA Cup final was played at London's Wembley Stadium. The first final there, on 28 April 1923, was an unticketed event and 200,000 people showed up to try to SQUEEZE into the stands: chaos ensued and the crowds swarmed on to the pitch. Kick-off was delayed for forty-five minutes, but when the WHISTLE blew David Jack scored the first goal for Bolton after just two minutes. Final score: Bolton 2, West Ham 0.

Fantastic facts: Wembley Stadium

- Wembley Stadium is the largest football stadium in the world. It can seat 90,000 spectators, all undercover.
- The giant screens in the stadium are each the size of 600 domestic television sets.
- The arch has a span of 315 metres/1,033 feet, making it the longest single-span roof structure in the world. It is so big that the London Eye could fit underneath it.
- The arch is 133 metres/437 feet at its highest point. It weighs 1,750 tonnes, the equivalent of 275 double-decker buses.
- The tips of the arch, known as 'pencil ends', are 18 million times as heavy as an average pencil.
- The arch is made up of 500 steel tubes, called straws, each one large enough to hold over 850 pints of milk.
- The paint needed to coat the arch is enough to cover Rome's Sistine Chapel ceiling more than 19 times.
- The arch has a special track on it for a cart to travel along and carry out repairs.
- The arch is lit at night and can be seen 21 kilometres/13 miles away at Canary Wharf.

LONDON FOOTBALL CLUBS

London football clubs are famously rivalrous, with fiercely loyal fans.

Arsenal

GROUND: Emirates Stadium, Highbury

TRADEMARK CHANT:
 'One nil to the Arsenal'

NICKNAME: The Gunners

RIVAL: Tottenham Hotspur

HOME COLOURS: Red and white

BADGE: A cannon, because the club was founded by the workers of the Arsenal Munitions Factory in Woolwich

Chelsea

GROUND: Stamford Bridge, Fulham Road

TRADEMARK CHANT:
 'Blue is the colour'

NICKNAME: The Blues

RIVALS: QPR, West Ham and Tottenham

HOME COLOURS: Blue and white

BADGE: A rampant griffin

Tottenham Hotspur

GROUND: White Hart Lane, Tottenham

TRADEMARK CHANT:
 'Come on you Spurs'

NICKNAME: Spurs

RIVALS: Arsenal, West Ham and Chelsea

HOME COLOURS: White shirt and socks and navy blue shorts

BADGE: A cockerel standing on a ball

West Ham United

GROUND: Boleyn Ground, Upton Park

TRADEMARK CHANT:
 'I'm forever blowing bubbles'

NICKNAMES: The Hammers; once known as the Thames Ironsides

RIVALS: Historically Millwall but now Chelsea and Tottenham Hotspur

HOME COLOURS: Claret and blue

BADGE: A castle and two hammers

Queen's Park Rangers

GROUND: Loftus Road, White City

TRADEMARK CHANT:
 'We are the Rangers boys'

NICKNAMES: QPR, The Hoops, The Rs

RIVAL: Chelsea

HOME COLOURS: Blue and white hooped shirt, white shorts and socks

BADGE: A heraldic crest with a football and a crown

Fulham

GROUND: Craven Cottage, Fulham

TRADEMARK CHANT:
 'We are Fulham'

NICKNAMES: The Cottagers, The Lilywhites

RIVAL: Chelsea

HOME COLOURS: White shirt with black shorts, white socks

BADGE: Red FFC letters on black-and-white shield

Crystal Palace

GROUND: Selhurst Park

TRADEMARK CHANT: 'Glad all over'

NICKNAME: The Eagles

RIVALS: Charlton Athletic and Millwall

HOME COLOURS: Red and blue striped shirt, blue shorts and socks

BADGE: An eagle atop a football and the Crystal Palace

Charlton Athletic

GROUND: The Valley, Charlton

TRADEMARK CHANT: 'Stand up if you hate Palace'

NICKNAMES: The Addicks; used to be The Valiants

RIVALS: Crystal Palace and Millwall

HOME COLOURS: Red and white

BADGE: A sword in a gloved hand

Millwall

GROUND: The Den, Bermondsey

TRADEMARK CHANT: 'No one likes us – we don't care'

NICKNAME: The Lions

RIVALS: Everyone

HOME COLOURS: Blue and white (based on their Scottish origins)

BADGE: A rampant lion

Brentford

GROUND: Griffin Park, Brentford

TRADEMARK CHANT: 'Hey Jude'

NICKNAME: The Bees

RIVAL: QPR

HOME COLOURS: Red and white

BADGE: A heraldic shield with swords and bees

Dagenham and Redbridge

GROUND: Victoria Road, Dagenham

TRADEMARK CHANT: 'Digger-Dagger, Digger-Dagger, oi oi oi'

NICKNAME: The Daggers

RIVAL: Leyton Orient

HOME COLOURS: Red and blue shirt, blue socks and shorts

BADGE: A heraldic shield topped by a knight's helmet

Leyton Orient

GROUND: The Matchroom

TRADEMARK CHANT: 'Oh there's only one team: Orient'

NICKNAME: The Os

RIVAL: West Ham

HOME COLOURS: Red and white shirt, red shorts and socks

BADGE: Two dragons

When two London clubs play against each other it is known as a London Derby.

Sport on the streets

Bowls, archery, football, tennis, rounders, cricket and boxing . . . every sport has been played on London's street corners for centuries. There were regattas on the river, rounders in Lambs Conduit Fields, archery competitions in Smithfield, cricket matches on White Conduit Fields and bowling alleys everywhere.

The big match: what's played where

Rugby – Twickenham

POLO – HURLINGHAM

Tennis – Wimbledon

cricket - Lord's and the oval

Football – Wembley Stadium

Anyone for tennis?

Wimbledon is the oldest tennis tournament in the world and has been played at the **ALL ENGLAND LAWN TENNIS AND CROQUET CLUB** since 1877.

The game was brought to London by Major Walker Clopton Wingfield in 1875 and was first called Sphairistike!

The first Wimbledon champion was Spencer Gore in 1877. In 1884, women first hit the courts and Maud Watson was the first Ladies' champion.

* The oldest velodrome in London is at Herne Hill. It was built in the 1890s, as a state-of-the-art Victorian facility. In the 1920s and '30s, cycling was at its peak of popularity, and the velodrome's great annual events attracted crowds of 10,000 people.

* Twickenham is the biggest rugby union stadium in the world, with a capacity of 82,000.

* The inventor of rugby football was the vicar of St Clement Danes Church, William Webb Ellis, who is said to have invented it in 1823.

* There have been cricket clubs in London since the thirteenth century. The most important is at Lord's, St John's Wood. The first Lord's cricket ground was in what is now Dorset Square.

* The first golf club in England was opened by James I at Blackheath in 1608.

* There was once a horse-racing track at Notting Hill, called the Hippodrome, in the mid-nineteenth century.

* Real tennis was a medal event in the 1908 Olympics.

* Rugby has been played as an Olympic sport only four times. In the London Games of 1908, only two countries put rugby teams forward and there was one match – the final. Australia beat Great Britain, 32–3.

Sport of kings

Real tennis was originally called ROYAL TENNIS and is known as THE SPORT OF KINGS. It is a game a bit like tennis but played in a large indoor court with a funny-shaped racquet. The court has a sloping roof on three sides and the ball is served on to one of these sloping roofs. There are lots of different ways to serve the ball, and they each have a different name, such as railroad, BOBBLE, poop, piqué, boomerang and giraffe. The oldest surviving real tennis court in England is at Hampton Court Palace. During the summer you can watch a match there.

The London Olympics

London is the only city in the world to have won the privilege of hosting the Olympic Games three times.

In **1908**, the Olympic Games were due to be held in Rome, but the **ERUPTION** of Mount Vesuvius put a stop to them and London stood in as host city. New stadiums at White City, near Shepherd's Bush, were built. Athletes paraded under their national flags for the first time.

The **1948** London Olympics were the first summer games since the Berlin Olympics in 1936. The Games of the XIV Olympiad, as they were called, had been put on hold during the Second World War. After the war, London was broke and nearly handed the 1948 games to the United States. George VI stepped in and declared it an opportunity for London to restore itself after the horrors of the Blitz.

The opening ceremony was suitably **MODEST**, with the release of 2,500 pigeons and the raising of the Olympic flag on a 10-metre/35-foot pole. The games were held at the Wembley Stadium, which was then called the Empire Stadium.

The **2012** London Olympics has transformed barren stretches of London's East End wasteland and provided exciting new sports venues for the City in the Olympic Park. Old London parks host some sports: beach volleyball at Horse Guards Parade, **EQUESTRIAN** and pentathlon events at Greenwich, open-water swimming in the Serpentine in Hyde Park and archery at Lord's cricket ground.

The velodrome at the 2012 Olympic Park is nicknamed the Pringle, as it is shaped like the famous crisp.

London's first . . .

- The first **PARALYMPIC GAMES** were held in London in 1948.
- The 1948 London Olympics was the first Olympic Games to be shown on **TELEVISION**.

The London Marathon

The London Marathon is one of the most important annual marathons in the world. Former Olympic champion Chris Brasher and another famous sportsman, John Disley, fired the starting gun for the first London Marathon on 29 March 1981. The race starts in Greenwich Park and ends at Buckingham Palace. In the first race, 6,255 people crossed the finishing line and in 2008 34,497 crossed the finishing line.

Mini London Marathon

Children from eleven to seventeen are invited to take part in the Mini London Marathon, a race on the final 5 kilometres/3 miles of the course on the same day.

Record breaker

The world marathon record of 2 hours, 3 minutes and 59 seconds set by Haile Gebreselassie of Ethiopia in 2008 is a full 51 minutes and 19 seconds quicker than the time of the winner of the marathon run at the 1908 London Olympics.

Fascinating facts: the London Marathon

- Two couples have been married on Tower Bridge during the race.
- The oldest woman to compete is Jenny Wood Allen, aged eighty-nine, of Dundee.
- The oldest man to run is Abraham Weintraud, aged ninety-one, of the USA.
- The male winners of the first London Marathon were American Dick Beardsley and Norwegian Inge Simonsen, who crossed the finishing line holding hands. They completed the race in 2 hours 11 minutes.
- The female winner of the first London Marathon was Joyce Smith, who ran the race in 2 hours 29 minutes.
- Celebrities who have run the London Marathon include Jo Brand, Anthea Turner, Jeffrey Archer, Floella Benjamin, Ronan Keating and Gordon Ramsey.

The story of the marathon

The marathon commemorates the story of a Greek soldier, Pheidippides, who ran from the Battle of Marathon to Athens in ancient Greece. The first marathon to take place in London was in the 1908 Olympic Games. Originally planned to be 26 miles long, the race was extended by 385 yards to make it the distance from Windsor Castle to the royal box in the Olympic stadium. The official distance of a marathon is now 26 miles and 385 yards (42.195 kilometres).

REGATTAS ON THE RIVER

The largest rowing club in the country is
Thames Rowing club, Putney.

London's oldest boat race

Doggett's Coat and Badge Race is the oldest rowing race, not just in London but in the world. It dates back to 1715, when the river was London's main road and watermen and lightermen were its taxi drivers. The race, organized by the Guild of Fishmongers, is a strenuous 7-kilometre/4 1/2 mile challenge up the Thames from London Bridge to Chelsea. The winner is presented with a smart scarlet coat and a silver badge.

Thomas Doggett, a London actor and manager at the Theatre Royal, Drury Lane, is said to have set up this race after a waterman saved him from drowning in the Thames.

London's newest boat race

The Great River Race, which has taken place on the river since 1988, is for boats of all shapes and sizes: gigs, skiffs, longboats – any boat will do as long as it has a minimum of four oars and flies a flag. In the tradition of boat taxis, each boat must also carry a passenger. It's a 32-kilometre/22-mile slog from Docklands to Ham and the race takes place every September.

London's traditional boat race

The Oxford and Cambridge Boat Race has been rowed annually on the Thames since 1829. The battle of the oars, originally raced at Westminster, today starts at Putney Bridge and ends at Barnes Bridge, running along a gruelling stretch of river, 6.77 kilometres/4 miles and 374 yards long. The loser has to challenge the winner to a re-match the following year.

The Head of the River Race is rowed on the same course but in the opposite direction every spring.

There is a pub in Isleworth called the London Apprentice,
after the apprentice watermen who used to row here.

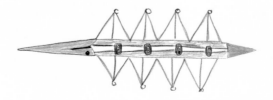

★ LONDON LINGO ★

'Below the belt' has come to mean 'not playing fair'.

Come out fighting

London has produced some of the world's finest boxing CHAMPIONS. For centuries, boxing was a popular London sport for both men and women. BARE-KNUCKLED prize fights were staged in London pubs. With no rules, it was a rough and DANGEROUS sport.

The father of English boxing is JOHN 'JACK' BROUGHTON, champion from 1729 to 1750. He first fought at the Adam and Eve pub on Tottenham Court Road. He went on to run his own boxing club called Broughton's Amphitheatre in Oxford Road in 1743 and wrote the much-needed first RULES of boxing in an attempt to make it fairer and less dangerous. He made these rules after he injured a man in a fight, who later died.

The London Prize Ring Rules of 1838 meant you had to fight in a ring and you were not allowed to bite, headbutt or hit below the belt.

Queensberry rules

In 1867, a man called the Marquess of Queensberry drafted more rules for the amateur championships at Lillie Bridge, London, to ensure a 'fair stand-up boxing match'. They are known as the Queensberry Rules and they still govern modern boxing matches.

London oldest . . .

The Lonsdale Belt, worn by boxing champions to this day, is the oldest CHAMPIONSHIP BELT in boxing and its origins started in London in 1909. Lord Lonsdale, patron to the National Sporting Club, was a keen boxing supporter and decided to present a gold and porcelain belt to every British boxing champion. The winner could keep the belt if he won three times. The belt was first won by lightweight Freddie Welsh in 1909.

The original heavyweight Lonsdale Belt, made from 22-carat gold, is at the Royal Artillery Barracks in Woolwich.

SECRET BOXING FACTS

* The oldest boxing ring in London is York Hall in Old Ford Road, Bethnal Green.
* A powerful female boxer known as Bruising Peg won a prize fight in Spa Fields, Islington, in 1768.
* In the National Portrait Gallery, there is a painting of the black American Bill Richmond. He came to London as a servant to Lord Percy in 1777 and became a famous London boxer, nicknamed the Black Terror. When he retired from boxing, he bought the Horse and Dolphin pub in Leicester Square and set up a boxing ring there.
* Londoner and heavyweight champion Henry Cooper was the first person to win three Lonsdale Belts outright in the 1960s and '70s, and the only British boxer to have done this.
* In the Lamb and Flag pub, Covent Garden, bare-knuckle fights took place on the cobbled front yard or in the back room, nicknamed the Bucket of Blood.
* Boxer Jack Broughton is buried in the West Cloister at Westminster Abbey, as he went on to become a Yeoman of the Guard.

It's just not cricket

The Gentlemen of London was the first cricket club in the city, playing on the Artillery Ground, Clapham Common and Kennington Park in 1700. In 1774, the laws of cricket were laid down by the LONDON CLUB, setting the pitch length at 22 yards, an over to 4 balls and limiting the batsman to one strike. The first club was the White Conduits Club who played in Barnsbury, Islington before moving to Dorset Square, Marylebone, as they were fed up with sharing the pitch with local ragamuffins. In 1806, the first GENTLEMEN VS PLAYERS match was played at Lords. The ground was named after the professional cricketer Thomas Lord.

The MCC stands for the Marylebone Cricket Club.

The Ashes

When England lost to Australia for the first time on home soil at the OVAL Cricket Ground in 1882, it was satirically announced by a journalist as the death of English cricket. An urn said to contain THE ASHES of a burnt cricket bail, symbolising its death, are kept in the museum at Lords. The Ashes tournament is played between the two rival countries.

LONDON TRANSPORT

Two hundred years ago, most Londoners got around on foot. Only the wealthy could travel by horse or sedan chair. The river was the fastest way to get around, with watermen carrying passengers in little rowing boats called wherries. By the 1850s, several million were travelling on the river in paddle steamers, and fashionable Londoners were nipping around in horse-drawn cabs. Horse-drawn omnibuses and trams gave ordinary Londoners a lift to work at a cheaper price. In 1900, 50,000 horses were needed to keep the city moving and the Tube rumbled underground. By 1915, everything had changed: motor vehicles and electric trams had taken over the streets.

London transport timeline

Sedan Chair

1700s Sedan chairs, horse-drawn cabs

1829 Horse-drawn buses

1830s Stream trains, paddle steamers

1863 First underground trains

1870 Double-decker horse-drawn trams

1903 First motor taxi

1910 Electric buses and trams

1911 Motor bus

1915 Motor cars for the rich

1925 Double-decker bus with covered top deck

1958 Iconic Black taxi

1959 Routemaster bus

1987 Docklands Light Railway

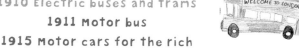

WELCOME TO LONDON

It has long been believed that every taxi driver has to carry a bale of straw in his cab, harking back to a time when taxis were horse-drawn. This is not true. Ask any London cabbie.

LONDON TAXI FIRSTS

- The first taxi drivers in London were the watermen on the Thames.
- The first London road taxi was a horse-drawn carriage, licensed for hire in 1662. These were called hackney cabs, from the French *haquenee*, which means 'an ambling horse'. They had no springs and no glass in the windows and were very uncomfortable to ride in. Londoners called them the hackney hell carts.
- Three years later, a man called Captain Bailey gave London its first taxi rank. He posted four hackney carriages at the Maypole in the Strand and charged by the hour.
- In 1834, Joseph Aloysius Hansom brought the racy Hansom cab to London from Paris. This was a light carriage pulled by a single horse, able to nip speedily in and out of the traffic. There was room for two passengers, who talked to the driver through a trap door. Folding doors covered their legs to protect them from being splashed and only once the passengers had paid did the driver release the folding doors to let them out.
- In 1903 the first motor taxi hit the streets.
- In 1958 the iconic black taxi Londoners love switched on its yellow light.

The Knowledge

In 1865, it was decided that every black-cab driver had to take a test, proving they knew the streets of London like the back of their hand. This was called the KNOWLEDGE of London Examination. This came about because London's taxi drivers could not find their way around London well enough when vast crowds came to visit London's Great Exhibition in 1851. They kept getting lost.

Taxi drivers today have to learn 320 routes, and all the LANDMARKS and places of interest along the way. They have to be able to drive these without looking at a map or using a sat nav. When a taxi driver passes the test, he or she is presented with a special green metal badge called the Knowledge.

Fascinating facts: taxis

- All black cabs have a small turning circle of only 8 metres/26 feet because of the narrow roundabout at the entrance to London's Savoy Hotel in Strand.
- Taxis are known as cabs, short for cabriolet. This was the proper name for two-wheeled horse-drawn carriages.
- The word taxi is short for taximeter, the name of the instrument that measures the distance travelled. It was invented by Wilhelm Bruhn in 1891.

The double-decker

The first double-decker bus with a covered top deck was introduced to the streets of London in 1925. Buses are different colours in different British cities. London buses are RED. They are painted with a special red called PANTONE 485. This is the same red as that of the London Underground sign and the Central Line.

The Routemaster

The iconic red Routemaster double-decker bus, designed by Douglas Scott, was exhibited in 1954 and made its first passenger journey in 1959. A FAVOURITE of Londoners for its jump-on-jump-off design, it was styled with shiny stainless-steel fittings, tartan seats, red leather cloth, soft lighting, a lovers' seat at the back of the top deck and wind-down windows.

To the regret of many, the ROUTEMASTER was phased out in 2004, but two routes survived the cull: the No. 9 from the Royal Albert Hall to Aldwych and the No. 15 from Trafalgar Square to Tower Hill. And a newly designed Routemaster by Thomas Heatherwick hit London's streets in 2012.

Stop the bus!

When you want to catch a bus, you have to wait at a bus stop. But buses don't stop at what are known as 'request stops' unless you wave them down by sticking your arm out into the street. You can tell you are at a REQUEST stop because the London Transport sign at the top of the stop has a red background with a white logo. All other bus stops have a white background with a red logo.

The same applies for getting off. If you want the bus to stop at a request stop, press the button and ring the bell before you get to the stop.

The longest bus route in London is 38 kilometres/23¼ miles

Lost property

Over 200,000 items of lost property are left on public transport in London. Last year the most commonly forgotten items were books (36,852), bags (28,550) and clothing (27,174 items). Some of the strangest objects include a stuffed puffer fish,

a HUMAN SKULL, breast implants and a lawnmower. The Transport for London Lost Property Office is in Baker Street.

The world's first bus station opened in 1924 at the British Empire Exhibition, Wembley.

London Underground firsts

The world's first underground railway opened in London on 10 January 1863. The first stretch of line was the Metropolitan line, which ran for 6.5 kilometres/4 miles below ground in trenches dug out from under the streets of London.

The first underground railway journey was made between Paddington station and Farringdon Street.

The first underground trains were steam powered and the tunnels became unpleasantly smoky. The wooden carriages lacked seats and had padded walls. Londoners called them 'padded cells'.

How the Tube got its name

In 1890, the world's first deep-level underground railway line opened. It was nicknamed the Tube. The City and South London Railway ran for six stops between King William Street in the City and Stockwell. It is now part of the Northern line.

The Tube map

London Underground grew so fast, with so many lines and stations, that it was decided to commission a good map. Harry Beck, a draughtsman, came up with the idea of designing it like an electrical circuit in 1933. He was paid just 5 guineas for his iconic Tube map, which has inspired underground network maps around the world. Each Tube line is a different colour.

Bakerloo
Central
Circle
District
London Overground
Hammersmith and City
Jubilee
Metropolitan
Northern
Piccadilly
Victoria
Waterloo and City

★ LONDON LINGO ★

The 1920s and 1930s suburbs, such as High Barnet,
Loughton and Amersham, that grew up at the end of the
Tube lines were nicknamed Metroland.

Baby boom

Three babies have been born on the London Underground:

- 1924 Thelma Ursula Beatrice Eleanor was born on a Bakerloo line train at Elephant and Castle. What do her initials spell?
- 2009 A baby girl was born on the Jubilee line to Julia Kowalska.
- 2009 A baby boy was born at London Bridge station to Michelle Jenkins.

Twenty facts about the London Underground

1. First Tube line: Metropolitan line
2. Number of Tube stations: 270
3. The first escalator: Earls Court station, 1911
4. Shortest escalator: Stratford with a rise of 4.1 metres/13½ feet
5. Longest escalator in Western Europe: Angel station at 60 metres/197 feet.
6. Total number of escalators: 422
7. Deepest station: Hampstead at 58.5 metres/192 feet below ground
8. Shortest tube line: Waterloo and City at 2 kilometres/1¼ miles
9. Longest tube line: the Central line at 55 kilometres/34 miles.
10. Distance travelled by a Tube train every year: 123,600 kilometres/77,000 miles.
11. Total length of network: 402 kilometres/250 miles.
12. Percentage of the Tube in tunnels: 45 per cent
13. Station with the most platforms: Baker Street, which has ten
14. Busiest station at rush hour: Waterloo
15. The shortest distance between stations: Leicester Square and Covent Garden on the Piccadilly Line at 0.3 kilometres/0.16 miles
16. Newest Tube line: the Jubilee line, opened in 1979
17. The Underground name first appeared on stations in 1908
18. London Underground has been known as the Tube since 1890
19. Every week the escalators on the London Underground travel the equivalent of twice around the world.
20. It takes an hour to complete a round trip on the Circle line.

Designer brief

In 1918, London Underground commissioned **EDWARD JOHNSTON** to design a modern typeface for the Tube's signs. He created the Johnston Underground font. He also designed the logo for London Underground, a red circle with a horizontal blue bar across it called **THE ROUNDEL**.

Platform for Art

The 1930s was a golden era for art on the London Underground. A man called Frank Pick set up a poster campaign called Platform for Art and commissioned artists and writers to produce posters, textiles and literature for the Underground.

- Man Ray and Graham Sutherland created publicity posters.
- Designer Paul Nash and artist Enid Marx designed special upholstery fabrics for trains, trams and buses.
- The poet John Betjeman wrote the Tube's leaflets.

LONDON FACT · LONDON FACT · LONDON FACT · LONDON FACT

DID YOU KNOW?

✳ Two Tube stations have been called Strand, one at Aldwych and one at Charing Cross. There is no Strand station today.

✳ The Bakerloo line is rumoured to exist purely to enable 'gentlemen' to get from their offices in the City to Lord's cricket ground as quickly as possible.

✳ A section of the East London line (now part of the London Overground) goes through Brunel's famous tunnel under the Thames. This is the oldest part of London Underground, built twenty years before the Tube.

✳ The great Victorian Prime Minister Gladstone and the champion of London's poor Dr Barnardo are the only people ever to have had their coffins transported by Tube.

Beneath your feet: London's secret railways

- There is a secret railway line under Postman's Park in the City that was once used to move letters around London as speedily as possible.
- A little round tower near the Tower of London was once the entrance to the world's first underground railway tunnel, built in 1870, called the Tower Subway.
- Camden Catacombs is a network of old long-forgotten tunnels deep under the streets of Camden. Once owned by the railways, they were built in the nineteenth century for horses who pulled railway wagons.
- Deep below high Holborn and Chancery Lane is a mile of hidden tunnels built by London Transport and used to shelter Londoners during the Blitz. Spy organization MI6 stored 400 tonnes of classified documents here until 1954. It was also the site of the hotline to the US President Eisenhower and the Soviet Leader Khrushchev during the Cold War. Entry was through a secret doorway on Furnival Street.

London's fastest train: on 14 November 1994 the London-to-Paris high-speed train, the Eurostar, made its first journey from Waterloo to Gare du Nord.

London firsts . . .

- The world's first PUBLIC RAILWAY was a horse-drawn train from Croydon to Wandsworth in 1803. It carried goods, not people.
- London's first STEAM TRAIN was called CATCH ME WHO CAN. It was demonstrated on a circular, funfair-style ride at Euston in 1808.
- London's first PASSENGER RAILWAY was from London Bridge to Greenwich in 1838. By the 1840s, two million people were travelling on the railway.
- The first HAIL AND RIDE BUS service in London was started in 1829 by coach builder George Shillibeer.
- The first LONDON OMNIBUS started its journey from a tavern in the Marylebone Road.
- In 1868, the first MANUAL TRAFFIC LIGHTS were installed outside the Houses of Parliament. They worked like railway signals with semaphore arms to control the traffic. Red and green gas lamps were used at night. These exploded a year later, injuring the policeman on duty.
- Between 1930 and 1932 electric traffic lights operated manually were introduced at Ludgate Circus. They were shortly followed by the first AUTOMATIC TRAFFIC LIGHTS in Europe at the junction of Cornhill and Bishopsgate.
- In 1937 the police force acquired its first two PATROL CARS.

In the 1950s, the average London street had five parked cars in it. By the 1970s, there were twenty parked cars on every street. Today there are nearly three million cars in London.

No Parking!

Parking tickets were handed out by the Lord Mayor of London even in the days of carts. You could get a ticket for parking on a street overnight.

You could also get a fine if your cart was longer than 7 feet 1 inch, if you drove faster than walking pace, if you didn't feed your horse with a nosebag on, or if you were under sixteen in charge of a horse and cart.

> The first parking meter was in Grosvenor Square in the West End in 1958. The first double-yellow lines were painted on the streets of London in the same year.

Where can I go from here?

ST PANCRAS: The Midlands and Kent
KING'S CROSS: North and east of England and Scotland
WATERLOO: South coast and the south-west
EUSTON: West Midlands, the north-west, North Wales and Scotland
MARYLEBONE: Commuter belt and Shropshire
VICTORIA: Kent, Brighton, Surrey, Sussex; Venice on the Orient Express
PADDINGTON: The West Country and Wales; Heathrow
CHARING CROSS: Kent
LIVERPOOL STREET: Eastern England
FENCHURCH STREET: East London and Essex

Trains to Europe:
ST PANCRAS INTERNATIONAL:
Brussels, Lille and Paris
VICTORIA:
Paris and Venice on the Venice Simplon-Orient-Express

Paddington

DID YOU KNOW? LONDON FACT · LONDON FACT ·

* Victoria station was built to carry thousands of visitors to the Great Exhibition in 1851.
* Paddington station has a children's story character named after it: Paddington Bear, who arrived at the station from darkest Peru and was found by the kind Brown family. There is a statue of the bear in the station.
* In Oscar Wilde's *The Importance of Being Earnest*, the main character was found as an infant in a handbag at Victoria station.
* Euston is London's oldest train station, opened in 1837.
* Marylebone is London's smallest mainline station.

London food

ondon's streets have always bustled with stalls and food cooked on street corners; chop houses, coffee houses, taverns and pubs are the stuff of London life. Many city streets still bear the names of the foods that were sold and traded there.

In the past, people ate just one hot meal a day, usually thin **VEGETABLE** stew, with a piece of meat or fish thrown in if they were lucky. People also ate simple food like bread and cheese. Ordinary Londoners did not have their own ovens and would take their dough and cakes to the nearest **BAKER** to be cooked.

Just outside the City walls were meadows, marshland streams and open countryside where Londoners would go and hunt for wild birds, rabbits and hares. Nearby farms sold their **WARES** at street markets every day. Milk was drunk fresh from cows and fish were caught live from the Thames or from ponds and moats specially stocked with carp and tench. Londoners ate fish on Fridays, as meat was banned by the Church one day a week.

Eat your way round the world in London

Turkish kebabs – Green Lanes

Middle Eastern baklava – Edgware Road

Indian curry – Brick Lane

Best Jewish bagel – Brick Lane

Nigerian food – Ridley Road Market

Caribbean food – Electric Avenue, Brixton

Chinese food – Gerard Street, Soho

Londoners have always been interested in trying new tastes and recipes. Since Roman times, ships laden with exotic cargoes have brought spices, oils, herbs and wines. In Tudor times, new foods from Spanish conquests in the Americas were unloaded: the potato, the tomato, the kidney bean, maize, corn, peanuts, vanilla, beans, red peppers, turkeys and tapioca. Later, delicacies such as pineapples, coffee, tea, chocolate and sugar came to London.

THE CHELSEA BUN

Made of rich dough with cinnamon, lemon peel and sweet spices rolled into a square spiral, these were created in the early 1700s at the Old Chelsea Bun House, Grosvenor Row, a favourite haunt of royalty of the time.

INGREDIENTS
500g/1lb bread flour
1 tsp salt
1 sachet dried yeast
300ml/10fl oz milk
40g/1½oz unsalted butter
1 egg
vegetable oil

FOR THE FILLING
25g/¾oz unsalted melted butter
75g/2½oz brown sugar
2 tsp cinnamon
150g/5oz dried mixed fruit

FOR THE GLAZE
A tablespoon of milk
A sprinkling of sugar

1. Sift the flour and salt into a large bowl. Make a well in the middle and add the yeast.
2. Warm the milk and butter in a saucepan until the butter melts and the mixture is lukewarm.
3. Stir the milk mixture into the flour and add the egg. Make a soft dough. Add extra flour if you need to.
4. Place the dough on to a floured worktop. Knead for 5 minutes or until the dough is smooth and elastic and no longer feels sticky.
5. Oil a bowl with a little vegetable oil and put in the dough, covering it all over with the oil. Cover the bowl with cling film and set aside in a warm place for 1 hour, or until the dough has doubled in size.
6. For the filling, knock the dough back to its original size and turn out on to a lightly floured work surface. Roll the dough out into a rectangle 0.5cm/1/4in thick. Brush all over with the melted butter, and then sprinkle over the brown sugar, cinnamon and dried fruit.
7. Roll the dough up into a tight roll, cut it into 4cm/1½in slices and place them on to a lightly greased baking sheet, leaving a little space between each slice. Cover with a tea towel and set aside to rise for 30 minutes.
8. Preheat the oven to 190°C/375°F/gas mark 5.
9. Bake the buns in the oven for 20–25 minutes, or until risen and golden brown.
10. Meanwhile, for the glaze, heat the milk and sugar in a saucepan until boiling. Reduce the heat and simmer for 2–3 minutes.
11. Remove the buns from the oven, brush with the glaze and then set aside to cool on a wire rack.

London first . . .

SUGAR first came to London from Venice in the thirteenth century in Henry III's reign. It was a rare commodity and most people still used honey to sweeten things.

Stone Pineapple

The **PINEAPPLE** took London by storm in the 1600s. The first pineapple was presented to Oliver Cromwell. Pineapples cost the equivalent of £5,000 each. The **WEALTHY** would decorate their homes and gateposts with representations of pineapples to show off. The pineapple became a symbol of hospitality.

The scientist and philosopher **FRANCIS BACON** wanted to prove that freezing food could preserve it through the winter. In 1626, he was driving in his open carriage through Pond Square in Highgate on a bitterly cold, snowy day. He noticed that where the wheels of the carriage had passed, the grass looked fresh and new under the **SNOW**. To test his theory, he jumped out, bought a hen and stuffed it with snow and ice. This was the first ever **FROZEN CHICKEN**. Sadly he didn't live to see if his experiment worked, as he caught a terrible chill and died a few days later.

London doctor **HANS SLOANE** brought the **COCOA BEAN** to London after travelling in Jamaica in the 1650s. There he was given a very bitter new cocoa drink. He added some milk to sweeten it and decided to bring his delicious recipe back to London. This **CHOCOLATE** drink was thought to be good for you and it was sold as medicine.

A few years later, the first chocolate shop in London opened in Bishopsgate in 1657. Opened by a Frenchman, it was called the Coffee Mill and **TOBACCO** Roll and sold **CHOCOLATE** cakes and hot chocolate.

Coffee came to London and the first coffee house was opened in 1652 in St Michael's Alley, **CORNHILL**, by an Armenian servant called Pasqua Rosée, who worked for a merchant who imported coffee from Turkey. **COFFEE HOUSES** became fashionable places to meet and each one had its own group of followers.

Coffee

Poets, politicians, artists and writers each had their own favourite haunt: lawyers met at the Grecian at Temple; clergymen at Child's in St Paul's Churchyard; **ARTISTS** at Old Slaughters in St Martin's Lane; authors at Buttons in Bow Street; men of fashion and politicians at the Cocoa Tree at Ozindas in Pall Mall. The most important insurance business in London, **LLOYD'S**, started in the Edward Lloyd coffee house in 1688. Its doormen are still called waiters from the days of serving coffee.

The story of . . .

THE SANDWICH The 4th Earl of Sandwich, an eighteenth-century aristocrat, is credited with the invention of the sandwich. While **GAMBLING** and playing cribbage, he ordered his valet to bring him meat tucked between two slices of bread. His friends followed his example, and began to order 'sandwiches'. The beauty of the **SANDWICH** is that you can carry on playing cards without getting your hands greasy or leaving the card table. This is mentioned in a book about London written in 1772 by a Frenchman called Pierre-Jean Grosley.

CURRY In the eighteenth century, curries from India, pilau rice and mango pickle came to London via the East India Trading Company. Curry first appeared on the menu of the Coffee House, Norris Street, in Haymarket in 1773. The first curry restaurant in London was the Hindostandee Coffee House, 34 George Street, which opened in 1809.

TEA Thomas Twining bought Tom's Coffee Shop on the Strand in 1706 and started selling tea. It was a perfect location for selling tea, a new and **FASHIONABLE** import from the Far East, as it straddled the border between the City of London and Westminster, and was where a lot of **RICH** people had moved after the Great Fire. Twining sold tea in packets for the equivalent of £160 per 100 grams/¼ lb. The shops were for men only, so society ladies would wait outside in their carriages while their **FOOTMEN** popped in and bought tea for them to drink with friends at home at tea parties. Tea was so precious that people kept their tea under lock and key in boxes called caddies.

> The East India company placed its first order of 100lb of china tea from Java in 1664. By 1750, annual imports had reached 4,727,992lb.

ICE CREAM Carlo Gatti, an Italian immigrant from Clerkenwell, brought penny ices to London for the masses in the 1840s. He imported ice from Norway by ship up the Thames and along the Regent's Canal. He kept it frozen deep in a special ice well in the ground near King's Cross. He opened a café serving ice cream and chocolate in 1860.

BOILED SWEETS Victorian London was awash with cheap sugar from the plantations in the Caribbean. Confectioners experimented with new ways of using sugar and invented boiled sweets. **SHERBET LEMONS**, pear drops, humbugs, rhubarb and custards and aniseed twists were proudly displayed to the world at the 1851 **GREAT EXHIBITION**, to the delight of London children.

LONDON CHEESECAKE

London cheesecake is not a normal cheesecake. In fact there is no cheese in it at all. It is essentially a puff pastry base with a dollop of jam and ground almonds on the top.

500g/1lb puff pastry	100g/3oz sugar
Jam	50g/1½oz butter
100g/3oz ground almonds	1 tbsp icing sugar
1 egg	1 tbsp dessicated coconut

1. Roll out the puff pastry and cut out a 9cm/3½in circle and place on a greased baking sheet.
2. Dollop a spoonful of jam in the centre and spread it evenly.
3. Mix the ground almonds with the egg, sugar and butter, and spread on top.
4. Preheat the oven to 200°C/400°F/gas mark 6.
5. Bake in the oven for 15 minutes.
6. Coat with icing and sprinkle some coconut on top.

French fancies

By the seventeenth century French cooking was all the rage. London high society filled their kitchens with chefs from Paris, who whisked up coulis, roux, ragouts and fricassées to delight dinner guests. They cooked with strange new tastes such as anchovy and capers. Salads and fresh vegetables became highly desirable on the London table for the first time.

London's first celebrity chef

Auguste Escoffier became the first chef at London's new and glamorous Savoy hotel in 1890 and was London's first celebrity chef. He created lots of new recipes for famous people. His Pêche Melba was named after an Australian opera singer called Dame Nelly Melba, who sang at Covent Garden in 1892.

The classic white tiered wedding cakes were inspired by the steeple of St Bride's church in Fleet Street. They were the idea of a pastry cook called William Rich, who worked in a bakery opposite the church.

St Bride's steeple

★ LONDON LINGO ★

London broil is an American method of cooking a boneless cut of beef, like a steak. If you order a London broil in a London restaurant, no one will know what you are talking about as it is unheard of here.

London's first domestic goddess: Mrs Beeton

Isabella Beeton is one of the most famous cookery book writers of Victorian London. She was born on Milk Street in Cheapside and married the boy next door. Her book *Mrs Beeton's Book of Household Management* (1861) was full of advice on how to run a household and included over 900 recipes, from elaborate jellies to boiled tongue and rabbit stew. It was a runaway success and sold 60,000 copies in its first year of publication. Mrs Beeton was a young and dynamic woman who died at the age of just twenty-eight.

London's favourite . . .

FAST FOOD From the eighteenth century street hawkers set up trestle tables on every corner to sell their wares. Londoner's favourite snacks were eel pies, PORPOISE TONGUES, hot meat pies, spiced London ale, ribs of beef, sheep's trotters, whelks, tripe, hot eels, steak and oyster pie, pancakes. In the Middle Ages good cooks were given nicknames such as Wife Mampudding of Tower Street.

LONDON OYSTERS were once the staple food of the Victorian London poor. They ate them pickled and drank them with stout. Whitechapel Road, one of the poorest parts of London, was famous for its oyster stalls. DICKENS wrote in *The Pickwick Papers*: 'It's a wery remarkable circumstance . . . that poverty and oysters always seem to go together . . .'

RULES Restaurant on Maiden Lane, Strand, was established by Thomas Rule in 1798 and is the OLDEST restaurant in London. It still serves the same British favourites, such as jugged hare, steak and oyster pie, woodcock and game, steamed puddings and pies. Actors Charlie Chaplin, Clark Gable and Laurence Olivier all ate here.

PIE AND MASH AND JELLIED EEL SHOPS have dished up cheap and nutritious food to London's East End working class since the eighteenth century. They sell pies, mashed potato and jellied eels. Eels were once plentiful in the Thames and boiled, chopped eels in jelly became a particular favourite. They are eaten with CHILLI VINEGAR. Pie and mash shops are traditionally only found in south and east London. M. Manze is the oldest surviving one with shops in Tower Bridge Road, Peckham and Sutton.

THE CRIES OF LONDON

Here's fine rosemary, sage and thyme.
Come buy my ground ivy.
Here's feverfew, gilliflowers and rue.
Come buy my knotted majoram, ho!
Come buy my mint, my fine green mint.
Here's fine lavender for your clothes.
Here's parsley and winter-savory,
And hearts-ease, which all do choose.
Here's balm and hissop, and cinquefoil,
All fine herbs, it is well known.
Let none despise the merry, merry cries
Of famous London-town!

Here's fine herrings, eight a groat.
Hot codlins, pies and tarts.
New mackerel I have to sell.
Come buy my Wellfleet oysters, ho!
Come buy my whitings fine and new.
Wives, shall I mend your husbands' horns?
I'll grind your knives to please your wives,
And very nicely cut your corns.
Maids, have you any hair to sell,
Either flaxen, black or brown?
Let none despise the merry, merry cries
Of famous London-town!

Anon., seventeenth century

★ LONDON LINGO ★

The fish-sellers at Billingsgate had a reputation for using bad language and swearing. The word billingsgate came to mean foul-mouthed.

London's main markets

NEW COVENT GARDEN – Fruit and vegetables; flowers
SMITHFIELD – Meat
BILLINGSGATE – Fish
COLUMBIA ROAD – Flowers

Billingsgate Market

To market, to market

In the days before refrigeration, live animals were herded from the countryside to London, staying overnight in the green fields of Islington before being taken to **SMITHFIELD** animal market the next morning for sale and slaughter. In Victorian London, a noisy 5,000 cattle and 30,000 sheep a week trampled through the high streets of Islington and Clerkenwell.

Meat eating was very popular: in 1844, Londoners consumed a staggering 110,000 oxen, 50,000 calves, 770,000 sheep, 250,000 lambs and 200,000 pigs.

Smithfield is still London's most important meat market, but there are no longer any live animals for sale.

London's oldest . . .

Borough Market, on the south bank of London Bridge, is the oldest **FOOD MARKET** in London, dating back to 1014. It sold grain, fish, vegetables and livestock. It's now a thriving **ARTISAN** and organic food market.

Fresh food

Before the days of refrigerators, ice was cut from lakes or ponds and stored in little round ice houses. The first **ICE HOUSE** was built in Greenwich as early as 1619. An ice house is a small, domed building, often in the shade of a tree, where ice was packed between layers of straw, keeping it **FROZEN** for as long as two years. There are old ice houses all around London, notably at Hampstead Heath, Home Park at Hampton Court Palace, Holland Park and the Winter Garden at Kew.

Golden Syrup was invented in 1883 at the Lyle sugar factory in East London. At first small quantities were sold in wooden casks to employees and locals. It soon became very popular and it has been packaged in the iconic gold and green tins since 1885.

Costermongers

Costermongers were the fruit and vegetable sellers of London who wheeled their barrows around the streets, calling out their wares as they went along. What they had to sell depended on the time of year:

April: wallflowers and sweet-scented stocks

May: herring

June: new potatoes

July: cherries and soft fruit

August: plums and greengages

September: apples

October: oysters

November: sprats

December: holly, ivy, and oranges for Christmas

Fishy facts

- In days gone by the fish traders at Billingsgate Market would wear **FLAT-TOPPED** metal hats with large brims. They would race with large baskets of fish in ice on their heads from Billingsgate to Leadenhall market. They had right of way on the cobbled streets, as the baskets were heavy and the **ICE** was melting – the brims on their hats caught the drips.
- St Mary-at-Hill Church in Lovat Lane near the old Billingsgate Market puts on a special fish harvest festival every year in October.

LONDON FISH

Bream

BROWN TROUT

carp

PIKE

London brews

Tankard

For centuries, most of London water was **FILTHY** and too bad to drink, so most ordinary Londoners, including children, drank beer and alcohol as we drink water. There have always been lots of pubs and **TAVERNS** in London: in 1589, there were an incredible 1,000 pubs crammed into the square mile of the City. The Victorians had one pub for every six houses in London.

London Pride, one of the world's most famous beers, is brewed at Fuller's Brewery in Chiswick. It has been making beer for 350 years.

London porter

Londoners used to drink a stout, a dark rich beer called London porter, so named because it was popular with the porters on the streets and river of London.

London's oldest pubs

The title for the oldest pub is hotly contested. These are the top contenders:

The Lamb and Flag, Covent Garden

YE OLDE CHESHIRE CHEESE, FLEET STREET

The Prospect of Whitby, Wapping

The George Inn, Southwark

London gin

London dry gin is a particular type of gin. At the end of the 1600s, Londoners were allowed to make gin without a licence. Imported alcohol was heavily taxed and expensive, while gin was **DIRT CHEAP**. As a result, soon six times more gin than beer was sold in London, and by 1740 over half of the drinking places in London were gin shops. The famous London Beefeater Dry Gin has been made in Kennington since 1820.

> ★ LONDON LINGO ★
>
> Gin turned many Londoners into alcoholics and became the ruin of the poor. Gin is still called 'mother's ruin'.

Mixed Media

The World's biggest library

The British Library on the Euston Road opened in 1988. It is the largest public library in the world and is the largest **PUBLIC** building constructed in the UK in the twentieth century.

It receives a copy of every publication produced in the UK and Ireland, including books, maps, magazines and music scores. Part of its collection used to be in the beautiful domed **READING ROOM** at the British Museum.

British Library facts

- The British Library holds over 150 million items.
- It has 625 kilometres/388 miles of shelves
- 3 million new items are added every year.
- The shelves grow by 12 kilometres/7½ miles a year.
- The British Library is made of 10 million bricks.
- 180,000 tonnes of concrete were used in its construction.
- It has fourteen storeys, five of which are underground.

If you were to take out five items a day, it would take you 80,000 years to look at the whole collection.

DID YOU KNOW?

- The first free public library in London was at St Martin-in-the-Fields church in Trafalgar Square.
- Karl Marx wrote his revolutionary work *Das Capital* in the Reading Room of the British Museum in rows J–P.
- The Russian leader Lenin also wrote there, registered under the name of Jakob Richter. He sat in seat L13.
- An original copy of Lewis Carroll's *Alice's Adventures Under Ground*, the original shorter version of *Alice's Adventures in Wonderland*, is on display in the Treasures' Gallery at the British Library.
- The London Library in St James's Square is the world's largest independent lending library.

Storybook London

The story of **PETER PAN** and his magical world of lost boys, pirates, Indians and ticking crocodiles was written by **J.M. BARRIE** who lived across the road from Kensington Gardens on Leinster Terrace. He was inspired to write his famous stories after meeting the Llewellyn Davies children in the park. The gardens were his favourite place to walk his dog Porthos. There is a statue of Peter Pan in **KENSINGTON GARDENS**. The Darling family home is set in Bloomsbury, where J.M. Barrie first lived when he came to London.

101 DALMATIONS is set at **REGENT'S PARK** near where the writer **DODIE SMITH** lived at St Andrews Place. Mr and Mrs Dearly walked their darling Dalmatians, **PONGO AND PERDITA**, in the park every day. When the dogs' puppies are **STOLEN** by the evil Cruella De Vil, the dogs head to the top of Primrose Hill to track them down.

There are eight stories about **MARY POPPINS**. They were written by **P.L TRAVERS**, who lived at 50 Smith Street in Chelsea. The strict but loving **NANNY** was brought in by the east wind to look after **JANE AND MICHAEL** Banks. The stories are set in a fictional London street called Cherry Tree Lane. P.L. Travers based Admiral Boom's ship-like house, with its quarter-deck and flagpole, on a house in Admiral's Walk, Hampstead.

The man who wrote the **PADDINGTON BEAR** stories, **MICHAEL BOND**, was a cameraman at the BBC who lived just off the Harrow Road in west London. The books tell of the hilarious scrapes of a **NAUGHTY BEAR** called Paddington. According to the story Paddington Bear was found one day by the kind Brown family at Paddington train **STATION** with a label round his neck saying 'Please look after this bear'. He had travelled from **DARKEST PERU**. The books are all set in and around the Portobello Road in Notting Hill.

Real haunts and hangouts from charles Dickens' stories

- **ST ETHELDREDA'S CHURCH, ELY PLACE:** David Copperfield meets Agnes Wakefield here (*David Copperfield*).
- **TEMPLE:** Tom Pinch works in an office at Fountain Court (*Martin Chuzzlewit*).
- **LONDON BRIDGE:** Nancy secretly meets Rose and Mr Brownlow on the steps (*Oliver Twist*).
- **OLD BAILEY:** Oliver Twist visits Fagin in Newgate prison (*Oliver Twist*).
- **LITTLE BRITAIN, SMITHFIELD:** Jaggers's office is down this alley (*Great Expectations*).
- **SMITHFIELD MARKET:** Oliver Twist and Bill Sykes pass through on market day on their way to burgle a house (*Oliver Twist*).
- **WESTMINSTER BRIDGE:** David Copperfield and Mr Peggotty cross the bridge in their search for Emily (*David Copperfield*).
- **ST BARTHOLOMEW'S HOSPITAL:** Bob Hopkins works as a doctor here (*Pickwick Papers*) and Betsy Prig is a nurse here (*Martin Chuzzlewit*).

Poets' corner

London has been home to some of the greatest writers and poets that have written in the English language. There is a special corner in Westminster Abbey dedicated to them. **GEOFFREY CHAUCER**, author of The Canterbury Tales, was the first to be remembered here. Look out for:

ROBERT BROWNING   Dr Samuel Johnson   Charles Dickens

RUDYARD KIPLING   THOMAS HARDY

Alfred, Lord Tennyson

There are also memorials to:

John Milton   William Shakespeare   WILLIAM BLAKE   John Keats

WILLIAM WORDSWORTH   **JANE AUSTEN**   Charlotte Brontë

T.S. ELIOT   John Betjeman

Headline news

London newspapers appeared for the first time during the drama of the English Civil War, when demand for news escalated. **THE DAILY COURANT** was the city's first daily newspaper, published in March 1702 and printed in the White Hart Inn on Fleet Street. By the 1720s, there were twelve London newspapers and by the 1800s there were a **STAGGERING** fifty two London newspapers. All Britain's leading national newspapers were written and printed in Fleet Street until the 1980s.

St Bride's church on Fleet Street is the journalists' church.

Read all about it: fascinating facts

- The world's first illustrated weekly newspaper, called the *Illustrated London News*, was published weekly from 1842 until 1971.
- The *London Evening News* was the first evening paper in London. It cost a ha'penny and was printed on light blue paper. It was published for 100 years from 1881.
- The *London Financial Guide* was launched in 1888 by Horatio Bottomley, and soon became the *Financial Times*, published on pink paper.
- *The London Gazette* is Britain's oldest continuously published newspaper. *The Gazette* was first published in 1665, to record the events of the Great Plague.
- *The Beano* is still published in Fleet Street, by D.C. Thomson.
- Newspapers are known as the press because of the early printing presses.

The Thunderer

The Times newspaper was first published in 1785 and was called **THE DAILY UNIVERSAL REGISTER**. It changed its name in 1788 and designed its own special easy to read typeface called **TIMES ROMAN**. It was the first newspaper to send correspondents to cover foreign wars. The **LONDON TIMES**, as the paper is known abroad, has lent its name to lots of other newspapers around the world such as *The New York Times*, *The Times of India* and *The Irish Times*. *The Times* newspaper's nickname used to be the **THUNDERER** because it was not afraid to disagree with popular opinion.

★ LONDON LINGO ★

★ When people talk about 'Fleet Street', they mean the newspapers and journalists, even though they have moved away.

★ When members of the armed forces are promoted, the London Gazette publishes the announcement. This has become known as being 'gazetted'.

★ The cheap offices in Grub Street near Moorfields (now called Milton Street) attracted impoverished writers and journalists, many of whom were prepared to make a quick buck by writing sensational stories to order. The expression Grub Street has come to refer to low-level writers and writing.

★ Journalists are sometimes rudely called hacks, after Hackney, the place where London's workaday horses were born and bred.

Broadcast news

The BBC, the world's first national broadcasting organization, was founded in London on 18th October in 1922. It started with a radio broadcast from **MARCONI HOUSE** in the Strand on 14th November. From January 1926, all announcers and performers on BBC Radio at Broadcasting House, near Oxford Circus, were told to wear **DINNER JACKETS** in the evening, even though no one could see them, as a sign of respect and good manners.

Children's Hour was first broadcast in 1922 and was one of the earliest radio programmes.

On the box

London was where British **TELEVISION** began. The first ever television audience gathered in the attic rooms of the inventor of TV, **JOHN LOGIE BAIRD'S** workshop in Frith Street, **SOHO** on the 26th January 1926, to watch this amazing new entertainment contraption. It just three years before the first public television broadcast was made on 30 September 1929 from a studio in **LONG ACRE**, Covent Garden via the BBC's London transmitter. By late 1930, half an hour of programmes were broadcast every weekday morning, and half and hour at midnight on Tuesdays and Fridays.

Fascinating facts: children's television

- *Blue Peter* has been on our screens continuously since 1958 and is the longest running children's television show in the world.
- The *Blue Peter* garden opened in 1974 at the BBC Television Centre in White City.
- The first episode of *Dr Who* was broadcast in 1963. It is the longest running science fiction show on television in the world.
- *Blue Peter's* first pet, a much-loved brown and white dog called Petra, first came to our screens on 17 December 1962.

DID YOU KNOW?

* Television broadcasts were cancelled during the Second World War as the engineers were needed elsewhere. Transmission stopped two days before the war started in 1939.
* The last programme to be shown before the war was a Mickey Mouse cartoon.
* Television programmes returned to the screens on 7 June 1946.

TV firsts

- The first sale of a television set in the world was from **SELFRIDGES** department store in 1928.
- The world's first scheduled television service was transmitted from **ALEXANDRA PALACE** in September 1936.
- The first children's television programme was broadcast for one hour on Sunday afternoons after the end of the war, in 1946. It featured the puppet **MUFFIN THE MULE**.
- The first **COLOUR TELEVISION** pictures were transmitted in November 1956.
- The first television broadcast of the **QUEEN'S CHRISTMAS MESSAGE** was on 25 December 1957.
- The world's first ever purpose-built television centre was the **BBC TELEVISION CENTRE** at White City in west London, built in 1960.

London's capital Radio was the first independent entertainment radio station for London and went on air in 1973 playing the British National anthem, God Save the Queen. This was followed by its catchy jingle:

Isn't it good to know, Capital Radio
You can turn on your friends, you can turn on the show,
you can turn on the world with Capital Radio.

In the 1970s, capital radio set up a charity to raise money for London's poorest children called HELP A LONDON CHILD.

LONDON'S TOP FM RADIO STATIONS

95.8 Capital Radio – pop music

97.3 LBC – NEWS AND TALK

106.2 HEART – OLDIES

104.9 XFM - indie

105.8 Absolute Radio – rock

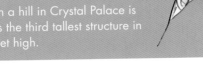

London landmark: crystal Palace

Towering over London's suburbs high on a hill in Crystal Palace is London's main television transmitter. It is the third tallest structure in London, standing at 219 metres/718 feet high.

Painting the town: art in London

London's art colleges make it the centre of some of the great art movements of the world.

THE PRE-RAPHAELITE BROTHERHOOD was a group of English painters, poets and critics. The Brotherhood was founded in 1848 by John Everett Millais, Dante Gabriel Rossetti and William Holman Hunt in Millais' parents' house in Gower Street. They wanted to return to a style of art using intense colours to create very detailed, complicated pictures.

THE CAMDEN TOWN GROUP was a group of sixteen artists including Spencer Gore, Charles Ginner, Harold Gilman and Robert Bevan who were brought together by Walter Sickert in 1911. They were British Impressionist artists inspired by the French movement, and they painted ordinary north London urban scenes.

THE LONDON SCHOOL is an art movement dating back to an exhibition at the Hayward Gallery in 1976. It refers to artists including Lucien Freud, Francis Bacon, Howard Hodgkin, David Hockney and Frank Auerbach.

THE YOUNG BRITISH ARTISTS appeared on the scene in the 1980s. Many of the painters, artists and sculptors associated with this movement studied at Goldsmiths in New Cross. Among the YBAs are Gary Hume, Damien Hirst, Tracey Emin, Sarah Lucas and Rachel Whiteread. Damien Hirst's 14-foot-long dead tiger shark immersed in formaldehyde at the Royal Academy's Sensation Exhibition in 1997 became the iconic symbol of Britart.

LONDON'S GRAFFITI ARTISTS are famous throughout the world. Banksy, the man behind guerilla art in London, has a secret identity, and has spray painted his subversive works of art on the streets of North and East London. Good places to look for a Banksy are Brick Lane and Essex Road.

LONDON'S MOST FAMOUS ART COLLEGES

Camberwell College of Art   GOLDSMITHS

chelsea   Central St Martin's

Royal College of Art

Slade School of Fine Art

Olympic art

Bombay-born London artist ANISH KAPOOR'S has created the tallest sculpture in Britain, higher than Nelson's Column and the Statue of Liberty, for London's 2012 Olympic Park. Officially called the ARCELORMITTAL ORBIT, it is nicknamed the helter-skelter. Take the lift all the way to the top to see London's awesome skyline and scramble back down the spiral staricase.

London's greatest artist: J.M.W. Turner 1775-1851

Londoner Joseph Mallord William Turner is one of the world's most famous landscape painters. He was the son of a barber and wig-maker and the family lived on MAIDEN LANE in Covent Garden. Turner studied art at the schools of the Royal Academy from the age of seventeen. He was a LANDSCAPE artist and mostly painted in oils. He is known as the painter of light. London was often the subject of his canvases. Turner sometimes sent his paintings to exhibitions at the Royal Academy unfinished and would complete them on Varnishing Day, which meant he had to finish them in front of a gathering crowd. It became a fashionable thing to watch the great master at work. Turner usually preferred to show his paintings himself, as he was so particular about how they were hung. He created his own art gallery in his DUSTY SITTING ROOM in Harley Street for exhibitions and painted the walls of the room dark red.

Turner died a RECLUSE at his last home in Cheyne Walk, where he was living under the pseudonym ADMIRAL BOOTH to avoid recognition.

One of Turner's most famous paintings, The Battle of Trafalgar, was commissioned by George IV for the walls of St James's Palace. It now hangs at the National Maritime Museum, Greenwich.

DID YOU KNOW?

Tate Britain has 300 oil paintings 30,000 sketches and watercolours and 300 of Turner's sketchbooks, many of which are hung in the Clore Gallery, which is dedicated to his work.
The annual Turner Prize, named in Turner's honour, is awarded each year to encourage young up-and-coming artists.
The National Gallery removed all its paintings in the 10 days before the declaration of war on 3 September 1939 as the government were sure London would be heavily bombed. Almost all of them were sent to Wales for safety.

What to see where

British art	Tate Britain
International modern art	Tate Modern
National art collection	National Gallery
Famous people's portraits	National Portrait Gallery
Summer exhibition	Royal Academy of Arts

The Fourth Plinth, Trafalgar Square has an empty statue plinth that has a constantly changing sculpture on top.

Famous paintings on show in London

Sunflowers by Vincent van Gogh	National Gallery
Pile of Bricks 'Equivalent viii' by Carl Andre	Tate Britain
Wham by Roy Lichtenstein	Tate Modern
The Laughing Cavalier by Frans Hals	Wallace Collection

The best street art in London

Antony Gormley's *Quantum Cloud*	On the river at Greenwich
Henry Moore's *Two Piece Reclining Figure*	Hampstead Heath
Barbara Hepworth's *Winged Figure*	John Lewis, Oxford Street
Elizabeth Frink's *Shepherd and Sheep*	Paternoster Square

GILBERT AND GEORGE are two famous London artists who always work together. They live in Spitalfields in the East End and all their work has been created there. According to George, 'Nothing happens in the world that doesn't happen in the East End.'

Fascinating facts: the Tate

Tate Modern

- The Tate Gallery is named after the family who owned the huge London Tate and Lyle sugar refinery in the docklands.
- The chimney of Tate Modern is 99m/325ft high and was deliberately built to be lower than the dome of St Paul's Cathedral. The building, originally a power station called Bankside, is made of 4.2 million bricks. The power station closed in 1981 and the building reopened, spectacularly transformed, as Tate Modern in May 2000.

SHOW TIME IN LONDON

London's first . . .

The first ever purpose-built **THEATRE** in London was an Elizabethan playhouse in Whitechapel called the Red Lion. Built by a grocer called John Brayne in 1567, it had a stage with trapdoors and towers for stunts. But the theatre did not last long. It was in what was then countryside, and was too far away for Londoners to come to. The only play to be put on was one called *The Story of Sampson*.

London's oldest theatres

Theatre Royal Drury Lane, 1663   SADLER'S WELLS, 1683

Haymarket, 1720   Royal Opera House, 1732

London's great opera house

The Royal Opera House is known to Londoners as **COVENT GARDEN**. There has been a theatre on this site since 1732 and it is now home to the Royal Opera and the Royal Ballet. The first ballet, **PYGMALION**, was danced here in 1734. A year later, a season of Handel's operas opened. Many of Handel's works were written especially for Covent Garden. For the first 100 years, Covent Garden was used mostly for plays and **MUSICALS** and was known as the Theatre Royal.

Spooky London

Theatre Royal Drury Lane is built on the site of three previous theatres and is the world's most haunted theatre. Its ghosts include an eighteenth-century gentleman in a three-cornered hat who watches daytime rehearsals and is called the Man in Grey; Charles Macklin, who killed a fellow actor with his sword; Dan Leno, a music hall comedian; Joe Grimaldi, the world-famous clown; and Charles Kean, a Victorian actor.

London's oldest music hall is Wilton's in Wapping, built in 1858.

Favourite London music-hall songs

- 'If It Wasn't for the Houses In Between' • 'The Lambeth Walk'
- 'Burlington Bertie from Bow'

The longest-running musicals in London

Les Misérables   PHANTOM OF THE OPERA   Blood Brothers

CATS   Starlight Express

The Mousetrap, an Agatha Christie murder mystery, is a record-breaking theatre show. It has been running since 1952.

Twelfth Night

Robert Baddeley was an actor at Drury Lane who died in the middle of a run of Sheridan's play *School for Scandal* in 1794. In his will he left money to be used to buy a cake, wine and punch for the actors at the theatre every Twelfth Night.

Puppets in London

1600 The earliest recorded puppet shows took place at Bartholomew Fair.

1650s Even when Cromwell closed the theatres, puppet shows flourished.

1662 Samuel Pepys saw Mr Punch in Covent Garden. This was the first recorded Punch and Judy show in London.

1672 Charles II saw a Punch and Judy show for the first time and ordered that Punch and Judy shows should be allowed to be performed at Charing Cross.

1777 There were four puppet companies in London's West End.

1850 After a decline, Punch and Judy shows took off again with the new public Bank Holidays, to entertain Victorian families.

1961 A troupe of puppeteers transformed a derelict hall in Islington into a magical puppet theatre especially designed for children, called the Little Angel Theatre.

1982 London's Puppet Theatre Barge opened at Camden Lock. In 1988 it moved to Little Venice.

The story of the circus

Philip Astley invented the circus as we now know it. He was a great horse rider and performed his riding tricks in front of crowds in Islington. In 1768 he famously performed in an open field in Waterloo, riding round and round in a circle rather than in the usual straight line. His performance was nicknamed the circus. He added a clown to fill the gaps between his riding sequences and later introduced jugglers, tightrope walkers and dancing dogs – the ingredients of what became the modern circus. He opened the world-famous Astley's Amphitheatre in London in 1773. His circus carried on for many years even after his death, not closing until 1893, and was mentioned in Charles Dickens's and Jane Austen's novels.

London's greatest clown: Joseph Grimaldi

Joseph Grimaldi (1779–1837) was born in London at Clare Market. His father, Joseph 'Iron Legs' GRIMALDI, was an Italian ballet master at the Drury Lane theatre and his mother was a dancer at Sadler's Wells. He gave his first theatre performance before he was two. Grimaldi made a name for himself as a pantomime clown and is considered the FATHER OF MODERN CLOWNING. His shows were full of great tricks, buffoonery and comic moments. He loved to make fun of the crowd and started the pantomime tradition of audience participation ('Oh no he didn't . . .'). He introduced the PANTOMIME dame to London's music halls. When he retired from the theatre, he famously said, 'It is four years since I jumped my last jump, filched my last oyster, boiled my last sausage and set in for retirement.'

HAHA!

Grimaldi would paint an upside-down smile on his face to make him look sad, as clowns do today. Londoners thought this was very funny and would tell this joke: A young man goes to see his doctor and says: 'Doctor, doctor, I am feeling very sad today.' The doctor says: 'Why not do something to cheer yourself up? Go and see Grimaldi the clown.' The young man answers: 'Ah, but, Doctor, I am Grimaldi the clown.'

SECRET LONDON

❋ Holy Trinity in Dalston is known as the Clowns' Church.
❋ Joseph Grimaldi's grave is in an Islington park named after him.
❋ Charles Dickens was such a fan of Grimaldi that he wrote his biography.
❋ Clowns are sometimes called Joeys, after Joseph Grimaldi.

Beatlemania: the Beatles in London

- The Beatles' first gig in London was at small Soho club called the **BLUE GARDENIA**.
- **ABBEY ROAD** in St John's Wood is where the Beatles recorded most of their albums.
- The Beatles set up their own record label called **APPLE RECORDS** at 3 Savile Row in the West End.
- The Beatles played their last ever live performance on the **ROOFTOP** of Apple Records on 30 January 1969.
- The Beatles opened the Apple Boutique in Baker Street in 1967s. **PAUL MCCARTNEY'S** vision was to create 'a beautiful place where beautiful people can buy beautiful things'.

London sounds

- Punk rock started in London in 1975, setting out to outrage and shock.
- Rock band manager Malcom McClaren and designer Vivienne Westwood ran an anti-fashion clothes shop called Sex at the **WORLD'S END**, Chelsea.
- Punk rockers paraded on the **KING'S ROAD** in ripped clothes, studs, spikes, safety pins and Dr Martens boots wearing hair spiked up in mohicans.
- The gig that brought the **SEX PISTOLS** to London's attention was supporting Eddie and the Hot Rods at the Marquee on 12 February 1976. The Sex Pistols signed their record deal outside Buckingham Palace.
- Their single 'God Save the Queen' was released to coincide with the Queen's Silver Jubilee celebrations in 1977.

London punk bands

SEX PISTOLS   The Clash   THE DAMNED

The Slits   Siouxsie and the Banshees   X-RAY SPEX

The Clash wrote a hit album called
London calling **in 1979.**

Lights, camera, action!

EALING STUDIOS is the oldest working film studios in the world. Directors have been shooting films here for over 100 years. Ealing is famous for black-and-white British comedies from its heyday in the 1950s and '60s, including the original St Trinian's films. They are known as Ealing Comedies.

PINEWOOD, SHEPPERTON AND TEDDINGTON film studios are famous for their extraordinary sets and underwater stages. Fictitious places like Wonkaville and Gotham City have been built here. Pinewood's cobbled street stars in *The Private Life of Sherlock Holmes* and the Scandinavian village at Shepperton features in *The Golden Compass*.

Famous children's films made at London studios

Chitty Chitty Bang Bang (1968) • *Bugsy Malone* (1975) • *The Spy Who Loved Me* (1977) • *Mamma Mia* (2008) • *The Dark Knight* (2008) • *The Prince of Persia: The Sands of Time* (2010) • *Harry Potter and the Deathly Hallows* (2010/11) • *The Chronicles of Narnia: Prince Caspian* (2008) • *The Chronicles of Narnia: The Voyage of the Dawn Treader* (2010)

The IMAX cinema at Waterloo has the largest cinema screen in Britain.

Children's films shot on the streets of London

The Golden Compass (2007)

STORMBREAKER (2006)

Sherlock Holmes (2009)

Batman Begins (2005)

GULLIVER'S TRAVELS (2010)

Peter Pan (1963)

Johnny English (2003)

LONDON FIRST

The first demonstration of cinema in London was by French brothers Auguste and Louis Lumiere in 1896 at a hall in Regent Street. The Empire Theatre, now the Empire Leicester Square, was the first theatre to screen films in London for the public, in 1896, screening the Lumiere brothers' movie. It is still the home of cinema in London and hosts all the big film premières in London.

London locations

- *The Dark Knight*: Dent and Bruce dine at the Criterion restaurant, Piccadilly Circus; the sinister warehouse scenes are filmed at Battersea Power Station.
- *Batman*: Arkham Asylum is the hotel at St Pancras station – at the time disused, now restored as the glamorous St Pancras Renaissance Hotel.
- *Monty Python and the Holy Grail*: Lancelot is arrested by police on East Heath Road in Hampstead.
- *The Golden Compass*: Jordan College dining room is the Painted Hall, Greenwich College; Mrs Coulter's carriage pulls up on Chester Terrace, Regent's Park; the Magisterium Palace is the historic Greenwich College.
- *Sherlock Holmes* (2009): the opening shot is of the spooky-looking Middle Temple Lane, off Fleet Street; Sir Thomas's House is the Royal College of Arms on Queen Victoria Street; the rioting scene is filmed at Greenwich College; the Reform Club in Pall Mall doubles as the Café Royal.
- *101 Dalmatians*: St James's Park stood in for Regent's Park for the massive dog chase where the owners fell into the pond.

The story of Charlie Chaplin

The star of black-and-white silent movies Charlie Chaplin (1889–1977) is thought to have been born in East Street in the slums of Camberwell. His family was very poor and he spent much of his childhood in the workhouse. His parents were music-hall performers and by the age of nine he had performed in his first show. From the time he was twelve Charlie lived with a troupe of young dancers. After touring America with a theatre company he headed to Hollywood and got into the movies, where his famous character the Tramp, with derby hat, black moustache, twirling cane and baggy trousers, was born.

One of the last films he made, *Limelight*, is about his London childhood.

Five JAMES BOND London movie moments

- ON HER MAJESTY'S SECRET SERVICE (1969) James Bond visits the College of Arms in the City.
- OCTOPUSSY (1983) M's London headquarters were filmed at the Old War Office building in Whitehall.
- THE WORLD IS NOT ENOUGH (1999) The 360-degree boat jump happens over the Royal Victoria Dock, Canning Town.
- DIE ANOTHER DAY (2002) James Bond parachutes over the Victoria Memorial to Buckingham Palace to receive his knighthood.
- CASINO ROYALE (2006) Bond travels through Trafalgar Square on his way to Downing Street.

Harry Potter on location

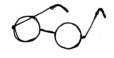

- Harry Potter is filmed speaking parseltongue to the boa constrictor who slithers out of the REPTILE HOUSE at London Zoo, Regent's Park
- Hogwarts Express puffs away from platform 9¾ at Kings Cross station, while the exteriors filmed are those of its rather more handsome neighbour, the gothic St Pancras Station.
- Australia House on the Strand plays the role of the goblin's GRINGOTTS BANK where Harry discovers the gold his parents have left him and the secret of Vault 713.
- Harry and Mr Weasley use the futuristic WESTMINSTER TUBE station to get to the Ministry of Magic, filmed at nearby Scotland Place, near Whitehall. The red telephone box on the street Harry uses to enter the Ministry was a film set prop.
- Professor Flitwick's magic spell classes were at HARROW SCHOOL, Greater London.
- Bull's Head Passage at Leadenhall Market is the way into the Leaky Cauldron.
- The muggle café where Hermione and Harry flee from the Death Eaters is in PICCADILLY CIRCUS.
- The Houses of Parliament, the London Eye, and the Millennium Bridge are the stars of the opening sequence of *Harry Potter and the Half-Blood Prince*.

Fascinating Film Facts

- The first-ever moving pictures shot on celluloid film were filmed in Hyde Park in 1889 by an inventor called William Friese Greene.
- In the 1930s, the entrepreneur Sidney Bernstein had the idea of building fabulous fantasy-style new cinemas to encourage Londoners to come to the movies, even in middle of the Great Depression. They were known as picture palaces and were built in Art Deco style. The designs took inspiration from the newly discovered tombs of ancient Egypt and had elaborately painted interiors and cubist zigzags. Lots of these old cinemas have been converted into bingo halls.
- The 1940s was the golden age of British cinema, with the success of the film studios of J.Arthur Rank and Alexander Korda.

James Bond author Ian Fleming named his character Goldfinger after one of his Hampstead neighbours. He disliked the man, an architect called Ernö Goldfinger, so much that he used his name for one of the most evil baddies James Bond has ever encountered: Goldfinger.

LONDON'S BEST

. . . .

Best free parades

A Guards Helmet

ALL YEAR **CHANGING OF THE GUARD**
The soldiers parade every day in summer, and every other day in winter, at the gates of Buckingham Palace and up the Mall to St James's Palace.

NEW YEAR **THE LONDON PARADE**
Follow the floats, marching bands and classic cars from Parliament Square to Berkeley Square on New Year's Day.

JANUARY **CHARLES I COMMEMORATION MARCH**
The King's Army (members of the English Civil War Society in authentic period dress) marches from St James's Palace to Banqueting Hall in the last weekend in January.

FEBRUARY **CHINESE NEW YEAR PARADE**
Follow the dancing dragon through Chinatown near Leicester Square.

MARCH/ APRIL **LONDON HARNESS HORSE PARADE**
Carts and horses parade through Battersea Park.

MAY **CAVALRY REGIMENTS MEMORIAL PARADE**
The cavalry parade in Hyde Park is on the second Sunday in May.

JUNE **TROOPING THE COLOUR**
Celebrate the Queen's official birthday in June by marching down the Mall with a band of soldiers.

SEPTEMBER **HORSEMAN'S SUNDAY**
Horses are blessed in Hyde Park on the third Sunday in September.

OCTOBER **TRAFALGAR PARADE**
The Sea Cadets march to Trafalgar Square and lay a wreath at the foot of Nelson's Column on the nearest Sunday to 21 October.

NOVEMBER **LORD MAYOR'S SHOW**
The new Lord Mayor rides in his golden coach from Guildhall to the Royal Courts of Justice.

Best races to cheer along

MARCH/
APRIL

THE OXFORD AND CAMBRIDGE BOAT RACE
Watch from the banks of the Thames anywhere along the river from
the start at Putney Bridge to the end at Barnes Bridge.

APRIL

THE LONDON MARATHON
This international race through London from Greenwich Park
to Buckingham Palace has become an annual event for tens of
thousands of runners. Best places to cheer them on are from the top of
the hill at Greenwich Park or from the Mall at Green Park.

NOVEMBER

LONDON TO BRIGHTON VETERAN CAR RUN
This is the longest-running motoring event in the world, first run in
1896. Once a year vintage cars rev their engines at Hyde Park at
sunrise and whoever gets to the seafront at Brighton by 4.30 in
the afternoon gets a medal. The best views are from Hyde Park or
Westminster Bridge early in the morning.

Best street entertainment is at Covent Garden and on the

South Bank, where there are jugglers, mime artists, variety acts, musicians and
other performers.

Best FREE fun things to do in London

- **WALK UNDER WATER** through the spooky Greenwich Foot Tunnel under the Thames.
  and **MUDLARK** for treasure on the banks of the river.
- Glimpse the **GIRAFFES** at London Zoo as you walk along the Regent's Canal from
  Camden to Regent's Park.
- Have your photograph taken with a **GUARD** outside St James's Palace.
- Take a shortcut from the City to the South Bank across the **WOBBLY BRIDGE**.
- Roar at the **DINOSAURS** in Crystal Palace Park.
- Feed the **DUCKS** in Regent's Park.
- Board the **PIRATE SHIP** at the Diana Memorial Playground, Kensington Gardens.
- Whizz down the **FLYING FOX** at Coram's Fields in Guilford Street.
- Fly a **KITE** on top of Parliament Hill in Hampstead Heath.
- **ROLLERBLADE** around Hyde Park.
- Sail a toy **BOAT** on the Round Pond at Kensington Gardens.
- Watch the feeding of the **PELICANS** at St James's Park each afternoon.
- Stalk the **DEER** in Richmond Park.
- **CYCLE** across Wimbledon Common all the way to Richmond Park.

Best things to spend pocket money on

- Take a BOAT out on the Serpentine in Hyde Park.
- Buy an ONION BHAJI on Brick Lane.
- SWIM in the ponds on Hampstead Heath (8+).
- Hire a whacky BIKE in Battersea Park for the afternoon.
- Get lost in the MAZE at Hampton Court Palace.
- Soar over the City on the LONDON EYE.
- Take a CLIPPER down the Thames from Westminster Pier to Greenwich.
- STRADDLE TIME at the Meridian Line in Greenwich Park.

Best hidden gardens in London

- **CHELSEA PHYSIC GARDEN**, Swan Walk, Chelsea
- **ISABELLA PLANTATION**, Richmond Park
- **CAMLEY STREET NATURAL PARK**, Camley Street, King's Cross
- **QUEEN MARY'S ROSE GARDEN**, Regent's Park
- **THE HILL GARDEN AND PERGOLA**, Inverforth Close, Hampstead
- **LITTLE CLOISTER GARDEN**, Westminster Abbey, Westminster
- **THE WALKS**, Gray's Inn, Holborn (weekday lunchtimes only)
- **INNER TEMPLE GARDENS**, Temple (weekday lunchtimes only)
- **THE MUSEUM OF GARDEN HISTORY**, Lambeth

Best ships you can clamber aboard

HMS BELFAST, Tooley Street
THE GOLDEN HINDE, St Mary Overy Dock, South Bank
CUTTY SARK, King William Walk, Greenwich

Cutty Sark

Best things to climb in London

- **THE MONUMENT**, Pudding Lane
- **PRIMROSE HILL**, Camden
- The dome of **ST PAUL'S CATHEDRAL**
- **THE SHARD**, London Bridge
- **THE JEWEL TOWER**, Westminster
- **KING HENRY'S MOUND**, Richmond Hill
- **THE ARCELORMITTAL ORBIT**, Olympic Park
- **WELLINGTON ARCH**, Hyde Park Corner

Best famous people's houses to snoop around

DR JOHNSON'S HOUSE, Gough Square, Fleet Street
SIR JOHN SOANE'S MUSEUM, Lincoln's Inn Fields, Holborn
KEATS HOUSE, Keats Grove, Hampstead
FREUD MUSEUM, Maresfield Gardens, Hampstead
HOGARTH'S HOUSE, Great West Road, Chiswick
HANDEL HOUSE MUSEUM, Brook Street, West End
BENJAMIN FRANKLIN HOUSE, Craven Street, Strand
KELMSCOTT HOUSE (William Morris's home), Upper Mall, Hammersmith
CHARLES DICKENS MUSEUM, Doughty Street, Bloomsbury
APSLEY HOUSE (Wellington's house), No. 1 London, Hyde Park Corner
CARLYLE'S HOUSE, Cheyne Row, Chelsea
ERNÖ GOLDFINGER'S HOUSE, 2 Willow Road, Hampstead

Best children's theatres

Polka Theatre, Wimbledon
The Little Angel Puppet Theatre, Islington

The Unicorn Theatre, Tower Bridge
The Puppet Barge, Little Venice

Best London farms and zoos

SPITALFIELDS CITY FARM

Mudchute Park & Farm

Freightliners Farm, Islington

HACKNEY CITY FARM

BATTERSEA PARK CHILDREN'S ZOO

London Zoo, Regent's Park

Best toy shops

HAMLEYS, Regent's Street
BENJAMIN POLLOCK'S TOY SHOP, Covent Garden
PETIT CHOU, St Christopher's Place
SNAP DRAGON, Crouch End and East Dulwich
AFTER NOAH, Upper Street, Islington
HONEYJAM, Portobello Road
MYSTICAL FAIRIES, Flask Walk, Hampstead
MIMI FIFI, Pembridge Road, Notting Hill
IGLOO, St John's Wood

London's best museums

MOST POPULAR: British Museum, Bloomsbury

BEST ON LONDON: Museum of London, Barbican,
Museum in Docklands, West India Quay

BEST FOR FASHION: Victoria and Albert Museum, Cromwell Road

BEST FOR DESIGN: The Design Museum, Shad Thames

BEST FOR DINOSAURS: Natural History Museum, Cromwell Road

BEST FOR TRANSPORT: London Transport Museum, Covent Garden

BEST FOR SCIENCE

WELLCOME COLLECTION, Euston Road, Bloomsbury.

OLD OPERATING THEATRE MUSEUM, Herb Garret, St Thomas's Street

ALEXANDER FLEMING LABORATORY MUSEUM, St Mary's Hospital, Paddington

HUNTERIAN MUSEUM, Lincoln's Inn Fields, Holborn

SCIENCE MUSEUM, Exhibition Road

FLORENCE NIGHTINGALE MUSEUM, St Thomas's Hospital, Westminster Bridge

BRUNEL ENGINE HOUSE, Railway Avenue

BEST FOR SOLDIERS

GUARDS MUSEUM, Wellington Barracks   **IMPERIAL WAR MUSEUM**, Waterloo

CABINET WAR ROOMS, King Charles Street   **NATIONAL ARMY MUSEUM**, Chelsea

ROYAL MEWS, Buckingham Palace   **HOUSEHOLD CAVALRY MUSEUM**, Horse Guards

WEIRD AND WONDERFUL MUSEUMS

PRINCE HENRY'S ROOMS, Fleet Street   **FOUNDLING MUSEUM**, Bloomsbury

LONDON CANAL MUSEUM, King's Cross   **FAN MUSEUM**, Greenwich

GEFFRYE MUSEUM, Shoreditch   **HORNIMAN MUSEUM**, Forest Hill

PETRIE MUSEUM OF EGYPTIAN ARCHAEOLOGY, Malet Place

BEST FOR CHILDREN

VICTORIA AND ALBERT MUSEUM OF CHILDHOOD, Bethnal Green

POLLOCK'S TOY MUSEUM, Scala Street

CABARET MECHANICAL MUSEUM, Covent Garden

Best museum shops for children

SCIENCE MUSEUM, Cromwell Road   **TATE MODERN**, Bankside

NATURAL HISTORY MUSEUM, Cromwell Road   **TATE BRITAIN**, Millbank

POLLOCK'S TOY MUSEUM, Scala Street   **MUSEUM OF CHILDHOOD**, Bethnal Green

BEST CHILDREN'S STORIES SET IN LONDON

Books set in medieval and Tudor London

THE LOAD OF UNICORN by Cynthia Harnett

An important cargo of paper goes missing and printer William Caxton's young apprentice is sent to uncover the mystery of its disappearance.

RING OUT BOW BELLS by Cynthia Harnett

A young page boy of a master of a City guild gets into scrapes as he finds his way around the City.

RAVEN QUEEN by Pauline Francis

A tale about Lady Jane Grey and the treachery, power struggles and religious turmoil of the Tudor court.

THE PRINCE AND PAUPER by Mark Twain

A chance encounter changes the lives of two boys.

KING OF SHADOWS by Susan Cooper

A twentieth-century boy actor goes back in time and meets William Shakespeare.

TREASON by Berlie Doherty

Young William Montague is plucked from a life of obscurity to become a page boy to Prince Edward, son of Henry VIII, at Hampton Court Palace.

BEARKEEPER by Josh Lacey

A thriller about a boy alone in Shakespeare's London.

Books set in Stuart and Georgian London

AT THE SIGN OF THE SUGARED PLUM by Mary Hooper

Sisters Sarah and Hannah run a sweetmeats shop and love it so much that they ignore the warnings of a terrible plague until it is right on their doorstep.

RAVEN BOY by Pippa Goodhart

A boy and his raven battle against injustice at the time of the London plague.

I, CORIANDER by Sally Gardner

A girl called Coriander starts an adventure in Cromwell's London when she slips on a pair of silver shoes.

JUPITER WILLIAMS by S.I. Martin

Set in 1800, this is the story of a wealthy, educated black boy who ends up on the streets alongside the poor black community of London.

CORAM BOY by Jamila Gavin

The story of two orphan boys who find themselves at Thomas Coram's Foundling Hospital and try to find their families.

THE DIAMOND OF DRURY LANE by Julia Goodling

An orphan girl who has been brought up backstage at the Drury Lane Theatre has action-packed adventures.

MARY ANN AND MISS MOZART by Ann Turnbull
One of the Historical House series, set at 6 Chelsea Walk: Mary Ann wishes to be an opera singer and meets the child prodigy Mozart at Ranelagh Gardens in Chelsea.

HETTY FEATHER by Jacqueline Wilson, illustrated by Nicholas Sharratt
Orphan Hetty Feather finds life hard at the Foundling Hospital and desperately searches for her long-lost mother.

THE TAR MAN by Linda Buckley Archer
An 18th-century villain, the Tar Man, is catapulted into twenty-first century London.

Books set in Victorian London

THE RUBY IN THE SMOKE, THE SHADOW IN THE NORTH and **THE TIGER IN THE WELL** by Philip Pullman
The dramatic adventures of Sally Lockhart, a sleuth in Victorian London.

JAMMY DODGERS GO UNDERGROUND, JAMMY DODGERS ON THE RUN and **JAMMY DODGERS GET FILTHY RICH** by Bowering Sivers
Three entertaining books about a gang of Victorian urchin children.

LIZZIE'S WISH by Adele Geras
Lizzie wants to be a gardener and when her strict stepfather sends her to stay with relatives in London she struggles to adapt.

SMITH by Leon Garfield
The adventures of a young boy who is being chased by murderers and scoundrels.

BLACK HEARTS IN BATTERSEA by Joan Aitken
The second book in the Wolves of Willoughby Chase series follows the adventures of a boy who goes to London to study painting but gets mixed up in intrigue.

JOE RAT by Mark Barratt
The fast-paced adventure of an urchin's struggles in the criminal underworld of Victorian London and the sewers of the East End.

THE LITTLE PRINCESS by Frances Hodgson Burnett
The story of a motherless child who is sent from India to Miss Minchin's boarding school in London. She has to work as a servant when the money runs out.

AROUND THE WORLD IN 80 DAYS by Jules Verne
In this story London gentleman Phileas Fogg makes a £20,000 bet that he could circumnavigate the globe faster than anyone ever has before.

Books set in 20th-century London

PETER PAN by J.M. Barrie
The story of Peter Pan and his magical world of lost boys, pirates, Indians and ticking crocodiles.

THE HUNDRED AND ONE DALMATIANS by Dodie Smith
The story of dalmatians, Pongo and Perdita, and their stolen puppies.

BALLET SHOES by Noel Streatfeild
Three orphaned girls attend a dancing school in London and are determined to become famous.

MISS RIVERS AND MISS BRIDGES by Geraldine Symons
Two young ladies find themselves caught up in the struggle of the suffragettes on the London streets.

THE PHOENIX AND THE CARPET by E. Nesbit
The story of the four Lamb children, who find an egg in an old carpet. It hatches into a talking phoenix and takes them on magical adventures.

MARY POPPINS by P.L. Travers
There are eight stories about the strict but loving nanny called Mary Poppins, who is brought in by the east wind to look after Jane and Michael Banks.

WHEN WE WERE VERY YOUNG by A.A. Milne
A collection of funny poems by the author of the Winnie-the-Pooh stories.

TIME TRAIN TO THE BLITZ by Sophie McKenzie
A young boy and a girl are given a mision to save a life. But with bombs falling on London they find they are counting down to disaster.

THIS MORNING I MET A WHALE by Michael Morpurgo
A boy spots a whale on the shores of the Thames.

KASPAR, PRINCE OF CATS by Michael Morpurgo
A story about the Savoy cat, Kaspar, and his adventures.

PADDINGTON BEAR by Michael Bond
The first in a series of hilarious stories about a naughty bear called Paddington, found at Paddington Station.

THE BFG by Roald Dahl
The Big Friendly Giant and orphan Sophie travel to Buckingham Palace to persuade the Queen to help them squash some fiendish plans.

THE MAGICIAN'S NEPHEW by C.S. Lewis
This story begins in a London terraced house where two children explore the attic rooms and discover a magical world.

London stories for older readers

A LONDON CHILD OF THE 1870S by Molly Hughes
The diary of a young girl growing up in Canonbury, Islington, in the Victorian era.

STONE HEART by Charles Fletcher
Misfit boy George is on a school trip to the Natural History Museum when he knocks into a dragon statue and breaks it, unleashing a strange new London: a world where statues move and talk.

TANGLEWRECK by Jeanette Winterson
A gripping time-travelling book in which weird things happen and a woolly mammoth is seen on the banks of the Thames.

THE DAY OF THE TRIFFIDS by John Wyndham
A scary science fiction book in which London is taken over by deadly plants.

WHEN I WAS JOE by Keren David
A boy called Ty witnesses a stabbing on the streets and puts his own life in jeopardy. This is the first in a trilogy.

STORMBREAKER by Anthony Horowitz
The first of a series of books about London teenage spy Alex Rider, who gets caught up in fast-paced Bond-style adventures.

THE OTHER SIDE OF TRUTH by Beverly Naidoo
This is the story of twelve-year-old Sade and her brother Femi, who flee from Nigeria to London. Abandoned at Victoria station by the woman paid to bring them to England as her children, Sade and Femi find themselves alone.

BURNING BRIGHT by Tracy Chevalier
A family moves to London and their shy teenage son, Jem Kellaway, befriends a streetwise local girl, Maggie Butterfield. Together they strike up a relationship with the radical artist William Blake and work for the nearby circus.

UN LUN DUN by China Mieville
Two twelve-year-old girls, Zanna and Deeba, discover a fantasy world where a discarded London exists in parallel.

TUNNELS by Roderick Gordon and Brian Williams
William Burrows' father disappears down a tunnel and when Will decides to investigate, he unearths a terrifying secret.

MORTAL ENGINES by Philip Reeve
Tom and Hester are stranded in a futuristic nightmare world and Tom is desperate to get back to his beloved London. The first in a trilogy.

THE LONDON EYE MYSTERY by Siobhan Dowd
A cousin comes to visit and disappears on a trip on the London Eye. An unputdownable spine-tingling thriller.

Best London picture books

THIS IS LONDON by Miroslav Sasek
A 1950s picture book about London with classic illustrations.
KATIE IN LONDON by James Mayhew
The story of a little girl called Katie who visits London with her granny.
MADELINE IN LONDON by Ludwig Bemelmans
The story of the French schoolgirl Madeline on an adventure in London.

Best bookshops just for children

VICTORIA PARK BOOKS, Victoria Park   **GOLDEN TREASURY**, Wimbledon
TALES ON MOON LANE, Herne Hill   **THE BOOKWORM**, Golders Green
CHILDREN'S BOOKSHOP, Muswell Hill
THE LION AND UNICORN BOOKSHOP, Richmond

Best bookshops with good children's departments

DAUNT BOOKS, throughout London   **LUTYENS & RUBINSTEIN**, Notting Hill
HATCHARDS, Piccadilly   **THE VILLAGE BOOKSHOP**, Dulwich
OWL BOOKSHOP, Kentish Town   **ENGLAND'S LANE BOOKS**, Belsize Park

Best cake shops

CAKE BOY, Battersea Reach, Battersea
COX COOKIES & CAKE, Brewer Street, Soho
GAIL'S, Hampstead High Street and branches around London
GINGER AND WHITE, Perrin's Court, Hampstead
HUMMINGBIRD BAKERY, Portobello Road, Notting Hill
J & A CAFÉ, Sutton Lane, Clerkenwell
KONDITOR AND COOK, Stoney Street, Borough Market
LOLA'S at Harrods, Knightsbridge, and Selfridges,
Oxford Street
MAISON BERTAUX, Greek Street, Soho
MELROSE AND MORGAN, 42 Gloucester Avenue,
Primrose Hill, and Oriel Place, Hampstead
OTTOLENGHI, Upper Street, Islington, and elsewhere
ROSE BAKERY, Dover Street Market, Mayfair
TINA, WE SALUTE YOU, King Henry's Walk,
Newington Green
TREACLE, Columbia Road
VIOLET'S, Wilton Way, London Fields

Cake

Best old-fashioned sweet shops

MR SIMMS OLDE SWEET SHOPPE, Ludgate Hill, Blackfriars
HOPE AND GREENWOOD, Russell Street, Covent Garden
MRS KIBBLES OLDE SWEET SHOP, St Christopher's Place, Bond Street
SUCK AND CHEW, Columbia Road Market
BREWODE'S CORNUCOPIA, Broadway Market

Best ice cream parlours

MARINE ICES, Haverstock Hill, Chalk Farm
SCOOP, Shorts Gardens, Covent Garden
FREGGO, Swallow Street, Piccadilly
GELUPO, Archer Street, Soho
WILLIAM CURLEY, Ebury Street, Pimilico
GELATO MIO, Holland Park Avenue
FORTNUM & MASON'S ICE-CREAM PARLOUR, Piccadilly
GELATERIA DANIELI, Queenstown Road, Battersea
CHIN CHIN LABORATORISTS, Camden Lock Place, Camden

Best pizzas

	close to
MALLETTI, Noel Street, Soho	Trafalgar Square
PRINCI, Wardour Street	Trafalgar Square
NONNA'S, Parkway, Camden	Camden Market
PIZZA EAST, Shoreditch High Street	Geffrye Museum
STORY DELI, Old Truman Brewery	Brick Lane; Spitalfields Market
PIZZA EXPRESS, Coptic Street	British Museum

Best hamburgers

	close to
THE DINER, Ganton Street	Hamleys, Handel's House
ED'S EASY DINER, Old Compton Street	Leicester Square, National Gallery, Nelson's Column
FINE BURGER CO., St Pancras Int. Station	Foundling Museum, Canal Museum
GOURMET BURGER KITCHEN, St Paul's Churchyard	St Paul's, Dr Johnson's House, Old Bailey

Best child-friendly places to eat

These are lots of these all over London, offering good children's menus and a decent meal for grown-ups. There are branches at all the major tourist sights in London: Royal Festival Hall, South Bank, St Paul's, Covent Garden, Shaftesbury Avenue, Tower of London, Tate Modern, the Globe Theatre, British Museum, Greenwich.

GIRAFFE	Stir fries, burgers, wraps
NANDO'S	Chicken any way you want it
CARLUCCIO'S	Italian food
STRADA	Pasta and pizza
WAGAMAMA	Noodles, rice and dim sum
YO! SUSHI	Sushi on a conveyor belt
PING PONG	Dim sum
LEON	Falafel, humous, lentil soups and the best hot chocolate brownies in London
EAT	Tasty sandwiches, soups and pies

Best places to eat pie and mash and jellied eels

CLARKS, Exmouth Market, Clerkenwell
A. COOKE, Goldhawk Road, Shepherd's Bush
COCKNEY'S, Portobello Road, Notting Hill
L. MANZE, Chapel Market, Islington
M. MANZE, Tower Bridge Road, Elephant and Castle
G. KELLY, Roman Road, Bow

Best places to eat fish and chips

GEALES, Farmer Street, Notting Hill
COSTAS FISH RESTAURANT, Hillgate Street, Notting Hill
GOLDEN HINDE, Marylebone Lane, West End
FAULKNER'S, Kingsland Road, Dalston
THE FRYER'S DELIGHT, Theobald's Road, Bloomsbury
GEORGE'S PORTOBELLO FISH BAR, Portobello Road, Notting Hill
GOLDEN UNION FISH BAR, Poland Street, Soho
THE SEA SHELL OF LISSON GROVE, Marylebone

draw a place in London you have visited

Places I've been to in London

stick tickets here to help you remember your visits

stick in a photograph of yourself in London

Exciting things I've done in London

write about your favourite London adventure

Secret facts I've discovered in London

INDEX

THE OLDEST THING IN LONDON

Probably the oldest thing you will ever touch is a large fragment of the Gibeon meteorite, on display at the Peter Harrison Planetarium in Greenwich, which plummeted to Earth, landing in the Namibian desert. It is 4.5 billion years old, about as old as our solar system.